D0266264

Lucky Break

First published in Great Britain in 2009
by Orion

1 3 5 7 9 10 8 6 4 2

A CIP catalogue record for this book
is available from the British Library.

ISBN HB 978 1 409 10492 6
     TPB 978 1 409 10493 3

Typeset at The Spartan Press Ltd, Lymington, Hants

Printed in Great Britain by Clays Ltd, St Ives plc

The Orion Publishing Group Ltd
Orion House
5 Upper Saint Martin's Lane
London, WC2H 9EA

An Hachette UK company

The Orion Publishing Group's policy is to use papers
that are natural, renewable and recyclable products and
made from wood grown in sustainable forests. The logging
and manufacturing processes are expected to conform to
the environmental regulations of the country of origin.

www.orionbooks.co.uk

The author and publisher are grateful to the following for permission
to reproduce photographs: Racing Fotos, Bill Selwyn, George Selwyn,
Matthew Webb, Bernard Parkin, Healy Racing, Graham Fisher, John
Grossick, Jim Meads, Ed Whitaker, Martin Alford, Brian Armstrong and
Lynn Keddie.

Every effort has been made to acknowledge the correct copyright
holders and the publishers will if notified by happy to correct any errors
in future editions.

Lucky Break

THE AUTOBIOGRAPHY

Paul Nicholls

with *Jonathan Powell*

*For my mum and dad who encouraged me
all the way from the moment I had my first pony
and have always been there for me.*

And for Paul Barber who gave me the chance.

CONTENTS

ACKNOWLEDGEMENTS

So many friends have helped in the telling of this story. My thanks to them all for taking the time to recall days and events from the past. My mum, dad, my sister Julie and her husband Geoff brought back happy memories from my early days.

Many others, too, had a part to play in this book. They include my first boss Dick Baimbridge, Mike and Jennifer Irish and their son Robin, Jenny Barons, Andy Hobbs, Peter Hobbs, Kevin Bishop, Robert Blackburn, Paul and Marianne Barber, Chris and Emma Barber, Marcus Armytage, Anthony Bromley, Clifford Baker, Ruby Walsh, Georgie Bown and Georgie Browne.

In addition I would very much like to thank Celia Marr and Geoff Lane who could not have been more helpful in explaining the complicated veterinary detail in this book.

Above all my thanks to Jonathan Powell who kept asking the questions over many months and somehow transformed my thoughts into a coherent narrative.

Paul Nicholls,
August 2009

FOREWORD

by Sir Alex Ferguson, CBE

One of the great benefits I get and one of my most pleasurable releases is watching other successful people at work as I can compare and relate their jobs to my own. When I first went to Ditcheat to watch the morning workouts I was interested not so much in those wonderful animals but in the way Paul himself worked.

One of the problems Paul has to deal with, of course, as in the case of all successful people, is one of expectation. As each big winner is unfolded so too is a further rising of the great expectation; not easy to deal with, but when you see the energy of the man and the enjoyment he is getting then you see a man in absolute control of the job. This is the point, I tell everyone, that you have to reach in order to be complete in your management of a successful operation. Once there, then responsibility, decision making and management of staff become natural to your everyday working. This is where Paul is now and, although he has to deal with many different owners with different personalities and commitments to his yard, he does so with an assured manner. His owners listen to him, and I have likened their response to him to that of many of the most successful people I have come across.

Paul works in an industry whose fragile nature requires a cool and decisive nerve, one that only huge experience gives you, as at any given moment on the racetrack fortune, or lack of it, has to be dealt with in a special way. Kipling's poem 'If . . .' was not wrong: when dealing with success and failure treat them both the same.

The other aspect that has impressed me about the man is his communication with his owners. I know that with today's technology it is easy to fax or e-mail your information but Paul always uses personal contact and telephones after your horse has run to give you the report on its health, performance and his plans for the next race. They don't all do that and it's part of his professional dedication and respect that he sees as a natural part of the job.

I wish Paul well and in his future challenge of remaining No.1 trainer in the country, and that's what we expect of him.

PROLOGUE

I used to be called all sorts of names in my days as a jockey. Not many of them were complimentary but I didn't mind because, against all the odds, I was living the dream by defying the laws of nature. I was the wrong shape altogether for riding over jumps, too tall and much too heavy. For much of my career I was riding at around two stone less than my natural weight, which is why I usually spent several hours a day sweating off unwanted pounds in my sauna at home in Devon.

Some people used to say that I rode like a policeman. They were closer to the truth than they realised because my dad Brian was a copper and so, too, was my granddad Frank who, for the record, was nineteen stone when he was nineteen. No wonder I struggled like hell from the start to do ten stone as a jockey, with or without a saddle!

Given my background I probably should have been a policeman, too. I was big enough for the job, no question, yet from a surprisingly early age horses were my passion and I set my heart on becoming a trainer. Well, we all have daft ambitions in our youth. Somehow, mine became a reality. I didn't have a clue how I was going to do it, or even if it was remotely possible, though I was dimly aware, watching racing on TV, that a trainer needed money, land, resources and someone to send him some horses. Nothing too daunting, then.

At that stage the right price about me becoming a trainer must have been a million to one. We were living in a police house and my parents worked all hours to give me and my sister Julie the chance to have ponies, which we kept in a field Dad rented behind the police station in Almondsbury, near Bristol. All our pocket money was spent on the ponies.

It was hardly the obvious launching pad for a successful career in racing, but long term I had no doubt that I would become a trainer

1

one day. It was up to me to make it happen. Although I've never been short on self-belief, there were many times along the way when the prospect of gaining a trainer's licence seemed no more than a mirage, a distant, absurd pipe dream. Deep down I knew that I had to find a way to become involved in the sport. Then maybe an opportunity might come up one day.

In my early teens I progressed from hunting and pony racing to full-time employment as a stable lad in a point-to-point yard. Later I rode in races as an amateur, eventually turned professional and managed 119 winners, though I never regarded myself as anything more than a journeyman jockey. For me it was a privilege to sit in the same weighing room as men like John Francome. I had huge respect for John and some of the others and never kidded myself that I was in their league or anything like it. I was just a policeman's son who had played around in gymkhanas and was scraping a living at the bottom end of the scale. Put it this way: if I was riding today I wouldn't employ myself as a jockey.

The strain of existing for years on a diet of little more than fresh air cost me my first marriage and eventually drove me to the brink of madness. Things deteriorated to the point where I felt so depressed from constant abuse of my body that I cried off my second ride of the evening at Towcester on 16 May 1989 because I couldn't do the correct weight of eleven stone. I can remember feeling utterly miserable as I headed west that night, knowing beyond doubt that my riding career was over.

That summer my weight spiralled out of control to well over twelve and a half stone by the time I returned from holiday. Standing on the scales at home gave me a terrible shock. However much I starved myself, whatever I tried I just couldn't get the weight off. I barely shifted a pound in the following two weeks once I returned to work for my boss David Barons. Looking back now, I realise I was in denial, crazily kidding myself that I could get myself in shape again for one last season. The opening of the new jumps campaign was less than a fortnight away when the problem was taken out of my hands.

One moment I was trotting down a narrow lane with the rest of the Barons string. The next I was in lying on the bank with a smashed left leg after taking a direct kick from the hind legs of one of the horses. The pain was indescribable as I waited for the ambulance. Pain is temporary but starvation had been a permanent companion for years. Already I was hallucinating about the big meals waiting for me in hospital. I could almost reach out and touch the tray carrying the food that I craved.

I should have known better. The nurses in casualty briskly told me I couldn't have anything to eat until surgeons operated on my leg. Twelve hours later the operation was cancelled without warning. That first never-ending night in hospital I was in despair, as low as I have ever been.

In time, however, I came to realise that the kick I sustained in that quiet Devon lane was the best possible thing that could have happened, because it took me away from the horrible cycle of wasting and starvation that had been my life for far too long. At last I could eat proper meals three times a day without feeling an overwhelming sense of guilt.

Most important of all, my broken leg forced me concentrate on my long-held ambition to become a trainer. But for that accident I might not be where I am today. It was my lucky break.

8th June 91 [stamp] 11 JUN 1991   ℅ The New Inn
                                         Morleigh
Tel: 0548 82386 (DAY)   Totnes
     0548 550006 (EVES)   Devon
                                         TQ9 7JH.

Dear Mr Barber

                Further to our telephone
Conversation on Saturday morning
I would like to express my interest
in your training establishment.
        As you know I left Mr Barons
at the end of April after working
as assistant to him after breaking
my leg two years ago, before that
I was Stable jockey for 4 years.
        Previously to that I spent 4 years
with John Lugford and before that
I was with Dick Bainbridge from
Berkeley who as you know is
the Countries leading point to point
trainer (along with Richard).
        From the Start I was always

more interested in the training side
of things but along the way I.
was lucky to ride alot of winners
for many different trainers.
        Since May my wife + I have
been looking at properties which
might be suitable but as yet
nothing has materialised, but we
have the support of several owners
and have some nice horses lined up
including Olveston who was favourite
for the Tote Gold trophy at Newbury
in the Spring (unfortunately it was
snowed off) and who I think could
possibly go right to the top over
fences.
        My wife Bridget is the daughter
of Mrs Rebecca Brackenbury and has
been involved with horses all her
life regularly hunting with the
Dartmoor Foxhounds and also riding
Successfully in point to points.
        Last Season we prepared two

horses for Bridget's mother (who has got a permit) and both horses won races. We have also trained point to point winners.

We are both totally dedicated to what we want to do + don't care how hard we have to work to make it successful but obviously we need some help + luck to get us on the way.

I have already been assured that I will be able to have a trainers licence, but the Jockey Club just need to know where + when.

Obviously we are principally interested in training jumpers but I would like to have a flat licence as well if it was possible so as to keep the operation going for twelve months of the year.

You asked on the phone whether we were interested in hunting.

We have both been hunting regularly this past season with the Dartmoor Foxhounds and the South Pool Harriers and have days with the Berkeley whenever we can.

Obviously you would like to see your yard built into a successful operation and I obviously want to go in that direction as well so perhaps we could help each other.

Look forward to hearing from you

Yours Sincerely
Paul Nicholls.

The letter to Paul Barber that changed my life.

1

One day I will be famous

One way and another, my weight has had an enormous influence in my life. Just about the only time I weighed in lighter than expected was when I tipped the scales at seven pounds two ounces at birth at the Cottage Hospital, Lydney, Gloucestershire, on 17 April 1962. As a horse-mad schoolboy I was small, slight and so short I could probably have ridden on the flat if anyone had been daft enough to give me the chance. When I started in point-to-points two days before my six-teenth birthday I was still so light I had to put around four stone of lead in extra-weight cloths under the saddle to make up the difference.

Then, suddenly, I shot up to six feet just as I made the decision to become a jump jockey. It would lead to years of starvation, gnawing, nail-biting hunger, depressing daily sessions in the sauna and a dangerous habit of devouring pee pills as if they were Smarties to help my constant battle with the scales. Looking back now, I realise I was living a lie as a jockey, pushing my body to the limit, trying and failing with all sorts of short-term diets that have had a detrimental effect on my long-term health.

On all known family form I was bred to be a policeman. My dad Brian, tall and powerfully built, was a PC in Stroud, Stow-on-the-Wold and Lydney before switching to traffic patrol duty at Staple Hill in the suburbs of Bristol. Soon he was recruited full-time to teach other policemen to drive cars in all situations. He also played as a second-row forward for the British Police rugby team and other local sides. He enjoyed his job so much that when he reached the point where he could have retired he stayed on for another ten years. Mum and Dad now live next to my home in Ditcheat. Even now, in his sixties, he is a commanding figure with a physical presence.

Dad hates being idle and helps me out in so many ways. He is always one of the first in the yard every morning and looks after our two all-weather gallops as if they were his own garden. He met my mum Margaret when she was working in a chemist's shop in Lydney in the Forest of Dean. They married in the village of Bream in December 1960.

Dad's father Frank was a village policeman all his working life in Lydney, Cinderford, Colford, Lydbrook and, finally, Yorkley. He was a giant of a man, twice the size of Dad and me, over six foot two inches, with a barrel chest as broad as the oaks in the Forest of Dean, weightlifter's shoulders and didn't stand any nonsense from cheeky kids.

Frank Nicholls, all nineteen stone of him, was already a fixture for the British Police rugby team in his teens. In full flight he would have taken some stopping. He was a larger than life, hard, no-nonsense village copper, walked miles on his beat every day, sometimes used a bicycle, and knew everyone in his area, including all the local villains who kept their heads down when he was in the vicinity. No one messed with Frank Nicholls. Lord knows what he would have felt about the job today in these politically correct times when policemen seem to have disappeared from the beat and spend all their time filling in forms.

When he retired from the force after twenty-five years, Granddad ran a village shop called the Tinman's Arms in Lydbrook, close to the River Wye. Sometimes I'd spend the day on the road with him in his little Austin A40 delivering bottles or crates of beer and cider to his customers around the Forest of Dean. Once he'd finished work he'd take me fishing on the Wye. He taught me to catch chub or eel and later I'd go off fishing on my own. I wish I had more time for it these days because it is a great way to switch off. Every summer I try to have at least one day's deep-sea fishing with a few friends. We'll hire a boat, load up with some beer and head out to sea without a care in the world.

Sometimes when we visited relatives in the Forest of Dean Dad would lift me on to a little pony called Sparky and take me for a walk on a leading rein. That was the start of a lifelong obsession with horses.

It was my granddad who introduced me to the delights of

horseracing. He was very friendly with Geoff Scudamore, father of Michael, who rode in sixteen consecutive Grand Nationals, and won it on Oxo in 1959, and grandfather of the multiple champion rider Peter Scudamore. My granddad would take Dad racing to Worcester and Hereford when he was a small boy. Frank Nicholls loved racing and used to talk to me for hours about the horses and jockeys of the past. As a regular punter he was quite knowledgeable, though it didn't make finding winners any easier.

Granddad never missed the opportunity to have a go at the most popular bet of the time, the ITV Seven on races shown on television each Saturday. He followed certain jockeys and allowed me an interest by giving me a Crunchie bar if my selection won. At the time Fred Winter had a series of top-class horses ridden by Richard Pitman. The combination was so dominant that I often relied on Pitman to deliver my afternoon snack. I nicknamed him Crunchie Pitman and have warm memories of shouting him home on quite a few decent winners.

I was only five or six at the time, but watching racing on television stirred my imagination. From the earliest age I can remember wanting to have a go on a pony. That posed a problem because none of my family had any connection with horses. Nor did Mum and Dad have the funds to buy me an expensive pony, but once they realised I was serious they backed me to the hilt. Basically we taught ourselves as we went along.

As beginners we experimented with some dodgy, cheap ponies who knew much more about the business than we did but we got lucky with our first one called Surprise, a small Welsh grey who quickly became part of the family. We kept him in a stable in the field next to the police house at Kingswood, where we lived. When we moved to another police house in Almondsbury in 1969, Dad rented a field behind the police station and built a couple of makeshift boxes.

Falling off ponies was all part of the fun. Some tried to dump me and others refused to budge when I jumped on their backs. Soon I was having riding lessons at Leyland Court, a riding school run by Mike and Jennifer Irish at Winterbourne, near Bristol. Mike was an ex-jump jockey who served his apprenticeship with Phil Doherty near Cheltenham at the same time as Richard Pitman. His claim to fame is that he rode the winner of the Grand National in Kenya.

I became great friends with Mike and Jennifer's sons Robin and

Martin, who were both keen on riding, particularly Robin. We'd charge round the cross-country course at Leyland Court, larking about, pretending to be jockeys. Naturally I used to call myself Crunchie Pitman, though we never imagined for a minute that we'd ever ride in a race.

Most lads at my school rushed off to play football and cricket the moment they left the classroom. I didn't have much of an eye for a ball, was rubbish at games and not much better at running. That didn't stop me being selected for the school's cross-country team with a lad called Nick Oakhill after a wheeze during training worked against us. One of the things I hated most about school was having to go for a cross-country run at the end of the afternoon. This involved two laps through the same wood. Nick and I worked out that life would be easier if we hid behind a tree on the first circuit and jumped in again second time round. This backfired on us spectacularly when we finished fifth and sixth and found ourselves selected for the school team. Needless to say, we never produced that form again and were swiftly dropped from the squad.

I hated school in so many ways and couldn't wait to get away once lessons were over. Some people believe their schooldays were the best of their lives, but for me they were a constant nightmare. All the time I wanted to be anywhere else but the classroom. Part of the problem was that I couldn't concentrate for more than a few minutes. I loathed maths, and wasn't much better at other subjects, but managed to scrape by with a minimum of effort. I made it so obvious I wasn't interested in French lessons that for two years I was allowed to spend the time working on a French racing project. In reality this involved nothing more strenuous than studying French racing, which was not too difficult as by then I was hooked on the sport. My homework basically involved cutting out articles from the *Sporting Life* and other newspapers and sticking them into an album.

All I ever wanted to do was spend time with my ponies and I quickly progressed to competing in gymkhanas every weekend. I could ride after a fashion and was fiercely competitive from the start. My sister Julie, eighteen months younger, rode too, so we both had ponies. One of the first gymkhanas I took part in was at a farm close to the River Severn where a canny character called Dick Baimbridge kept a big flock of sheep. I was already friends with his two children, Ann and

Mark, through the Berkeley pony club. Dick had a big reputation in the point-to-point world and would become my mentor in the years ahead.

I used to be badly bullied at school for preferring ponies and horses to other sports. Because I showed no interest in kicking a ball and seemed to be the only one keen on riding, some boys decided I was the odd man out and a bit of a girlie. They were not slow to point out their view that riding was a girl's sport. Because I was small, chirpy and not slow to stand up for myself I used to get a fair bit of stick, particularly at primary school. If anyone gave me any gyp I'd fire straight back like a terrier. Even then I would never walk away. On a couple of occasions my reaction led to a bit of a hiding but you soon learn to duck and dive when your tormentors are much bigger than you.

Julie would cry when the bullies hit me. I didn't enjoy it much either because they wouldn't leave me alone. It was not a happy time but it didn't bother me as much as Julie and I managed to deal with it without any dramas. I'm probably stronger for it. All the teasing and cheap shots just made me more determined to be a better rider.

The next step was to go hunting with the Berkeley. The first time, aged seven, I spent the day on my little grey pony, Surprise, on a leading rein with Buster Daniell, the wife of John Daniell, who is a great Berkeley man and a point-to-point legend in that part of the world. They swiftly took me under their wing. I loved everything about my first experience of hunting and couldn't wait to do it again. To this day I am a huge supporter of hunting and the point-to-point scene. I keep a few pointers in a livery yard and on the rare occasion I have a day off at the weekend I enjoy nothing more than an afternoon at Larkhill, Badbury Rings, or Charlton Horethorne. It is a brilliant way for me to switch off.

Our family's friendship with Mike and Jennifer Irish developed to the point that when they took a holiday we would all move into Leyland Court to look after the place. They used to leave their boys Robin and Martin behind so that they could continue at school. For me it was a huge bonus to have the chance to be riding for hours each day with like-minded friends. Even better, I had dozens of decent ponies to choose from. Mum has never had much to do with ponies and horses but after some initial reluctance she has supported me all the way.

Apparently she threatened to leave Dad if he bought a pony for Julie and me. Luckily, she wasn't serious and was soon involved in the planning of all our days out at the weekend shows. Mum has always been a calming influence on the rest of us. Dad can be quite fiery and I had my moments, too, so she had a fair bit to put up with. I knew I could always talk to her about any problems. They were strict parents, but always fair, and taught us the value of honesty and hard work.

Money was pretty tight back then for our parents to be indulging us with ponies. Yet if we wanted a better saddle or bridle for our ponies, they would always try to help out, though we were encouraged to make a contribution from our pocket money. We were also expected to share the daily tasks of mucking out and feeding the ponies. Dad had an ordinary job in the police and we lived in a police house without any frills.

Because I was so small I was always getting run away with on my ponies. The more I fought them the more they enjoyed carting me. If I had to bail out, or fell off anyway, I loved it even more. At that age you are fearless; you'd try to jump big hedges and rails without hesitation. If you got buried you just picked yourself up and remounted. Though I didn't suffer any bad injuries I more than made up for it when I started race riding. Mum and Dad used to run the gymkhana ring at Almondsbury Show each summer but there was no favouritism involved when the judges awarded me the annual trophy for the most sporting rider after a wild Shetland pony dropped me at least six times during the afternoon. Apparently they chose me because I kept remounting. Four years ago my life turned full circle when I returned to the Almondsbury Show to present the same cup.

My progress in the saddle came to an abrupt halt when I was ten after I set off a fire extinguisher at the guest house where we were staying on holiday in the Isle of Wight. Bored at being sent to bed early with Julie, I started playing with the extinguisher at the top of the stairs. The next moment it went off with an almighty explosion that must have terrified the neighbours.

My parents rushed out of the sitting room to discover an avalanche of foam and water cascading down the stairs. I was caught bang to rights on the landing as my mum and dad fought a losing battle to limit the damage. What made it worse for me was that Mum was wearing a smart new outfit she'd bought for the holiday. By the time she had finished clearing up her trouser suit was ruined and my dreams of a new pony with it. I crept back to bed with the words of my dad ringing in my ears: 'Your pony is going and you will never ride a horse again.'

He said it and he meant it, which left me feeling miserable for the rest of the holiday. But time is a great healer and, shortly after we returned home, Dad relented. It helped, of course, that he enjoyed messing around with the ponies as much as I did. Although he was a late starter he was involved in everything I did at that stage. By punishing me he discovered that he was punishing himself, too. Soon we were ready for the next stage in my riding education.

Most of the ponies Dad bought me had question marks about them because he couldn't afford the finished article. Since we both like a challenge, we enjoyed bringing them along, making them into better ponies and sometimes selling them on. When Dad bought a really fast pony, a chestnut mare, from Mike Irish called Hint of a Tint for £300, we decided to take the plunge and try our luck at pony racing, which was rather frowned on in those days. Just to be on the safe side Dad suggested that I rode under the disguise of Paul Frank, Frank being my middle name. This might sound a bit dramatic but we were new-comers to the twilight world of a sport widely known as flapping and didn't want to take any risks.

We headed for Brockenhurst in the New Forest with high hopes. With a livewire pony like Hint of a Tint there was no need for long tactical discussions. I jumped her off in front, made all the running and won with something to spare. All the winners that day ran again in a grand final with a staggered start. As the youngest rider on the smallest pony I was in pole position. The starter then told my dad that I should ignore his flag and go the moment he touched his tie. Maybe he had a few quid on Hint of a Tint. I followed my instructions, pinched a dozen lengths when he touched his tie, and never saw another pony. Hint of a Tint proved a wonderful schoolmistress for me. We shared so many victories, though all our winning was done well away from home in case of repercussions. At the time I was tiny, extremely light and not very stylish but I was pretty sharp in a race and quickly became hooked on pony racing.

Our next move from Almondsbury to Olveston was highly signifi-cant because it was the first house my parents had owned. When I was eleven I was sent to Marlwood School, which is not an experience I recall with any pleasure. Looking back now I think school was a complete waste of time; the exams I passed don't seem to have done me any good. Whatever I've set out to achieve I've always relied on common sense to help me through.

In Olveston we rented a paddock and two old-fashioned stables for our ponies in a barn within easy reach. To help towards the cost of the ponies Julie and I started an egg round. Each Thursday after school Dad would drive us to a local farm where we'd collect twenty dozen eggs, maybe more. We'd then set off on foot round the village delivering half a dozen here and a dozen there. Naturally we were paid in cash. Quite soon we built up a thriving little business. Given the time I reckon I could have made a decent living as an egg salesman.

Julie and I progressed to taking part in midnight steeplechases at Leyland Court but, to Dad's dismay, she wasn't quite as competitive as me. Once, as she was winning, she eased up a fraction just before the line to pat her pony called Paddy. This allowed Mark Pitman, later a successful jockey, to nip past and snatch the verdict. Julie was thrilled to finish second; Dad was furious that she had allowed herself to be caught. I had a lot of fun with Robin Irish in pony races at night on the greyhound track at Brean Sands under such feeble floodlights that we had to rely on the headlights of Land Rovers placed at strategic points to see where we were going. The course was narrow and the bends incredibly sharp but our ponies seemed to have terrific eyesight and didn't hesitate as they charged flat out into the first turn. Hint of a Tint was almost unbeatable at Brean and won many a cup for me.

Already I was set on a life with horses, to the dismay of my teachers who urged me to reconsider. One of them, David Goldring, frequently poured scorn on my dreams of becoming a jockey. Fully aware that I got through each day doing the minimum in class, he was convinced I was a waster. Mr Goldring, who was also our careers officer, once told me, 'You will never make a living out of horses.' His words acted like a red rag to a bull.

Drawing myself up to my full height of five foot four, I replied in icy tones, 'Nobody believes me but I am going to be a jockey one day and I will be famous!' A couple of years ago he asked me back to Marlwood to give a talk on my career in racing. I began by saying that I honestly believed the time I spent at school was the worst of my life; and followed up by adding that, although the meals were consistently bad, they would be pleased to see that I'd finally got over my anorexia!

Days spent hunting with the Berkeley increased my ambition to work in racing. I loved jumping at speed and wasn't put off by a series of falls. Once, spectacularly, a sparky mare called Flyby, owned by Mike Irish, buried me as she tried to gallop through a five-barred gate. The plan was to stay with the huntsman all day, but that came to an abrupt and painful halt when Flyby turned a somersault. I was lucky to escape with a split lip and a bleeding nose. You don't expect any sympathy in the hunting field so I dusted myself down, wiped my face, jumped back on and set off again.

I didn't necessarily set out to become a jockey or become addicted to racing. It just happened. The man who made it all possible was Dick Baimbridge, already at that stage in the mid 1970s a master at training point-to-pointers. Dick had a gift for buying difficult horses at rock-bottom prices and turning them into prolific winners. In 2008 he reached a notable landmark when he trained his 500th point-to-point winner at the age of seventy-eight and is particularly proud of his exploits with Mendip Express, who won thirty-eight races for him. He maintains that Mendip Express was the thinnest horse he ever trained, so light that he resembled an anorexic teenager. The horse, which had come from the knacker's yard, and was prone to colic, was transformed by regular drenching with milk, eggs, cod liver oil and vitamins. Dick still farms at Hill, a mile or so from the River Severn.

He also had a gift for bringing along decent young jockeys, most notably Alison Dare, who became champion lady rider six times while working for him and rode more point-to-point winners than any girl in the sport. But he had his hands full in trying to convert me into a jockey. I started working for him at weekends and in the school holidays, when I was barely thirteen, and joined him full-time as soon as I left school at sixteen. Sometimes my dad would drop me off at his farm early in the morning. When he wasn't free I'd jump on my bike and cycle the nine or so miles through narrow country lanes to his yard.

Dick Baimbridge had a well-deserved reputation as a hard taskmaster. To this day he is a perfectionist who expects every job in the yard to be done properly. There were no short cuts or skiving off work and he wasn't slow to hand out bollockings to lads who earned his displeasure. Some couldn't take it and walked out; not many survived for long. I think I was the only one who stayed because I never minded long hours or hard work and when he told me off in sharp tones, as he frequently did, it was just like water off a duck's back. Dick was a hard chap who used to bollock me every other day. He laughs now when he tells his friends that he used to cuss me 'something terrible' and call me all sorts of things. Though he blew his top a fair bit, he never held a grudge and it was all forgotten in two minutes. That was just his way because he wanted things done right with up to eight point-to-pointers in training at any one time.

The truth is that all the bollockings didn't bother me at all. I'd spend many happy hours at his farm riding the horses, mucking them out, fencing, haymaking and repairing the schooling jumps. We also broke in horses and took hunters at livery. I didn't quite manage to master the art of sheep shearing, but was pretty useful at rolling up the fleeces into bundles and putting them in a big bag. You had to fold them, roll them into a ball, then wind up the cord and tighten the knot. That was hard work. We didn't have regular hours and you didn't last long if you had one eye on the clock. You simply kept going until all the jobs were finished.

A tough, no-nonsense countryman, Dick had a huge influence on me. The bonus was that I got to go hunting twice a week on his horses with the Berkeley, which boasted big, blackthorn hedges and deep ditches. I was so lucky to join Dick Baimbridge at an impressionable age and have no doubt that I learned more from him in the next five years than from any of the trainers I subsequently rode for. To this day I use many of the methods he taught me, in particular making sure all my horses have plenty of rugs in their boxes. When they were out at exercise he never put a sheet on them. That changed once they were back in the yard. 'They can't keep themselves warm when they are still,' he told me on numerous occasions. It was brilliant advice.

Dick had all sorts of tricky horses through his hands. He called the most difficult ones villains and always said the only way to make them civil was to get them as fit as possible. He did this by breezing flat out round Berkeley Park for up to two miles and with short, sharp work up the steep banks on his farm. He says he can still remember the excitement in my voice when I rang in June 1991 to tell him that I had found a place to train with a hill just like his.

My first, adventurous gallop as a tiny thirteen-year-old came following Dick in the park. On his farm we'd jump rails, hedges, gates and all sorts of other obstacles on the way round. I thought it was fabulous. We didn't use hard hats or crash helmets in those days. Instead we used to whizz along with our cloth caps turned round so that they didn't fly off our heads. I don't mind admitting I got carted every time. Not that it bothered me much.

I was very light in my early teens, and quite weak. All too aware that I was struggling to hold one side of any horse I rode, Dick encouraged me to relax my vice-like grip on the reins. 'Don't fight them, just try to ride them on a long rein and they will eventually switch off. If you fight them they will fight you,' he'd call out as I was about to disappear over the horizon. If my mount was still running away he'd suggest I virtually let go of the reins. What's more, it worked. I soon discovered that holding hard-pulling horses is not so much about strength as knack and confidence. Dick rode everything himself, shod his own horses and fed them four times a day.

Although my mum harboured doubts about me working with horses for a living, my mind was made up by the time I was fifteen. I loved every minute of the days I spent with Dick Baimbridge at weekends and holidays. To further my education my parents suggested I spent part of my summer holidays working for John Haine, who trained a team of flat horses near Stroud.

The month I spent as a lad with Haine almost put me off racing for life. I stayed in lodgings a couple of miles from the yard, cycled to work and hated every minute, partly because I was constantly homesick and lonely and partly because just about everything I rode tried to run away with me. I couldn't hold anything, had no interest in flat racing, and was thrilled when the month was over. Although Haine had been a wonderfully gifted jump jockey, he hardly ever seemed to be around in the mornings. Nor did he ride out or appear when we dressed the horses over at evening stables. It was so different from the hands-on approach of Dick Baimbridge and I couldn't wait to return to the familiar routine at his stables.

There was an added incentive to work hard as winter approached. After a family conference my parents agreed to buy a schoolmaster for me to ride in point-to-points when the new season came round in the spring of 1978. None of us had much of a clue about buying racehorses back then; nor did we have any capital to finance our new venture. We started looking for a suitable old jumper with the intention of training him ourselves from the field we rented near home. Once we'd done the preparatory work he'd be transferred to Dick Baimbridge for a racing campaign.

We bought Lucky Edgar from his owner, Lord Ullswater, on the advice of Captain Rollo Clifford, a joint master of the Berkeley. The horse was twelve with a lot of mileage on the clock but that didn't put us off one bit. Dad and Dick Baimbridge both felt I needed a safe conveyance to start on and he fitted the bill because he was such a sound, careful jumper. Hopefully, he'd be an ideal tutor for me. Lucky Edgar had been a decent horse in his prime, winning on the flat, over hurdles and fences before landing the 1976 Grand Military Gold Cup at Sandown ridden by Sandy Cramsie. But he finished in the rear in the same race twelve months later, always wore blinkers and had become increasingly unreliable, which was probably why he was for sale. Encouraged by Captain Clifford and egged on by me, Dad rang Lord Ullswater and agreed a price of £300 for Lucky Edgar on the understanding that he was going to a good home.

I can still recall my excitement as we collected Lucky Edgar from stables not far from Wincanton, and loaded him into our trailer. He was a powerfully built chestnut, with a bold head and surprisingly clean legs after almost one hundred races, though I realised he was far from a young jockey's dream. His most recent form suggested he was quite slow, in decline and no longer interested in getting involved at the business end of a race. He was also cheap and, best of all, he was now mine and would be my launching pad as a jockey. To help spread the costs, Dad passed on third shares to two friends, Alan Taylor, our local newsagent, and George Deverson. We turned Lucky Edgar out to grass for a summer's break at Olveston while my grandmother, Lucy, set about knitting a jersey in my soon to be registered racing colours of gold with red sleeves and cap. My life would never be the same again.

2

A master class in training

My dad supported my involvement with horses in so many ways. He never seemed to mind going without certain things as long as I did my share of the work. To help towards the cost of Lucky Edgar's keep, I started a part-time job in the local bakery. It was a strange episode in my life. I was fifteen and impatient to break free from the shackles of school. My weekend egg round wasn't enough on its own to make a meaningful contribution. I needed another regular source of income to go towards the bills that would be incurred by my new racehorse during the point-to-point season.

I'd reached a crucial point in my education. Since horses dominated my thoughts my plan was to muddle through my O levels, leave school and work full-time for Dick Baimbridge. Naturally, my mum had different ideas. Like so many mothers she was determined that her son should pass his exams before learning a trade which would provide a steady living. Only then, she insisted, could I indulge my dreams by working with horses, though she'd have much preferred me to stay at school for another two years until I was eighteen. What's more, she explained, if I didn't get at least six O levels I wouldn't be leaving school. Instead, I'd have to take the exams again. As usual, Mum only had my best interests at heart. Dad was more pragmatic and backed my plan to join Dick Baimbridge. Eventually we agreed an uneasy truce.

I didn't fancy following the family tradition as a policeman. Nor did I wish to continue my studies in higher education. I was set on working with horses, despite opposition at home. At the time Mum used to help out in the shop at a bakery run by Chris Curtis at Olveston. Chris had an opening for a young part-timer prepared to work unsociable hours. It was hardly the job opportunity I craved, but it did offer a timely compromise.

After a fair bit of bargaining on my part, Mum eventually agreed that I could work at the bakery during weekends and school holidays, then head off to Dick's yard as soon as my early shift was over. I am sure she hoped that I'd enjoy the work sufficiently to take up a trade myself as a baker or shopkeeper. Deep down, however, she must have realised there was no chance of that happening. She knew I wasn't going to do anything else because I had a one-track mind. I'd learned to cook at school and, though I say it myself, I was quite handy around the kitchen even if I was never going to become a master baker. Those four hours I spent each morning baking cakes and making doughnuts nearly drove me crazy. I'd be up at 4.00 a.m. and flat out at work by 5.00, dressed in the usual baker's kit of apron, trousers and white hat. As the newest employee I became the general dogsbody, cleaning up behind others. The only thing that kept me going was the knowledge that my modest wages were helping to pay for Lucky Edgar's keep.

It was hot work, mind-numbingly tedious and I counted the minutes every morning until I could escape. After months of this purgatory I reached the limit of my patience and can remember telling Dick I had to escape from the bakery. There was nothing subtle about my plan; it was simple and destructive and I achieved my objective just as I hoped. One of my jobs was to prepare and cook doughnuts by filling each one with jam then rolling it in sugar. Not on my last day working for Chris Curtis. That morning I rolled them all in salt, then left the shop confident that I wouldn't be welcome back. My life as a baker was over!

I spent the late autumn of 1977 preparing Lucky Edgar for a programme of races in the spring. I'd ride him most days, sometimes before school, sometimes afterwards, and we'd also go hunting with the Berkeley most weekends, though he was a bit of a mule when it came to jumping the bigger fences. Then I'd spend at least an hour strapping and grooming him every evening. I looked after him and the other point-to-pointers that followed as if they were Gold Cup contenders, which, in a sense, to me they were.

Much of Lucky Edgar's work was done on the roads and grass verges around Olveston. We'd trot briskly up Vicarage Lane, a steep hill going out of the village, walk down the other side then trot back up again. For the next stage I used to do lots of sprinting on the same two grass verges. He proved to be a terrific jumper when I popped him over some fences, but we had our disagreements because he liked to have his own way. Early in January 1978 I applied for my point-to-point riders' certificate. It arrived around the same time we transferred Lucky Edgar to Dick Baimbridge. The rules then prevented anyone under sixteen riding in point-to-points. I waited impatiently on the sidelines and managed to slip under the radar by making my debut at the West Somerset Vale meeting on 15 April 1978, two days before my birthday.

We paid £1 to enter Lucky Edgar in a hot-looking Open race that offered £40 to the winner and I changed into my racing colours in the corner of a cramped little marquee. I remember that weighing out was quite a performance because Lucky Edgar was set to carry twelve stone seven pounds and I was probably a little over eight and a half stone wet through. Dick Baimbridge solved the problem with a heavy weighted saddle and two additional weight cloths loaded with pieces of lead to make up the difference. Standing on the scales with that lot in my arms convinced me I'd never become a weightlifter.

I knew a couple of the riders as I'd led them up at the races. Others taking part included several of the leading names in the sport. It was a bit scary waiting for the call to the paddock, although I had a fair idea what to expect after taking many of Dick's runners to the races over the previous three years. I was nervous at what lay ahead but also thrilled to be involved. I'd been waiting half my life for this moment and received plenty of advice from Dad, Dick and friends in the Berkeley Hunt. Our expectations were not high but that didn't prevent Dad having a fiver on Lucky Edgar on the Tote at huge odds. With twenty-one runners, including some decent, in-form hunter chasers, we had no chance of winning. My horse would definitely benefit from the outing and, as for the jockey, well, I just planned to do my best, keep out of trouble and hopefully finish.

The race lasted six minutes and ten seconds. For me it passed in a blur and it was just as well Lucky Edgar was a lot wiser than me. He dropped himself out at the start, hacked round at the back, jumped soundly and brought me home safely in fourteenth place. I got a rear view of it all, hung on for dear life at the fences and wasn't fit enough to hit him to try to wake his ideas up. By the end we were almost walking. I'd been pushing for so long on Lucky Edgar that I was speechless as Mum, Dad and Julie rushed up to greet us. I was tickled pink to finish and couldn't wait to do it again.

Over the following month Lucky Edgar and I raced together three more times. We got a bit more involved in the early stages before finishing last of nine at the North Ledbury. Next came the highlight of my first season in the Berkeley Hunt race. The opposition was modest and Lucky Edgar had the form in the past but unfortunately I lacked the skill to motivate him. We were fifth at halfway but he didn't want to know and we soon lost touch before finishing a distant fourth. I knew then that I was never going to win a race on Lucky Edgar, because it takes two to tango and I couldn't manage it on my own.

A week later, on 13 May, we had our final outing of the campaign over four miles at Larkhill. We might as well have stayed at home as Lucky Edgar trundled round in the last trio, never out of first gear. The more I pushed, slapped and shouted at him the less he was inclined to exert himself. Eventually he pulled himself up four fences from home. I was red-faced, angry and frustrated. He couldn't care less. At least he'd given me a safe introduction to a sport that would dominate my life, but I knew it was only a matter of time before Lucky Edgar would be on the transfer list. It was a sobering end to a forgettable first season. The authors of *The Hunter Chasers and Point-to-Pointers Annual* didn't mince their words on Lucky Edgar: 'Doggy now and wears blinkers. Used as a schoolmaster in 1978 and took his diminutive rider round safely'.

After the crushing disappointment of Larkhill I settled down to serious revision before taking my O levels. Normally I skipped homework without a moment's hesitation, but to keep the peace at home I knew I had to make an effort on this occasion. At the back of my mind was the fear that, if I failed to come up to scratch in the exams, I'd have return to school for another year to take them all again. That terrified me.

Once my last term at school was over in the summer I started working full-time for Dick Baimbridge. The results of my final exams were surprisingly good, given that I'd spent most of the past couple of years daydreaming in class. I achieved six O levels and left Marlwood

School without a backward glance. The next day we began haymaking at Dick's farm. My life in racing was about to begin.

I earned around £18 a week for long hours that would horrify today's trade union leaders. When I was needed I'd be there seven days a week. It got to the point on my rare days off when I hated not being at the yard. If you worked hard and pulled your weight, it was a really rewarding way of life. I was hooked on it all. I loved the work, the sport, the training, the hunting and the way Dick got his horses fit up the hill. I enjoyed every moment of my time with Dick and his wife Joyce. They treated me like one of their own sons. Dick's attention to detail was unbelievable. Though I didn't know it at the time, I was receiving a master class in the art of training horses to win races. It was a brilliant education. I know Dick regrets not taking the plunge and setting up on his own full-time as a professional. He was certainly tempted more than once but wasn't sure he could handle the pressure of the job. I have no doubt that he could have trained plenty of winners, but as a private man who likes to do things his own way he wouldn't have taken any nonsense from difficult owners. That would have made life difficult for him.

We used to canter up the hill banks, turn straight back down and do it all again several times. Dick would also take horses for a twenty-minute canter, then sprint them along the ridges of some fields. I cannot tell you how much work we used to do on them. As he couldn't afford an all-weather gallop he created the next best thing by taking out a hedge on an uphill stretch of ground and then spreading the muck and shavings from the stables on the grass. Then we could go straight up over the top of the hill. Dick got his horses jumping a variety of obstacles, including hunt jumps, poles and rails. When the ground was suitable in the meadow he'd also build two schooling fences. More often than not we'd be cantering round the farm and he'd say 'Follow me' and take on three or four hedges in a row.

My daily journey from Olveston to Hill took less time once I spent some of my wages on a 50cc motorbike that was little more than a puddle jumper. It was quicker than my bike, just, and reached the dizzy speed of 25mph with a following wind. A year later I moved up in the world by changing to a little yellow Honda SS50. I used to fall off it every other day!

Once the horses were back in training I'd spend hours strapping them in the afternoons. That used to be standard practice in every racing yard in the country in the dim and distant past. Not any more because there is simply not enough time. Dick taught me how to strap horses. He'd take a wisp of hay in his hand and then slap and brush them on their quarters for twenty minutes at a time to tone up their muscles. It was a bit like giving them a massage and did them the world of good.

My second season riding in point-to-points wasn't a great deal better than my first. I was a year older, a little bit stronger and had more firepower after some friends got together to take shares in a couple of horses bought cheaply by Dad to give me more chances. One of them, French William, had some pretty desperate form in Kent, but we hoped we might improve him. At the price we were prepared to take a chance. He ran in the name of Chris Curtis, my old boss from my days at his bakery in Olveston. Clearly I had been forgiven for the doughnut incident.

French William fell on our debut, jarring my collarbone, but gave me hope for the future by finishing fourth in his next race. He then ran out with me at the last fence with victory in sight in a decent Open race on Easter Monday 1979, at Hackwood Park. It was an incident that left me with two lasting impressions. I still have an ugly lump on my left thigh from the haematoma I collected as he crashed through the wing of the fence. And I have never forgotten the bollocking I got from Dick for allowing French William to be squeezed out just as we were coming to win. It was no more than I deserved.

Much to my surprise, French William travelled like a dream in the leading group that day. This was an entirely new experience for me and I couldn't resist poking up at the fences between the two front runners ridden by Robert Alner and John Dufosee, two of the canniest riders on the West Country point-to-point circuit. They didn't appreciate this cheeky young pup snapping busily at their heels and retribution was not long in coming. As Alner's mount weakened on the run to the last I made my bid for glory and went for a gap on the inside of Dufosee and Hesitation. Given a good jump we'd probably have won. But the opening suddenly narrowed in the final strides before the fence as Dufosee edged over as he sensed the threat appearing beside him. With nowhere to go, French William panicked, dived violently through the wing and turned upside down.

I was shocked, upset and in terrible pain after colliding with the upright of the fence. I was also lucky not to have broken my thigh and as my parents rushed up a woman standing by the fence told Mum that she had never heard language like it from a small boy. If I expected Dick to console me I was in for a nasty shock. He was furious that I had thrown away a winning opportunity. He told me exactly what he thought and left me to pick up the pieces. It hurt at the time but when things are said in that manner it makes you pay attention. I took my medicine and learned a valuable lesson. After seeing that fall my poor mum was frantic with worry every time I hit the deck. To ease her fears I promised I'd wave a white flag to let her know I was OK.

French William fell with me again next time while going well in the Berkeley Members race and failed to sparkle in his final two outings. *The Hunter Chasers and Point-to-Pointers Annual* showed no mercy in describing him as doggy and a reluctant jumper. But that didn't prevent them carrying a photograph of the pair of us on the front cover jumping a fence at the North Warwickshire Open. I am sitting up his neck just like a flat jockey, lean and light and surprisingly small. Well, they say a picture never lies!

By this stage I knew quite a few of the riders on the point-to-point circuit. One who took me under his wing was a tough-as-teak character called Bob Woolley, a square, short-legged figure with long, shaggy sideburns, a broad grin and a passionate love of hunting. Bob often took the time to offer me a word of encouragement. He worked for years as a coalminer, was an incredibly tough competitor and a diamond beneath the rough exterior. He was first offered rides after making a habit of catching loose horses that had fallen and hacking them back to their owners near the horsebox park. It was a novel introduction to race riding but he progressed to win ninety-nine races in a long, colourful career. I thought the world of him and was devastated when he broke his neck in a fall in May 1985 which led to his premature death four years later.

I also had three rides in 1979 on Lucky Edgar, who'd earned a brief reprieve in the hope that a break might rekindle his interest. He was fourteen by then and much too long in the tooth to be competitive, so we sold him on. It was an early example of something else that Dick Baimbridge taught me. Racehorses are not pets, he insisted. You can't become too sentimental about them. Lucky Edgar was my first horse, he was bought to do a job and it was time to move him on.

In the autumn of 1979 Dick and Dad bought two more horses at the Ascot Sales which we hoped might finally deliver my first winner. Both ran in my name but we could not have done it without the loyal support of people like Chris Curtis and Alan Taylor. Lahzim, well-bred and imposing, cost only 360 guineas and we soon discovered why. He fell with me at the first fence on his debut, then pulled up lame on his only other run for us. He had a tremendous engine but his fragile legs couldn't stand training. Energy Saver, who cost 1,200 guineas, was more promising. He'd had at least half a dozen trainers down the years, including Jack Berry and Eric Cousins, without showing much ability, but his victory in a maiden point-to-point persuaded us to buy him at Ascot.

I made a bad start on Energy Saver when we fell heavily at the Beaufort on 1 March 1980. Somebody must have spotted some promise before we parted company because, two days later, Energy Saver started favourite in a division of the Restricted Open at the North Herefordshire. He ran well, too, in finishing a clear second after we chased the winner in vain for the last mile. We raised our sights next time by running him in a hunter chase at Chepstow. Although Energy Saver was a 25–1 shot, he didn't let me down by finishing second to Tartan Prince ridden by a pencil-slim amateur jockey Nigel Twiston-Davies, who has been training horses much longer than me.

The fact that Energy Saver was running on stoutly at the finish at Chepstow over three miles and three furlongs confirmed my view that he stayed really well and relished muddy conditions, so my hopes rose as we arrived at Nedge for his next race on 22 March to discover that the ground was heavy. Energy Saver, the favourite, was fit and in form so I was determined to make use of his stamina. We jumped out among the leaders, were always in the first three, took up the running at halfway and squelched home in front by two lengths. The first winner is the hardest of all. After so many disappointments you think it will never come. It was a brilliant feeling to win on Energy Saver, but Dick made sure it didn't last long by putting me to work mucking out half a dozen horses as soon as we got back to his yard. Which was just as well as I had to wait for almost a year before the next winner came along.

It didn't take me long to discover the downside of racing. Just over a fortnight later I was marched in front of the stewards after making a fool of myself on French William. He'd lost all interest in racing that spring and had become a pig of a horse. In four races he didn't try a yard with me. When he refused to try at Upton-on-Severn I lost my temper halfway through the race and gave him a hiding. It probably looked worse than it was because at that stage I didn't have a clue how to use the whip, let alone hit one in the right place. I was summoned before the stewards with Dick Baimbridge acting as my defence counsel and was lucky to escape with a severe warning.

Worse followed a week later at the same course when a nice old horse called Crushed Oats dropped dead moments after we finished fourth in the Open. I sensed something was wrong as we pulled up, and jumped off his back just before he keeled over. It was a horrible shock for me and even nastier for his owner, Bob Forsyth, a friend of my dad's, and all the racegoers standing close to the finishing line. A few minutes earlier he'd been sailing along in the lead, ears pricked, without a care in the world. He was fourteen, had enjoyed a great innings with the best of care and died doing what he loved best. I felt then and still do that there are many worse ways to go.

I ended the season by trying to break the land speed record on my first ride at Cheltenham on a horse called Rosy Can, trained by Robin Matthew. I was probably mad to take the mount but when you are a lad you'll do anything for a ride round a place like Cheltenham. I wasn't aware of the risks then and thought it was all a bit of fun. Rosy Can had no obvious ability, nor any brakes, but at least she could jump. She used to go like the wind until she was exhausted. She dumped me before the start and I barely had time to remount before she tore off into the lead at a hundred miles an hour. I was pretty much a passenger as we soared over the fences at a pace I had never experienced before. You can't sustain that tempo for very long and when the whirlwind had run its course she stopped very quickly and pulled herself up. I will never forget that hairy ride. As for Cheltenham, it made no impact on me at all.

Since Dick Baimbridge didn't employ me in the summer, when the horses were turned out, I furthered my racing education by working for Toby Balding for a few weeks. During a long career Toby enjoyed no end of success at the highest level but his lasting legacy has been the legion of jockeys he produced from his yard at Weyhill, near Andover. He is one of racing's greatest enthusiasts, loves to encourage young people to do well in life and knows just about everyone in the game. I have huge respect for Toby and relished the time I spent working for him. It was fun to be part of his team.

Before I left to return to Dick Baimbridge I walked into Toby's office and put him on the spot. 'You've seen enough of my riding here every day. Is it worth me trying to become a professional jockey and making a career of it or am I wasting my time?' I asked. I was quite expecting him to say I had no chance of making the grade; or, perhaps, let me down gently. So you can imagine my surprise and delight when he encouraged me to give it a go. I can still remember his words now.

'You need to improve your riding but you are keen enough to do it and basically you've got a future. The more rides you have the better you will become. I think you should go for it and if I can help I will,' he said. It was a generous offer and he was as good as his word. Once I received my amateur permit he gave me my only ride on the flat at Ascot on Casabuck in September 1980. I can't have made a complete fool of myself because Toby soon gave me another chance on The Vinegar Man, who finished third under top weight in a three-mile chase at Lingfield. I wasn't getting carried away at this stage. I never rated myself as a jockey because I knew I was far from a natural rider and didn't look great in the saddle. I was also the wrong shape and still weak, particularly in the closing stages. I tried to make up for that by attempting to think like a jockey through a race even if I didn't look much like one.

My growing ambition to make a career in racing was shaken after seeing an amateur called Ray Callow on the receiving end of the most terrifying bollocking from Ron Hodges, a trainer, who, ironically, is now one of my best friends. Ron is a lovely man, warm-hearted, generous and amusing, but on this occasion he lost it completely after Ray was beaten on one of his called Yalo Boy in a novice chase at Hereford.

Perhaps I was still a bit wet behind the ears but in all my years involved with horses I have never heard anyone cussed like it. Ron called Ray every name under the sun. It so nearly put me off to the point that I remember saying to Dad, 'If that is typical of racing I don't think I want to be involved in this.' So you can imagine how I felt a few weeks later when I was chosen by Hodges to ride Yalo Boy at Exeter after Callow was injured. It was Toby Balding who put me in for the ride. The first I knew of it was at about five o'clock in the morning of the race when I returned home after a wild night out to discover a note from Mum on the fridge. If I'd heard about it the previous day I'd have been in bed by nine. Instead, I had to face the ferocious Hodges with hardly a wink of sleep. I drove to Exeter quaking in my boots but he put me at my ease, told me how to ride the horse and, to my immense relief, didn't offer a word of criticism when Yalo Boy finished unplaced.

My final year as a point-to-point rider in 1981 brought two more wins on Wynsor House 11 and an injury that could have ended my career before it had really started. We bought Wynsor House 11 cheaply on the advice of his previous owner, Bill Walter, and started him off in hunter chases. We might have won the second one, too, but for falling in the lead. Jumping was an issue with him throughout the season. If he met a fence on a stride he was fine but if he was wrong he tended to plough through them as if they didn't exist. His form definitely improved with Dick Baimbridge; he had bags of stamina and when he stood up he was usually involved in the finish. We survived several blunders before winning for the first time together at the Mendip meeting on 28 February in the colours of Chris Curtis, my old boss at the bakery.

A month later I had a painful introduction to the darker side of racing on my first ride for Kevin Bishop, one of the youngest trainers in the country. Not Lightly, a 50–1 shot in a hunter chase, crashed out heavily at the third fence, leaving me with a dislocated left shoulder and a broken arm between the shoulder and the elbow. I was in agony as I waited for the ambulance on the far side of the course. The journey back to the medical room was more painful than I care to say. The going was so rough and bumpy that every yard felt like a mile and long before the end my shoulder popped back in on its own.

Alan Taylor had come down to Devon with me for the day. He drove me to Exeter Hospital, where we waited around for ages in casualty before anyone saw me. Eventually X-rays confirmed the break in my upper arm. They strapped me up, gave me some painkillers and sent me home. I worried that the damage was serious enough to prevent me riding again, but the doctors assured me it would heal in time, though to this day I still cannot lift my left arm much above shoulder height. Although it was incredibly painful for months, it didn't put me off racing at all. I remember thinking that it was a badge of honour, that I was a proper jockey at last after such a serious injury.

I spent a frustrating month moping around at home and trying to help out with a few minor jobs at Dick's yard. It gave me time to consider my next move because it was clear as crystal to me that in the future Dick was going to give all the good point-to-point rides in the yard to Alison Dare, who was already making a name for herself in the saddle, particularly in ladies races. She was well ahead of me in the queue and definitely prettier than me. On both counts it was no contest.

I learned so much from Dick but at that stage I can't say I was set on following his example as a trainer one day, though the idea was lurking somewhere in the depths of my brain. Back then I didn't know anything about trainers, bar what I'd learned from Dick, and I assumed that you needed loads of money to set yourself up. The prospect seemed so far-fetched that I couldn't see a chance of it ever happening. For the time being I wanted to concentrate on my modest plans as an amateur jockey. Dick felt that I hadn't progressed that much as a rider and had his doubts that I could make it as a professional. But I loved the thrill of riding at speed, felt I was beginning to get the hang of things and was ready for the next step.

If you are young, ambitious and hungry for success you can't sit around forever waiting for a chance that might never come. You have to go out, bang on a few doors and try to make it happen. It was time to spread my wings. I spoke to Dick, who understood my reasons for wanting to move on and gave me his full blessing. We agreed that I should leave at the end of the point-to-point season early in June.

A crucial period in my life was about to come to an end. But before then I had one final ride on Wynsor House 11 in the Open race at the North Warwickshire meeting at Lowsonford on 25 May. During my enforced absence, he'd run in three hunter chases without distinction. My arm was still uncomfortable and I was far from fit after only a few days riding out, but I was determined to have one last go and no one was going to stand in my way. I managed to pass the scales without any awkward questions and, though my arm hurt like hell, and got worse by the minute through the race, Wynsor House 11 took me safely round and carried me to my last victory as a point-to-point rider. It was a great way to go out.

3

A red-letter day

I didn't have to wait long for my first job offer. It came from Kevin Bishop, trainer of Not Lightly, the horse which had buried me at Exeter. Kevin was still riding a few point-to-pointers while expanding his team of horses at Kilve, on the north Somerset coast. I bounced up to him at an end-of-season race meeting, asked if he had any vacancies and found myself agreeing to join him in the autumn as his pupil assistant.

First, though, I took a well-earned holiday before riding out most mornings for Richard Holder, who had just taken out a full licence to train not far from the M5 at Portishead. Richard was quite a character who often made a book at Epsom Downs on Derby Day and liked nothing more than spending the night playing cards with a few chums in Bristol. At the time he was fiddling around with a few horses with the help of his daughter Louise, who I took out on a number of occasions. She was probably my first girlfriend. My sister Julie says I used to teach all her girlfriends to kiss. Naturally I was delighted to help out, but girls didn't feature too much on my radar at that stage because I was so heavily into horses.

By the time I joined Kevin in August I'd ditched my pea-green Simca builder's van, which cost me my last £200 and had been my constant companion for eighteen months. I settled into digs at Kilve with Jean and Geoff Coles a mile or so from Kevin's yard. They had no children of their own and looked after me well. Geoff was a farm labourer while his wife was housekeeper to John Thorne, another trainer in the village. Once again my dad did his bit by sending two horses, Tabacco and Wynsor House 11, to Bishop for me to ride. We suspected they were not good enough to win races but at least they gave me some much needed practice over fences. Bishop was only a few years older than me and beginning to attract more owners. I was expected to do just about every job in the yard, from mucking out and riding work to helping the trainer put a new roof on his lorry. I was already starting to fill out and put on weight and kept myself as busy as possible to sweat off unwanted pounds.

Naturally I was anxious to kick off the jumps season with a few rides for my new boss but my first chance came from an unexpected source. Richard Holder had entered up Jock's Bond at Newton Abbot on 2 September. The horse had a string of duck eggs against his name and was miles out of the handicap but Richard sounded hopeful and was keen to use my seven-pound claim to reduce his weight to nine stone seven pounds. This left me with a serious problem as I was already ten stone and needed to shift the best part of ten pounds if I was to make the weight on a light saddle.

For guidance I turned to a more experienced amateur, Peter Hobbs, who lived close by, near Minehead. He laughed at my concern, handed me a couple of pills, told me to take them on the morning of the race and I would be fine. I was really naïve in those days and knew nothing about sweating and saunas. I swallowed the pills and, bang, they worked a treat. I spent most of the day peeing and lost enough weight to do nine stone seven pounds by the skin of my teeth. No wonder I felt weak and light-headed as I set off on Jock's Bond. It was the first of many times when I used to feel little more than a passenger after taking pee pills.

Jock's Bond, the outsider of five, was in front after the second fence and romped home by six lengths. That first victory was indescribable, mainly because I wasn't in control from start to finish. I don't know who was more surprised, me or Richard's daughters, Louise and Kate, who were in charge at Newton Abbot. He had given the girls £20 to cover the cost of the diesel. They promptly blew it on champagne as we celebrated in the racecourse before they ran out of fuel on the way home, so their dad had to turn out to rescue them. A couple of weeks later I won on Jock's Bond again at Warwick.

Encouraged by these early successes, I began badgering Kevin Bishop for a chance. It came at Exeter in November in a competitive novice chase on Easter Carnival, a smart mare who would go on and win three times over fences. But not with me, though we were in front and going well when I had a rush of blood to the head, asked her for an extravagant jump and suddenly found the ground rushing up to greet me. After that I was swiftly put back to yard duties.

Those wins on Jock's Bond proved to be a false dawn. I rode a few ordinary horses but none with a chance and all the time my weight was worrying me. Every time I was offered a light ride I'd starve myself, take several pee pills and feel like death by the time I reached the racecourse. Often when I used pills I was just a passenger. The horses half took off with me and I wasn't in total control but normally I could just about steer them. More often than not adrenalin took over. I hoped no one was aware that I was getting through these pills at an alarming rate, yet on light weights I had no alternative but to use them. I thought I knew how far I could push my body and tried to make sure I didn't cross the line.

If I was starting my riding career today at the same age and weight, there is no way I'd survive because diuretics, quite rightly, are banned. Without them I would have been lost because I rode for nine years at least two stone below my natural weight. Pee pills allowed me to pursue a career that would not have been possible today. I was already six foot and my days of doing nine stone seven pounds wouldn't last long. When I did force myself to get down to the minimum weight, I always felt worse for the experience. I used to think it was just me being weak but, in truth, a combination of factors left me some way short of what was required from a jockey. Until I was twenty-one I was never strong enough to push one for three miles and it took me long enough to do that efficiently. That's why I keep telling the boys with me now not to be in such a hurry.

Once you start taking pills to help you lose weight you find yourself locked into a vicious cycle. At first Peter Hobbs supplied me with a few of his own. When I ran out I made an appointment with my doctor and told him I needed a plentiful supply of diuretics because I was struggling with my weight. He immediately gave me a prescription for them. As easy as that. In the early days a couple of pee pills did the trick for me. I'd lose up to half a stone quickly, though you had to plan the best time to take them or you could find yourself caught short in the most embarrassing circumstances. Leave it too late in the morning and you'd be forced to stop on the side of the road every twenty minutes with your pals hanging out of the car windows laughing out loud at you. I worked out that the best time to take them was just before going to bed. OK, you had to get up in the night at frequent intervals but at least that way you had a chance to adjust to feeling dehydrated in the morning.

The worst thing about using those pills on a regular basis was that you soon needed more and more to have the same effect. At first one or two would be sufficient to help me lose half a stone pretty rapidly. Later I needed to take as many as six to shed four or five pounds. No wonder I felt like death most of the time. Once I got caught short just as we arrived at the start of a race at Exeter. I handed the reins to one of the other jockeys, jumped over the rails, relieved myself behind the nearest hedge and emerged to loud cheers from the other riders.

I've always tried to be positive but by late November I hadn't had a sniff of a winner for months, felt hopelessly weak when I did get a ride and couldn't see how to turn things round. In addition, I didn't appreciate being away from home. I was new to the area, didn't have any friends there and remember sitting in my room at my digs one evening wondering where it was all going wrong. Two victories in four months was hardly setting the world on fire. It was time to go on the offensive.

Peter Hobbs' older brother, Philip, had earned the nickname Buzby in the weighing room for his habit of ringing up trainers asking them to give him a ride. Some of the older jockeys thought this was bad form, but in the days before agents took such a tight grip on the business I felt there was a lot be said for Philip's enterprise. If it was good enough for him, it would do for me.

I made it my business to buy the racing calendar each week and began ringing trainers with entries in races for amateurs. It was tedious, expensive work and nineteen times out of twenty I got short shrift if I managed to get through to a trainer. Les Kennard, in particular, turned me down time and time again, which was hardly surprising since he'd never met me. Things reached the point where I became almost too embarrassed to call him any more. I swallowed my pride and kept pestering him because he was a local trainer with a reputation for giving boys a chance. Except this one.

Not all my calls fell on fallow ground. I struck lucky straightaway with Josh Gifford. Spotting that he had Ridan Tower in an amateurs' race at Folkestone on 30 November, I called his office and two minutes later found myself booked for the mount. I also picked up three more rides on the card for Ron Shaw, a larger than life City figure who loved a punt.

I set off for Folkestone in high spirits and returned home a few hours later exhausted and deeply depressed. I ended up on the floor in the first race, then made a spectacle of myself by falling off Mr Darkie just after passing the winning post in fourth place in the long-distance chase. By starving myself to make the correct weight of nine stone eight pounds I left myself so weak and light-headed that, long before the end, I was running on empty.

I was so knackered as we pulled up that when Mr Darkie spooked as we passed the water jump shortly after the line I tumbled clumsily from his back. I literally fell off. No one else realised what had happened, but I knew and felt highly embarrassed. In those days you didn't have to wear body protectors. So, if you were doing light, you just pulled on your colours, often made of silk, and by the time you had been standing around in the paddock for a few minutes in mid-winter you were frozen. I used to get so cold, dehydrated and hungry. It wasn't exactly the perfect platform for an athlete to per-form and after my debacle on Mr Darkie I felt like hiding rather than going out to hear my instructions from Josh Gifford. Ridan Tower came to my rescue by carrying me safely into fourth place.

I thanked Josh for the chance, trudged back to the weighing room and barely had the energy to change colours for my final performance of the day on Heirline, a 50–1 shot for Ron Shaw. I was too tired to give him any help but, thankfully, we were still together at the finish a furlong behind the rest. Back in Kilve that night I had a long, hot bath at my digs and doubted if anyone would be offering me rides in the future.

Snow, frost and heavy rain wiped out most meetings around Christ-mas and the New Year and racing finally came to a halt for ten days on 7 January. Out of the blue I had a phone call early one Monday morning that turned my season on its head. Roger Hoad, who trained in Sussex, urgently needed an amateur for a race that afternoon at Fontwell because Dermot Browne, his original choice, was stuck in freezing fog in Yorkshire. Was I interested? Is the Pope a Catholic? Pausing only to check that I'd have to do ten stone on a horse called Bash Street Kid, I popped a couple of pee pills and set off, praying that the meeting would survive a late inspection. It was touch and go, but in the end Fontwell was the first meeting to be held in England for a while. In the paddock, Hoad was bullish. Since Bash Street Kid was a good jumper he wanted me to encourage the horse to attack the fences. It worked a treat. We jumped into the lead setting out on the second circuit and came home unchallenged.

Two days later Les Kennard rang. It was the first time he had called me. I held my breath as he explained that he was running two in an amateurs' race at Kempton on Saturday. He'd already booked Kay Rees for one and wanted me for Lord Leighton. My persistence with Kennard had finally paid off but this was hardly a ride to set the pulse racing. Lord Leighton hadn't run for ages and was dismissed as a no-hoper in the morning pages, which didn't stop the pair of us bolting up at 33–1.

It was a modest race on a bleak, mid-winter afternoon in front of a sparse crowd. Ours was the last race of the afternoon and by then many racegoers had left for home. But this was a red-letter day for me, the one above all others that kick-started my career as a jockey. All of a sudden I was the new kid on the block. A young, in-form jockey claiming a weight allowance for his inexperience is a mighty valuable asset to a trainer. Les Kennard starting using me whenever he could, and other trainers, too, suddenly began to take an interest in P. Nicholls.

One minute I couldn't buy a winner. The next I was in constant demand so, after I won two races in quick succession for Les on Tudor Road early in February, I took the plunge and turned professional. Just to be sure, I rang Gifford. He encouraged me to take the plunge as things were going so well. I've always been decisive and there was no hesitation about this decision after talking to him . . . apart from the nagging worry that I might not remain light enough for much longer. What was the point in continuing as an amateur if I could be earning £41.50 a ride?

Dad would always try to come to support me at the races, work permitting. Sometimes, with some skilful juggling, he managed to do both at the same time. My last victory as an amateur on Tudor Road at Wincanton on 11 February was memorable for the sight of my dad waving frantically at me from his patrol car parked by the racecourse perimeter fence at the point where we pulled up. It was brilliant to know he was behind me all the way. No son could ask for more.

On my first day as a professional, 16 February 1982, I found myself back on Easter Carnival taking on the subsequent Gold Cup winner Burrough Hill Lad at Newton Abbot. If it had been a boxing match the referee would have stopped the fight long before the end. Burrough Hill Lad, a 5–2 chance, romped home by thirty lengths while Easter Carnival struggled round in the rear before finishing sixth. Four days after joining the paid ranks I enjoyed my first double at Chepstow on Lord Leighton and Two Coppers. Their trainer, Les Kennard, was proving to be a tremendous ally. His horses were fit, healthy, kept going when challenged and took their races remarkably well. I remember my surprise when I won on Tudor Road at Hereford. As I picked up my whip he just took off with me, pretty much bolted. I didn't even hit him. Les's horses seemed to know what they were there to do. You only had to threaten them with the whip and they'd be gone. Perhaps they'd had a few cracks around the ribs at home to sharpen them up.

Les was hard and tough and so were his horses. His success was amazing really as he didn't have what you might describe as conventional gallops to work his horses. I never rode out for him but from what I hear he'd use a hill here and a field there to give them a spin and would canter them up banks on the Quantock Hills time and again. You could do it with the numbers he had, twenty-five or thirty horses, but not with 120. Les was a resourceful fellow who utilised whatever facilities he could find. He gave them plenty of hard graft and, I'm told, wasn't averse to slipping round a neighbouring farmer's field while he wasn't looking.

Though I'd left it late in the season to turn pro, I had such a good run in the spring that I almost won the conditional jockeys' championship. Every night I'd go through the racing calendar and then be on the phone to every trainer with entries in the boys' races. One evening I called Stan Mellor asking to ride Charlie Muddle in the final of the Daily Mirror Conditional Jockeys series at Lingfield. He rang me back the next day confirming the booking, but that was before I was ironed out by a crunching fall on Lord Leighton at Cheltenham on Thursday, two days before Lingfield.

Once I came round I felt as though I'd just been run over by a steamroller. I hurt everywhere and for a while was totally gaga. I can't remember how I found my way back to the weighing room but, once there, I collapsed again and passed out. That night I hurt so much I barely slept before struggling to get out of bed in the morning. It was a relief to get off my rides at Fakenham, but I felt Charlie Muddle had a brilliant chance the next day and had no intention of missing out.

As Stan Mellor had seen the fall at Cheltenham, I wasn't surprised when he rang on Friday morning to check on my condition. When I assured him I'd be fit, he told me I must prove it by riding a bit of work on Charlie Muddle that very afternoon. I headed for the sauna, had some physio and asked Mum to drive me to Lambourn. I still felt like death but managed to disguise it sufficiently to pass inspection on Charlie Muddle under the critical eye of his trainer.

That evening I persuaded my doctor to pass me fit, then did a few, half-hearted press-ups to convince myself I was up to the task. I arrived at Lingfield with my leg heavily strapped from knee to thigh and took painkillers at regular intervals through the day. Eagle-eyed punters watching me limp round the course beforehand would probably have been put off backing Charlie Muddle, but the result was never in doubt as we hacked up by ten lengths. My percentage of £8,458 eased the agony of the past forty-eight hours and there was a bonus when I received a cash prize of £100 from *Daily Mirror* editor, Mike Molloy.

I ended my first season as a professional with sixteen winners. After such a modest start I was tickled pink, but my success left me facing a tricky choice for the following autumn. For several weeks Les Kennard had been pressing me to join him full-time as his conditional. I was flattered that he wanted me but also aware that he had a record of dropping his young jockeys once they had run through their claim. I enjoyed my time with Kevin Bishop, a nice guy who has done really well. I was ambitious, in a hurry to make a name for myself and needed to move on if I was going to progress as a jockey. I'd worked hard for him and learned plenty but my situation had changed.

I was still considering Kennard's offer when Josh Gifford came in with a counterbid. Josh had been champion jockey four times before taking over the reins from the legendary trainer Ryan Price at Findon in Sussex. I'd had a few rides for Josh without success, but his was one of the most powerful stables in the land. I'd be working in the yard, doing my two or three horses and hoping to be given the chance to prove myself.

I've always believed in being upfront with people so I immediately told Les of my decision, explained my reasoning and made it clear that I was keen to continue riding for him whenever possible. With that, I headed off on holiday to Malta. I knew I was bound to be piling on the pounds over the summer break that used to last for two months. Lying beside a swimming pool under a cloudless Mediterranean sky, my weight problems seemed a million miles away. They would return to haunt me in the coming years.

4

Everyone thought it would kill me

In all my years as a jockey I was only once asked to stop a horse. It happened at Taunton in March 1983, towards the end of my first season at Findon. I arrived at the track with high hopes of at least two winners. John Thorne's Beau Ranger, later a prolific chaser, had a favourite's chance in the novices' hurdle, but my nap was Carflax in the selling hurdle. I'd won a seller on him at Taunton two months earlier and he'd run right up to form at Newton Abbot on the day the racing world was captivated by Michael Dickinson's extraordinary feat in training the first five in the Cheltenham Gold Cup.

Racing sometimes seems to run on whispers and my confidence in Carflax was slightly dented when several people at the track warned me that he was not expected to win. At least the horse looked the part in the paddock. His trainer, Mark Stephens, seemed on edge as he pulled me aside so that he could not be overheard, then told me, 'Not today, do anything but don't win.' I was so shocked by his instructions that for a moment I was speechless. As I stood there dumbfounded Stephens repeated, 'Not today.'

I was furious that he expected me to play his dirty little game and also that just about everyone on the course, except me, seemed to know about his intentions. I looked him in the eye, told him that was not my style, turned on my heels and headed back towards the weighing room. It was his turn to be shocked. He chased after me, caught up with me at the paddock gate me and said, 'No, no, no. You've got to ride this horse. Just don't win.'

I shook my head and continued towards the weighing room with the intention of crying off the ride with the excuse that I was unwell. After a short confrontation, Stephens talked me round though I made it clear I'd be going all out to win. With that, he legged me up on

Carflax. By that stage I was so furious I was determined to win by as far as possible so you can imagine my feelings when Carflax blundered so badly at the second last that I almost fell off. Luckily for me we stayed together before pulling clear to win by fifteen lengths. I walked back into the winners' enclosure with a big smile on my face, jumped off and told Stephens never to ask me to ride for him again. I ended a rewarding day by winning on Beau Ranger.

That first season with Josh Gifford proved to be my best as a jockey by far, although working in a big racing yard for the first time was quite a culture shock for me. I can't say I enjoyed it much, particularly in my early days at Findon. New lads were often greeted with an ambush that left them trussed up in a muck sack hanging from the ceiling of the hay barn. Some ended up having their private parts covered in hoof oil.

Cruel initiation ceremonies used to be part of racing's culture. I managed to avoid anything too savage when I arrived by hiding in the broom cupboard when the lads were looking for me. You needed to be alert at all times or you'd find the horse you had just brushed over would be covered in manure and shavings and your grooming kit turned upside down in the box just as Josh was approaching. I got on well enough with the other lads but there was always an undercurrent of jealousy. If you tried hard to score a few brownie points with the guv'nor, the others would slag you off.

Head lad Ron James was a hard stableman of the old school who ruled the place with a rod of iron. Josh left the running of the yard to him; Ron's word was law. If you took him on, there could only be one winner. I still can't believe the way he treated some of the lads. I remember the shock of seeing him armed with a shovel waiting round a corner to ambush a lad who turned up late for work. Times have changed, definitely for the better, and if head lads today behaved like Ron they would probably find their victims taking them to an industrial tribunal. In those days fighting between lads was the norm in racing. You heard terrible stories of bullying, too. It was a sad existence really. My head lad Clifford Baker and I will not tolerate any bullying or fighting at Ditcheat. Our lads know that they are out if there is any sign of fighting.

Josh's stable jockey, Richard Rowe, was quite a prankster. I fell asleep in the car on one of my first trips to the races with him and woke up to discover that he'd tossed my shoes out of the window several miles back. That irritated the hell out of me. The next time my tie went missing when I nodded off on the way home. Peter Double, another claimer who often travelled with us, was just as bad as Richard. Together they were lethal.

Josh was a decent guv'nor and, true to his word, gave me plenty of chances, particularly that first season 1982–3. I kicked off the new campaign with two winners in quick succession early in August on Quazar Light for Les Kennard. The second victory, at Worcester, was notable for the fact that my claim was then reduced from seven to four pounds. That could only be good news in my struggle with the scales. Josh's team didn't usually hit its stride for another couple of months and it wasn't until early November that I rode a double for him at Towcester on Moonlight Express and Buck and Wing.

When you are trying to make a name for yourself you have to take the good with the bad. One of the most terrifying rides of my life came out of the blue at Wincanton where a young trainer needed a substitute jockey at the last minute. I volunteered and found myself on a thing that didn't have the first idea how to jump. It was so clumsy I doubt if it had ever seen a flight of hurdles. It galloped straight on at the first and was all but down, then never raised a leg at the second and nearly fell again. The horse was too thick to be frightened but by now I was thoroughly alarmed, travelling at upwards of thirty miles an hour on something that clearly hadn't a clue how to get from one side of a hurdle to the other. My ordeal ended painfully at the third flight where we turned a somersault. As the wretched horse picked itself up it trampled all over me. I was steaming by the time I got back to the weighing room, furious at being put at risk on something that had blatantly never been schooled.

I relished every chance to head back to the West Country and enjoyed a rewarding afternoon at Taunton in January with a double on Carflax and The County Stone. A couple of days later The County Stone's trainer, John Thorne, handed me a £5 note as a present from the horse's owner, Anona Taylor. Any help towards my travelling expenses was always welcome but I drew the line at £5, gave it back to John and suggested Anona needed the money more than me! A couple of years ago she asked me to help her find a suitable horse from Ireland for around £30,000. I spent a fair amount of time trying to pinpoint one to suit her before coming up with a nice youngster that I thought would be ideal. Anona then left me speechless by asking if I minded if she sent the horse to Philip Hobbs!

The highlight of the 1982–3 season was my first visit to the Grand National meeting. It was a curious few days. As I had a ride in the Topham Trophy on the Thursday and another in the race after the National on Saturday, I asked Josh if I could stay at Liverpool for the three days. 'Certainly not,' he replied. 'Get yourself on the lorry coming back here after racing on Thursday and travel up again on the big day.'

I set off from Findon in his car on Thursday, anticipating a character-forming introduction to the big Aintree fences on Moonlight Express, a horse who had fallen on his first three runs in the autumn. It was such a horrible jumper everyone thought it was going to kill me and the lads in the yard were taking bets on the fence where it would happen. I needed to be at my strongest if I was going to survive, so I didn't take any pee pills and put up seven pounds overweight, at ten stone three pounds. Moonlight Express flew the first and soon settled into a rhythm before finishing a close fifth. I couldn't wait to tackle the fences again.

As I unsaddled I told Josh I'd see him on Saturday. He replied, 'Why the hell are you going home?' I reminded him of our conversation twenty-four hours earlier. 'Don't worry about that. You'd better stay now that you are here,' he suggested. Suddenly I had the freedom of Liverpool for two nights. What I didn't possess was a change of clothes or a hotel. Mel Fordham, a young photographer, heard I was looking for a bed and offered to share his room. We've been friends ever since and I hope I've repaid his generosity by training lots of winners for him.

Grand National day was quite an experience. I'd have given anything to join the rest of the boys on that short, nervous walk from the weighing room to the paddock. Instead, I watched with the rest of the world on television as Corbiere landed a historic victory for Jenny Pitman. She was probably still giving interviews when I won the following race for conditional jockeys on a smashing old chaser called Approaching. I couldn't have asked for a better introduction to Liverpool. I ended that first season with twenty-three winners from 239 rides. I hoped it would be a launching pad for a rewarding career as a jump jockey but a reality check was just around the corner.

Of all our jumps tracks Cartmel is the most unusual. Tucked away in narrow lanes not far from the M6 in Cumbria, it attracts huge crowds and has the friendly atmosphere of a country fair with all sorts of sideshows and attractions. Visitors will come for several days, pitch their tents, park their caravans and enjoy the wonderful scenery with picnics and barbecues. I don't remember much about my first trip there in August 1983 because I had a gravedigger of a fall on Fanta's Girl. I landed head first on ground which was officially hard and eventually came round to discover Dad bending anxiously over me with a First Aid man. They were trying to make sure I hadn't broken any bones. Seeing that I wasn't making any sense and aware that I had some decent rides for John Thorne on the Monday, Dad took over, delved into the First Aid man's medical bag, found some smelling salts and shoved them under my nose.

By the time the doctor arrived I was just about OK, apart from a splitting headache. I told him I was fine, limped back to the weighing room and managed to escape before anyone else started to ask awkward questions which might have led to an entry in my medical book ruling me out for at least a week. I found one of those old-fashioned red telephone boxes in the car park and rang Thorne's partner, Roxy, to check that his horses were running two days later. Dad then drove us all home, with me spark out on the back seat with shocking concussion. When you are young and fit, you can bounce back amazingly quickly from the worst falls. It would be stretching the truth to say I felt 100 per cent but jump jockeys are usually carrying one injury or another and I was able to achieve a double on Thorne's pair, Winterland and A Little Tipsy.

Winterland was my first winner for Paul Barber, a jumping enthusiast who would play a massive part in my life in the years to come. He was missing that day. Harvesting was in full swing so Paul was at the wheel of Thorne's combine at Kilve so that John could saddle his runners at Newton Abbot. I must have summered well because I put up six pounds overweight on A Little Tipsy at ten stone three pounds. It made no difference as he ran home an easy winner. It was a notable landmark for me because I had finally run out of my claim. From now on I would be riding on level terms with the best in the business. The period after losing your allowance can be tough for young riders. Many disappear without trace. Others struggle to make an impact. Full of self-belief, I hoped I'd be one of those who kept on winning. I was in for a rude awakening though I enjoyed the odd decent success that season, mostly for Josh Gifford, and managed a high-profile double for him at Ascot in November on Homeson and Approaching.

One of my first interviews as a jockey wasn't read by many racing enthusiasts as it appeared in the parish magazine in Olveston. I talked of my early days in the pony club, the years spent with Dick Baimbridge, the long hours working for Josh and my desire to be a top jockey. I ended the interview by revealing that, long term, I was looking forward to becoming a trainer.

Since I was only twenty I didn't have a clue how it could be done or how I was going to finance it. Yet even at that early stage I knew beyond doubt that somehow, some way I would have a go at training racehorses. Fitness, I felt sure, was the key. Most of the fancied horses I rode then and in later years got beaten through lack of fitness rather than for any other reason. Dick Baimbridge's horses rarely if ever failed because they weren't ready and he was the benchmark by which I rated all other trainers. It's fair to say that there are several ways to bring a horse to peak fitness. Josh's horses always seemed to hit form in November. They tended to need a race or two and definitely improved for runs, but he had a shedload of winners every season and came within an ace of being champion trainer.

For the last couple of years at Findon I shared one of Josh's bungalows with Peter Hobbs and Paul Hacking. The absence of door handles in the house made life interesting and we used pliers to turn on the cooker. But it was home to us and we had a lot of fun though we all had to be incredibly secretive about our girlfriends or everyone in the yard would know your business within five minutes. Once, just to be sure no one knew what was going on, Peter and I locked our girls in the bungalow when we set off for work in the morning!

We often travelled to and from the races with the guv'nor. He tended to drive there and allow one of us to drive him home. Whenever possible, he liked to stop in Guildford on the way back for fish and chips, which wasn't great for my diet, and then we usually enjoyed a drink at one of his favourite pubs, the Lyme Grove. Peter and I used to plan the final run to Findon with military precision when we were at the wheel for the good reason that, if we arrived back at the yard before six, we'd be pressed into action at evening stables.

With Josh safely asleep many is the time we'd ease up approaching the village to kill five or ten minutes. If things were really tight we'd circle the roundabout near Findon up to a dozen times to waste another few seconds. Anything to avoid reaching the yard before six and getting an earful from Ron James. If we mistimed things and got there too soon, we'd be forced to help feed the horses in our best clothes.

By this stage I was using a sauna as well as pee pills to lose weight. Peter and I spent a fair bit of time at the White Horse at Storrington. It was one of those rare pubs with a sauna but too often the benefit of a good sweat was followed by a long drink, which promptly put back on most of the weight. I've never been a big drinker, then or now, but when you are in a pub and people want to buy you drinks they can get quite offended if you say no. Rather than sound impolite, I'd accept a glass of whatever was offered then quietly tip its contents into the nearest flowerbed.

Successive injuries early in the New Year played havoc with my weight. It couldn't have come at a worse time. With the stable jockey Richard Rowe out of action with a shoulder problem, I was set to pick up plenty of decent rides. That prospect ended with a bone-crunching fall on The Thatcher on his debut over fences. He was a horrible horse, who no one in the yard wanted to ride. I got the short straw at Windsor and paid the price by smashing my collarbone for the first time and dislocating my shoulder. I felt sick all the way home, much to the amusement of Josh who suggested I was going soft. Mum and Dad collected me so that I could recover at home and, after the best part of a month off, I managed a welcome success at Sandown on Paddy Boro, the 49th winner of my career. Just as I was getting my confidence back I broke the same collarbone again.

My 50th winner finally arrived at the end of April on Beni, courtesy of Martin Pipe, the man who became my arch rival when I turned to training. I doubt if Martin had even heard of me in those days but Beni belonged to a well-known West Country character called Tim Handel and I was offered the ride because I was trotting out with his daughter Hilary at the time.

Pipe wasn't quite a household name then but he was already

making an impact. In the paddock it was obvious that Beni was as fit as a butcher's dog. This one wouldn't fail through lack of condition. Unbeknown to me, money was pouring on to Beni in the ring. In the space of a few minutes his odds tumbled from 8–1 to 4–1. I jumped him out in front and never saw another horse as we raced home unchallenged by twenty-five lengths. No wonder the man was having winners. Just over a fortnight later we won again at Newton Abbot, but I wasn't getting carried away. It was an interesting interlude but there was no danger of my being offered a job by Martin Pipe or a present by Tim Handel.

When I was taking out Hilary I'd sometimes stay overnight in the family's caravan in a field near their house. Once I was woken at two in the morning by a fearful pounding on the door which gave me a hell of a fright. I stumbled out of bed to discover the irate figure of Tim Handel on his way home from a late night at the pub brandishing a big walking stick. Perhaps he was expecting to catch me out with his daughter. Had he done so, I might not have lived to tell the tale. Luckily, she wasn't with me and after a brief exchange Tim grumpily withdrew.

For a bit of light relief that summer I found myself involved in a chat show on a handful of occasions during Butlins Racing Holiday weeks at Minehead and at Saltdean, near Brighton. I've never minded talking, on or off camera, but readily admit to some embarrassment at seeing the events advertised as 'An Evening with Paul Nicholls'. It was all down to a good supporter of mine, Ray Gould, a journalist who organised these racing breaks. We'd sit on stage in front of a couple of hundred racing enthusiasts and chat about horses and jockeys for an hour before inviting questions. It was a fun way to earn a few bob.

Shortly after I split up with Hilary I got together with Tarnya Davis, who had gorgeous curly ginger hair. We met through a great pal of mine of mine, Mark Richards, an amateur jockey who later joined the SAS and was tragically killed by friendly fire. My new girlfriend's dad, Joe, trained under permit at their home in Feckenham, near Droit-witch, an hour north of Bristol. I remember spending some of that summer in 1984 helping him put in a new equine swimming pool. Soon Tarnya and I began messing around with a few of their horses, notably a handy mare called Princess Hecate. It ran under her dad's name, but we did all the work with her.

Although Princess Hecate was not very talented, she tried her best, was consistent and finally won over hurdles with me at Towcester in October. It would be stretching the truth to say I trained her but she was certainly the first winner in which I had been heavily involved with all the preparation work. We won again together at Market Rasen a month later, which was just as well as I didn't have much else to celebrate in that final season with Josh Gifford.

Competition for rides at his yard was greater than ever and I seemed to have slipped down the pecking order partly through injury and my never-ending struggle to maintain a racing weight. From my point of view there were too many jockeys in the yard. I wasn't enjoying it much at Findon and was barely earning enough to pay for my car and other expenses. You always like to pretend that you are one of the lads in the weighing room but, deep down, I knew by then that I wasn't good enough to make it to the top. I was exactly the type of jockey I would not employ now.

Two or three times on bad days I was tempted to give up riding and try something else. Yet I had no savings, no obvious prospects. It was too early to consider training and I hadn't a clue what else to do. I knew for sure I couldn't stay at Findon for another season. It was time to go. My weight problems prevented me chasing rides, injuries hadn't helped and opportunities had dried up since I'd lost my claim. If I didn't change tack quickly, I had no future as a jockey. Training was still the long-term plan but before then I wanted a few more years riding before my weight ballooned out of control.

I began looking around for a suitable opening and found one in unusual circumstances. Sitting in the weighing room between races I overheard David Barons' jockey Hywel Davies telling Colin Brown of a possible job in the yard near Plymouth. I pricked up my ears when I heard him say Barons was importing a large contingent of young horses from New Zealand and was looking for another jockey to help out and ride them all. The more I thought about it the more I liked the sound of it. You don't get far in life if you don't help yourself, so that night I wrote to Barons applying for the job.

His wife, Jenny, replied inviting me down there to have a look at the set-up. It turned out that Barons was a businessman and farmer as well. He held the licence but it didn't take me long to realise that Jenny's input on all matters to do with training was essential to their success. Together they made a highly effective team. Jenny was an outstanding horsewoman who had left boarding school at fifteen to train the family's racehorses once her father became ill. She was a first-rate jockey, became champion ladies point-to-point rider five years running between 1954 and 1958 and won forty-one times on a horse called Lonesome Boy, nearly all of them over banks. In the late 1960s and early 1970s Jenny and David sent out upwards of fifty winners a year as a matter of course. Once they achieved a half-century before Christmas, but the numbers of winners and horses had begun to dwindle. That was when they decided to change things by importing young stock from New Zealand.

A Sunday morning spent with David and Jenny Barons left me sensing that a revival in their fortunes might be around the corner. I was thrilled at the thought of being back in the West Country and felt the stable was on the up again, though, crucially, they didn't have runners every day of the week. Given my weight, that could only be a bonus. I hoped that I'd be involved in the training and riding without having to starve myself full-time. We reached an agreement that I'd go down there two or three times a week in the late summer to ride out and then move into lodgings once the season got under way. I would ride most of the horses, but Hywel Davies would have first call on the better ones. As I headed for home after my interview I couldn't wait to start.

First, though, came my debut in the 1985 Grand National on the 150–1 shot Roman Bistro, who'd been out of form all year. I was thrilled to be given the chance by Josh to tackle the race that has brought me more heartache than any other over the years. I can't say I had any great expectations on Roman Bistro particularly after walking the course in the morning. Maybe it was my imagination but the fences looked massive, a fair bit bigger than I anticipated. That was one day I didn't care about putting up overweight.

I don't mind admitting to feeling nervous beforehand. There is a unique tension among the jockeys crowded into the weighing room on National day. It isn't fear, more a sense of apprehension. I tried to convince myself the race was no different from any other apart from forty runners and the size of the fences. At best I hoped for a clear round. There was a fair bit of carnage at the early fences but tucked in, just behind the leaders, we missed most of the trouble. I let Roman

Bistro bowl along, he winged Becher's Brook and after a circuit we were bang in contention in seventh or eighth place. Then, as if a switch had been turned off, he ran out of puff; our race was over. Next day the newspapers reported that Roman Bistro had refused but I pulled him up because he was choking. The poor horse ran once more a fortnight later, was sent for a breathing operation and died.

I ended that season with the miserable score of seven winners. It was horribly clear to me that I'd be forced to seek alternative employment if my switch to the West Country in the autumn didn't start paying dividends soon.

5

A fresh start in Devon

My first working day for David Barons set the pattern for the years to come. I spent the morning riding out and the rest of the time helping out during harvest. My new boss had a large farming empire, well over 1,000 acres, so there were always jobs to be done once the horses had been exercised. I didn't mind that we were all expected to get stuck in because I badly needed to be losing some weight and stacking bales on a hot summer's day is a better way than most to sweat off a few pounds. It was a useful diversion but long term I made it clear to David I didn't wish to be involved with the farm work because I wanted to concentrate on the horses.

The career of one young amateur working in the yard nearly came to an abrupt end that harvest. Marcus Armytage, later to win the Grand National on Mr Frisk in 1990, was driving the cart that collected the corn from the combine when he failed to close the tailgate properly. As he drove across the field on his way to the farmyard, tons of Barons' precious wheat were pouring out of the back of the trailer. The trainer, at the wheel of the combine, had a fit when he realised what had happened.

While there was harvesting and late autumn drilling to be done, Barons tended to leave racing matters to Jenny who was more than capable of running the show on her own. She was bright, extremely knowledgeable, full of common sense and experienced in the ways of racing. Andy Hobbs, the head lad, was a year younger than me and clearly knew what he was doing. Even then Jenny and David would leave the day-to-day decisions on work and feeding to him. Andy and I were both mad keen to have as many winners as possible and soon began working closely together to try to make that happen.

David Barons had lots of nice youngsters, either in training or ready to come in. He bought them in New Zealand and used to bring a planeload over at a time. He could see the benefit of importing a reasonably cheap product and selling it on whenever the chance arose. Some were passed on to other trainers, but many were sold to stay in the yard, including Playschool and Seagram, two horses that would have a huge influence on my life. Seagram was bought very cheaply as a three-year-old by Jenny on her own judgement, unbroken and unnamed. I felt the stable was full of potential and was pleased to be part of it, though it would often be October before David shut the farm gate and put on his trainer's hat. That first season I spent two or three nights a week lodging with the Barons' housekeeper in Woodleigh. As the stable tended not to have early runners I was short of rides for the first three months.

The horse that helped put me on the map was one of only a handful in the yard that wasn't bred in New Zealand. Broadheath was a grand, old-fashioned, raw-boned chaser, bred in Ireland and owned by Michael Marsh, one of the nicest people in jumping. I got my chance on Broadheath at Chepstow early in November when Hywel Davies rode two others for the stable at Sandown. Broadheath started a warm favourite against ordinary opposition in a three-mile handicap and finished powerfully to land the prize. It was great to be sitting on a decent horse again. He could be ignorant at times at his fences and make desperate mistakes, but was usually clever enough to recover and genuine as they come. Although Hywel was available next time at Wincanton, to my delight Mr Marsh said that I could keep the ride. We romped home in the Lord Stalbridge Memorial Gold Cup and shared two more victories that season.

I was just hitting my stride in my new job when I was forced on to the sidelines again with a broken collarbone at the start of December. I tried to come back in time for the Welsh National on 21 December but failed to pass the doctor so had to wait impatiently until Newton Abbot on Boxing Day, when I'd be reunited with Broadheath. The downside was that I put on so many pounds during my enforced break that I was in danger of logging a serious amount of overweight.

My fears eased when I spotted the friendly figure of Graham Welcome in charge in the weighing room. Some clerks of the scales appeared to relish making your life a misery. They had no charity in their souls as they resolutely refused to offer you any leeway. The worst in my time was an ex-military type called Ian Manning who couldn't wait to catch us out. Given half a chance he'd march you in front of the stewards for the most trivial offence and more often than not you'd end up with a suspension.

The boys all hated Manning and with good reason, though he was only doing his job. There was much celebrating in weighing rooms around the country when the story filtered through that John Francome had slipped a couple of pee pills into Manning's mid-afternoon cup of tea and added some even more disgusting ingredients. That made us all feel better.

Graham Welcome was the opposite – a warm, generous human being with a well-developed sense of humour. I pulled him aside at Newton Abbot, explained that I'd missed the last three weeks, had done myself rather too well over the festive season and was fearful of the consequences when David Barons discovered that I was going to be least half a stone overweight on his three runners. I can remember Graham's response as if it was yesterday. 'Well,' he said, his eyes twinkling with amusement as he consulted his racecard, 'what weight would you like to do?'

The form book offers lasting testimony to his kindness. I was set to carry eleven stone on my first mount, a pound less on Broadheath and an alarmingly light ten stone ten pounds on my final ride of the day. Let the record show that I didn't put up overweight on any of them, even though I couldn't possibly have been an ounce under eleven stone stripped. Barons was none the wiser and Broadheath gave me a late Christmas present by winning the feature race. I was weak from a combination of wasting and lack of fitness after my injury and Broadheath was so full of himself that I couldn't hold one side of him. He ran away with me, loved being out in front and won well.

My girlfriend Tarnya Davis would often ride out with me for Barons. She was developing into a smart amateur jockey and won twice that spring over fences on Spider's Well, a horse given to me by Josh Gifford. In his youth Spider's Well had won four races on the bounce but after that he didn't seem able to stand training. I felt he still had tons of ability if we only could keep him sound, which was never easy. I brought him home to Olveston, gave him time off, nursed him back to health, sold a half-share to our long-time friend Alan Taylor and gave the other half to my mother. Dad discovered

My grandparents Frank and Lucy Nicholls with my dad Brian as a toddler.

PC Frank Nicholls. By the age of nineteen he weighed nineteen stone.

I could have been a contender.

Once a cowboy, always a cowboy.

Part of the family...
my first pony Surprise.

A collection of some
of the trophies won by
my sister Julie and I at
gymkanas and shows.

Under starter's orders... on my first point-to-pointer Lucky Edgar. I was fifteen at the time.

Dick Baimbridge taught me so much. He has had a huge influence on my career.

Showing the style on French William (left) upsides the present Lord Leigh on Gallivanter 11 at the North Warwickshire Open in 1979.

My first winner on Energy Saver at Nedge on 22 March 1980.

Posing with the trophy afterwards closely attended by twins Liz and
Jan Rundle from Dick Baimbridge's yard and Alan Taylor.

Winning on Approaching at Aintree on Grand National Day, 1983.

Way out over Becher's Brook on Roman Bistro on my first Grand National ride in 1985 – when Becher's used to be a proper fence.

Broadheath helps put my career back on track with a timely success
at Chepstow in November 1985.

Posing for the cameras as Seagram heads for victory at Sandown in March 1987.

Playschool lands the 1987 Hennessy Gold Cup at Newbury.

With the trophy a few minutes later.

Close to disaster at the last fence on Playschool... but we survived to win the Vincent O'Brien Gold Cup at Leopardstown in February, 1988. It was the biggest success of my career.

Left With the trophy a few minutes later beside David Barons.

Playschool in a classic pose on the gallops in Devon.

that Spider's Well was supposed to suffer from an iron deficiency, so we started feeding him watercress to balance his diet. We also put pads under his shoes, which made a big difference. A spell out hunting seemed to rejuvenate Spider's Well and he landed quite a touch in a novice hunter chase at Fakenham, ridden by Tarnya and trained by her father Joe Davis.

The journey from Devon to Bangor-on-Dee is not one to be recommended, particularly when you are in a hurry, but Tarnya and I had good reason to celebrate after we both rode winners at the course on the same day in March. An hour after Tarnya won on Spider's Well it was my turn for victory on Scotch Princess, owned and trained by Robert Chugg, a notably successful breeder of jumps horses. Normally he is a sound bloke: not on this occasion, when he seemed to go haywire in the twenty-four hours leading up to the race. I'd ridden Scotch Princess a couple of times before but that didn't stop Robert giving me so many sets of orders that I was dizzy with confusion by the time I left the paddock. I've never had so many different instructions.

It started the night before when he rang to tell me exactly what I needed to do on his filly, continued in the morning with another long lecture on the phone and resumed when I walked into the paddock. I remember thinking, what is this bloke on, as he rambled on and on. God knows what he would have been like if he trained twenty horses. I tried not to laugh but in his anxiety to make sure I didn't cock things up on Scotch Princess he was just making things worse. I'm surprised he didn't write me a letter, hand it to me in the paddock and tell me to open it at the start!

At least Scotch Princess had been well schooled over fences. We won comfortably and Robert wasn't complaining afterwards. I've been teasing him about that day ever since. In his defence it's fair to say that he'd ridden plenty of winners and was probably finding it hard to let someone else do the job in the saddle.

I ended the season with what proved to be my last ride in the Grand National on Another Duke, trained by Joe Davis. In normal circumstances no one would have taken the slightest interest in a 200–1 outsider who hadn't won for several seasons and was clearly, at thirteen, past his best. Things changed when he was leased for the day by Des Lynam, anchorman of *Grandstand* for so many years and the face of BBC TV at Aintree. One of his tasks each spring was to interview the winning jockey, though there was never much chance of his talking to the one wearing his own green and white colours afterwards.

Another Duke was one of those horses who used to pull like hell, so I opted to try to settle him by tracking something safe down the inner. The horse I chose to follow was the previous year's winner, Corbiere, ridden by Ben de Haan. So much for the best-laid plans. We were nicely in Corbiere's slipstream when he took the fourth fence by the roots and turned over. Another Duke nimbly sidestepped the fallen horse and rider but this left us virtually in front on the inside.

Once he saw daylight he took off with me and headed for Becher's Brook like a five-furlong sprinter. We were flat out, really tanking as we approached the most famous fence in racing. I thought, here we go, this looks like the end so I might as well die the brave way, but Another Duke met it on a good stride, flew over it and survived the drop despite half stumbling on landing. My excitement at surviving Becher's didn't last long. We jumped three more fences safely before we were brought down at the tenth.

I ended that first season back in the West Country with nine winners. It was hardly a stunning revival in my fortunes but I felt I was part of a team that was going places, I'd ridden some nice horses with potential and believed the best lay ahead . . . if I could control my weight. The icing on the cake came when David Barons told me that I'd be his first jockey once racing resumed in August. With the job came the chance to live in one of his farm cottages. Things were definitely on the up.

Further ahead, I was sure I'd train horses myself eventually and began to wonder if the opportunity to do it might arise at Woodleigh. I could see that David's time was increasingly taken up with his farm business for months at a time and Jenny was busy doing other things, too. Aware that they didn't get on brilliantly I had this mad idea that, two or three years ahead, I might have a chance to become the trainer there. It was fanciful in the extreme but at least I was learning all the time about getting horses fit and I was beginning to have an input in the training.

After a summer's break I moved into my new home at Woodleigh with Tarnya. We'd got engaged in June and planned to marry a year later yet I had some nagging doubts all along which often surfaced as I sat in the new sauna I installed at the house in an attempt to ease my battle with the scales. I kept thinking the year would never pass and tried to put my fears out of my mind. Deep down, the thought of marriage frightened me to death.

The start of the new campaign was memorable for a hair-raising experience on Billy Bumps in a novice chase at Newton Abbot. He'd lost his jockey at the start on his debut and was listed in the papers as the outsider of seven. In the paddock his trainer, Chris Popham, explained that Billy Bumps was blind in one eye. Nor, as I discovered shortly after, could he see too well out of the other one! Billy Bumps blundered his way round, led briefly when the odds-on favourite fell and somehow managed to finish second. I was amazed we were still together at the end.

My trusty old friend Broadheath resumed on a winning note with me at Chepstow, but our interest in the Mackeson Gold Cup ended when we were brought down. It was only a temporary setback. Five days later we put the record straight with a stylish success at Wincanton. Since Broadheath was in the prime of his life we aimed him at the Hennessy Cognac Gold Cup, one of the most competitive long-distance chases of the year. There was one snag that gave me sleepless nights in the run-up to the big race. Broadheath was set to carry the featherweight of ten stone five pounds, lighter than I'd managed for ages.

I starved myself for a week, took pee pills regularly, walked for hours every evening and somehow managed to make the correct weight with the help of my smallest saddle and some custom-made, wafer-thin cheating boots I reserved for special occasions. When things were really tight they could save me a pound. Once I passed the scales I'd pop back to the weighing room and change into my regular boots. If I was caught wearing them by the clerk of the scales, I'd be forced to ride in them, which was seriously uncomfortable even with a racecard stuffed inside them.

Broadheath made it all worthwhile by carrying me to the first major success of my career. He travelled through the race like a dream, but he was always capable of making a howler without warning. It came just as we edged into the lead at the final ditch three from home. He clouted the fence so hard that I almost went into orbit. Luckily for me when I came down I managed to cling round his neck as he pitched on to his nose on landing. For some horses that would have spelled the end, yet Broadheath was going so well it barely stopped his momentum. He was not for passing that day and kept on strongly to hold the persistent challenge of Two Coppers.

After two or three years muddling along it felt brilliant to win a race like the Hennessy, but as we came back to unsaddle I needed my wits about me to weigh in without drama. As I walked in carrying the saddle I managed to slip off the surcingle and girth and pass them to our travelling lad, Darius Harding, who stuffed them under his coat. That probably made a difference of only one pound but I didn't want to alert anyone by weighing in heavy. One of my rewards for winning on Broadheath was a case of Hennessy Cognac. The bottles I took home that night helped solve a few problems with presents that Christmas.

Half an hour after the Hennessy Gold Cup I had further cause for celebration after Playschool's eye-catching debut success in the Hopeful Chase. He gave me such a good feel that day I told the press afterwards that he'd be back in twelve months' time to land the Hennessy. That didn't go down too well with David Barons, who later gave me a minor bollocking. He didn't really approve of me talking about his horses in public but I've always been upfront with people and meant what I said. Nor did I lose confidence when he fell on two of his next three starts. All he needed was more practice.

Playschool's jumping was much better as the season progressed and he was a leading fancy by the time we arrived at Cheltenham for the Sun Alliance Chase. My hopes were high when we set sail into the lead down the hill, but we couldn't hold off an old rival, Kildimo, who appeared at my shoulder full of running and eventually beat us by seven lengths. That was the closest I ever came to riding a winner at the Cheltenham Festival.

Barons' other big white hope, Seagram, wasn't the biggest but had a great attitude. We won a minor novice chase at Wolverhampton on firmish ground but he then buried me when he stepped at a fence at the same track next time. I hated riding at Wolverhampton, chiefly because I had so many heavy falls there. It was a flat, sharp track which suited speed horses and caused the slower ones to make mistakes. It was a tip of a place, so I wasn't heartbroken when they dug it all up and built an all-weather track, which eventually put an end to jumping there.

At one stage that season David Barons switched Seagram back to hurdles, a decision that was rewarded with a fluent success at Sandown. They say the camera never lies, but it did on that occasion because the next day's papers carried shots of me perched athletically up Seagram's neck at the last flight, looking like the most stylish jockey in the world. If I didn't know better I'd say John Francome had pinched the ride.

The move to team up with David Barons was beginning to pay dividends. I'd enjoyed one of my best seasons, with eighteen winners, including several major races, and I hoped the best was to come. Tarnya, too, had won more races on Spider's Well whose long-term target remained the Grand National in twelve months' time. There was so much for us both to look forward to but as the summer break beckoned I began to have cold feet about our wedding plans. We'd got on fine at first but things weren't so smooth once we moved in together at Woodleigh and we'd often end up squabbling over the most trivial things. It wasn't a good omen.

A week before the big day I warned Dad that I was going to call it off and set off in the car to tell Tarnya it was all over. By the time I arrived at her parents I'd changed my mind. I'm not a great one for upsetting people and couldn't face the hurt I'd cause by putting an end to our wedding plans. We were married on 13 June 1987 and spent our honeymoon in St Lucia. Cracks soon began to appear in our relationship and our marriage was over after eight or nine months. We were together for a total of three years but it ended when Tarnya walked out. I don't point a finger at her for what happened because most of it was my fault. Looking back now it's obvious we were both too young.

A lot of it was down to the fact that, because of my non-stop battle with the scales, I was such a miserable bastard. When Tarnya tried hard to cook light meals that would help my diet I'd often push the food around the plate without tasting anything. On Saturday nights she'd be wanting to get dressed up and go out and have a good time at a disco, clubbing or at a party somewhere. I didn't want to do it. In fact, I couldn't do it. Eating and drinking or clubbing were the last things I felt like doing because I knew I'd wake up the next morning several pounds heavier and have to go straight back into the sauna. You get in a depression because you are in a state struggling against nature all the time.

Of course, she became exasperated with that, we'd start arguing again and sometimes she'd storm off on her own and not come back until hours later. Part of the problem was that she was fed up with me because I was addicted to racing and riding. Wasting had taken over my life to the point that I was lousy company for her, particularly at home. We should never have got married. It wasn't the right time and we both made a big mistake. In many ways riding over jumps is a single man's game.

Long before the end we were fighting like two cats in a sack. The final break came shortly after the lead-up to the 1988 Grand National in which I was due to ride Spider's Well, who'd found his form with a vengeance. In a joint recorded interview for the BBC's National programme on *Grandstand* we both made it clear we expected to be riding the horse on the big day at Aintree. I insisted that I would be his jockey but Tarnya wasn't convinced and pluckily argued her case. We ended up sparring on camera like Punch and Judy. It was probably just as well for both of us that the piece was never shown because Spider's Well returned lame after giving me my 100th win as a jockey at Hereford a week before the National.

When the end came after yet another row, Tarnya packed her bags and left. There was no going back, particularly when she declared that she wasn't going to speak to me for ten years! What's more, she was true to her word. The process of divorce was unpleasant, but time heals and I get on fine now with Tarnya and her husband, Oliver Sherwood, a trainer in Lambourn. She always wanted to be a trainer's wife.

One night at dinner last year after the Doncaster Sales they told me a great story about the birth of their second child, which, to Tarnya's undisguised horror, was due on my birthday. When she was in labour she promised Oliver she'd do everything in her power to wait until after midnight before giving birth. The decision was taken out of her hands when the doctors chose to do a Caesarean section. So Archie Sherwood and I now share the same birthday!

Later that same evening at Doncaster Anthony Bromley, who helps me buy so many horses, couldn't take his eyes off Tarnya's impressive cleavage, particularly when her top button slipped open. I looked across, then blurted out loud, 'Bloody hell. They were never like that in my day!' Once the laughter died down Tarnya admitted that her new boobs had cost £2,500 each, to which I replied, 'It cost me double that for my girlfriend Georgie to have the same op last year. Talk about inflation!'

When I told Tarnya I was writing this book she suggested the title *Tunnel Vision* because of my obsession with racing and training to the exclusion of everything else.

6

Food was like a drug to me

Trying to live a normal life on my own fully two stone below my natural weight nearly drove me round the bend. I wish I'd done better as a jockey but was never in the same league as some of the guys I used to ride against. They were proper jockeys. Given my shape, I wasn't designed to be a jockey. I've got such big bones I couldn't get into anyone else's riding boots and needed an extra large body protector to go round my shoulders.

For weeks at a time I existed on a diet of little more than fresh air and on the days I was racing I'd often eat nothing and manage barely half a cup of coffee. I'd be up at five, spend a couple of hours in the sauna before going into work, then jump off whatever I'd ridden on the gallops and walk or jog back to the yard afterwards. Walking was always a useful way to control my weight. Whenever I could, I'd take off with my two dogs, Carly and Buster, for miles in the evenings.

Travelling to the races with David Barons proved a further ordeal. When we set off for places like Plumpton, Fontwell or Kempton we'd barely be out of Devon before he'd reach for his picnic box and start on his packed breakfast with a nice steaming cup of coffee. What made it worse was that he'd often ask me to open his sandwiches and pass him snacks. He'd be chatting away full of the joys of spring and I'd be sitting beside him, tongue hanging out, drooling, stomach rumbling, starving hungry. A couple of hours later he'd get to work on his packed lunch. It was a routine that used to send me up the wall.

Before racing was over David would appear at the door of the weighing room, hand me his picnic box, and ask me to fill up his flask with coffee and take any sandwiches that were still on show!

Then we'd repeat the whole frustrating exercise on the way home when I was usually expected to take over at the wheel, the last thing I needed after a long day without food or drink. Sometimes, after a fall, I'd stay down longer than necessary, or wait for the ambulance to pick me up and acquire a limp when I stepped out of it. That way I'd climb into the back seat of David's car and lie down, saying I had a bad back or a headache. Then he had to drive us back to Devon while I slept!

Back at home before going to bed I'd spend half an hour in the sauna, jump into a cold bath, then lie on the floor before doing it all again. If I was still too heavy when I went to bed I'd take a couple of pee pills. By that stage of my career I was tending to put on twice as much weight as I'd lost once the pills had worked their way through my system. The sauna helped a bit. Then, the next morning, I'd get up feeling absolutely starved knowing we'd be off again to another distant racecourse with David beside me working his way through another bloody great picnic. When I drove myself I'd often wear two tracksuits, and a thick coat under a bin liner with two holes cut out for my arms. With a woolly hat on my head and the heater going at full blast I'd arrive at the races with a great puddle of sweat on the floor.

Aware that I was never going to be a top jockey I used my time in the saddle as a means to getting somewhere else and pinned my hopes on training one day. That's not to say I didn't enjoy the riding when I was on a good chaser at a manageable weight because I was naturally competitive. But I was always hurting myself. You feel absolute shit back in the weighing room knowing you have got to go through it all again in a few minutes.

Many a time, after coming back in the ambulance, I'd wonder how I was going to get through the day. Sometimes I couldn't even stand up and limp to the scales. Then the adrenalin kicked in, you'd look at the paper and sense you had a chance, so you'd go out and ride four more and life was brilliant again. To satisfy my craving for food I'd stop at a garage on the way home and gorge myself on Mars Bars, chocolate, Lucozade and sweets, then regret it an hour later when I started feeling sick as a dog. No wonder I was such a miserable sod. The hungrier I became the more I used to fantasise about a decent fry-up. Once or twice I gave way to temptation and then beat myself up within minutes of bolting down a plateful of eggs, bacon and chips.

I wouldn't want to go through all that again and don't doubt it has had a detrimental effect on my health. I tried different varieties of pills to help me to shed weight as quickly as possible. They all worked after a fashion but the worst thing was you'd soon swiftly put back on five, six, even eight pounds and be up shit creek again. The constant cycle of starving myself and taking all those pills can't have done me any good. I used to have the familiar symptoms of stomach cramps, lack of energy and not being able to sleep. I had so many nightmares about my weight I'd jump on and off the scales twenty or thirty times a day. I was obsessed with it, knowing that if I ate one biscuit with half a cup of coffee I'd put on a pound. It was a terrible time, though I realise I wouldn't be where I am today without it.

Cheating became second nature to me. There were so many ways to pass the scales without revealing your true weight. I used to think I was the king of cheating but, looking back now, I wasn't in the same league in the art of deception as John Francome, Graham McCourt, Steve Smith Eccles and Mike Williams. With their tricks they could have ridden on the flat. Hereford and Bangor had weighing rooms that lent themselves to a bit of subterfuge. At Bangor the scales were right by the table where the clerk sat. So you could jump on the scales with your saddle, look innocently at him and he couldn't see what you were up to with your feet. Manipulating the scales there with a well-placed toe became second nature; making the correct weight was never a problem. If you were struggling to weigh in after a race you'd ask one of your mates to stand by the scales and use his foot to nudge the arrow in the right direction.

We are only talking about two or three pounds here but that was a lot to me because I was always on the limit. Crucially, I never carried less than my horse was set to carry. Given my figure that would have been impossible. I wasn't cheating the punters, only the system. Believe me: a pound or two extra makes no difference to the result of a jumps race. So if I knew I was heavy coming back in I'd slip off the girth, the leathers and the stirrup irons, if necessary, and anything else I could lose before weighing in with just the bare saddle. Once when I was hopelessly heavy I followed John Francome's example, tossed my saddle through the window and weighed in with a number cloth disguising the evidence of my crime.

The first time I rode in the Grand National on Roman Bistro I weighed out on a tiny saddle, then rode on the biggest, most comfortable one I possessed as no one was expecting us to finish in the money. If I'd been forced to weigh in there is so much chaos after the National that I'm sure I'd have smuggled myself through at the correct figure by feigning exhaustion and shaking wearily on the scales. The art of it was never to vary your weight too much. The clerks knew my lightest was ten stone five or ten stone six pounds so I had a fair chance of getting through at that level. If I'd suddenly tried to do ten stone, alarm bells would have started ringing. Most clerks were a little bit flexible; others, like the dreaded Major Manning, watched your every move. Digital scales have put an end to cheating now. I would be in serious trouble nowadays at Kempton where the winning jockey is escorted to the most public set of scales in the country, set in a glass-fronted kiosk in full view of punters and officials. Even John Francome couldn't have found a way round that one.

Today's jockeys have dieticians and nutritionists helping them with the right sort of food available in most weighing rooms. By contrast, my wasting attempts were totally unscientific. I always tried to have one good meal a week, normally Sunday lunch, either at Mum's or, failing that, wherever I happened to be that day. Then, an hour or two later, I'd start regretting it. Food became like a drug to me. I imagine my suffering was a bit like that experienced by anorexics. I hated it in the end. If only I'd been two stone lighter like Nigel Hawke or Adrian Maguire. If only. Life would have been a breeze.

There were days when I felt so dreadful I imagined it was how people suffer when they are terminally ill. I can honestly say that for the last three years I was riding I felt permanently ill. I know I shouldn't have been doing it, and can't imagine how I managed to ride all those winners in such a poor state of health. Once I finally packed up riding I had a glimpse of heaven when I was able to eat what I liked and not worry about my weight. It felt just like starting a second life.

All those years of wasting put me at a greater risk of injury. Most times I fell, which was quite often, I'd land on my head and end up with concussion. The Jockey Club's doctor, Michael Allen, explained to me more than once that, if you are really fit, the fluid around your brain acts as a shock absorber. By sweating or using pee pills I was getting rid of that vital safety net. Reaching a state of dehydration, which I did on a daily basis, definitely increased the dangers when I did get a bang on my head.

No wonder I was knocked out so many times. By the end I was like a boxer who couldn't take a punch. One tap and the lights would go out. I get stomach cramps to this day and I'm sure I pee more often that I should. If I drink more than two pints of beer, I'm absolutely bursting. I'm convinced that is caused by all the years of wasting, but at least the really bad headaches that came quickly from nowhere on a regular basis have all but gone.

Everyone says jump jockeys are the bravest but I never saw it like that. To me riding over fences was something I enjoyed doing. I didn't worry about the downside of the falls but that doesn't mean I was particularly brave. I tried to use my common sense on horses that were iffy jumpers or downright dangerous. If you are brave and stupid you will end up getting hurt. No question. Some people are naturally fearless; others are brainless.

I viewed riding over jumps as a sport. I didn't really see it as a job. I covered my costs, drove a nice car and made a bit of pocket money, though it was hardly a living. As the risk of an accident is much greater when you are driving lots of miles I always made sure I had a decent car. That took up a fair bit of my income until things improved when I took charge of a smart Toyota Celica GT after fixing up a sponsorship deal with a garage in Bath.

If I hadn't had horses like Playschool, Broadheath and Seagram to ride, I would probably have packed it all in earlier because I never expected to be anything more than an enthusiastic amateur when I started in racing. Then I found a bit of success, turned professional and couldn't step off the treadmill. Having been twelve and a half stone in the summer I somehow got down to ten stone five pounds at one stage after a sustained push in October 1987, but I felt so dreadful I didn't plan to repeat it. Playschool started the new season by falling with me at the last fence in the Charisma Gold Cup at Kempton. He jumped badly left-handed the whole way before diving so violently left at the last that we parted company. When I came back in I warned David not to run him on a right-handed track again.

Playschool picked up a knock that day, missed a lot of work and was badly in need of the run when he was narrowly beaten by Kildimo at Cheltenham a fortnight before Newbury. I told his jockey Graham Bradley we'd turn the tables in the Hennessy. Andy Hobbs and I knew Playschool would come on a bundle for the run and between us we made sure he was at peak fitness next time. Andy always liked a bet and went for a big touch in the Hennessy, which paid for a two-week holiday in Florida. Barons felt I should stay loyal to Broadheath after winning the Hennessy on him the previous year. I argued that I should ride the one I felt had the best chance. If Broadheath had been at his best, it would have been a tricky choice but he was well below par that autumn and when I spoke to Michael Marsh he understood my reasons for switching horses.

My big race hopes were in ruins when I cracked a bone in my right wrist in a fall at Plumpton three days before the Hennessy. Somehow I managed to convince the doctor I was OK and left the course without a red entry in my medical book. Persuading David Barons I was fit wasn't quite so easy but he gave me his backing after watching me ride out on Saturday morning. Whenever I picked up an injury I turned for help to my physio, Mike Ash. He'd patch me up at his clinic in Newton Abbot, work on the problem area with ultrasound treatment and strap me up so that I could ride again in double-quick time. Mike gave me intensive treatment on the wrist for two days, strapped it up securely with a metal strip between thumb and forefinger and sent me off to Newbury in high spirits.

Playschool helped me out with a faultless round of jumping. We took up the running five fences from home and won with plenty to spare by five lengths from Contradeal, with Kildimo, the 2–1 favourite, a weary fourth. It was quite something for the same stable to win one of the biggest races of the season two years running and I felt there was definitely more to come from Playschool.

The situation at Woodleigh had begun to change in my final two years as a jockey. David and Jenny Barons were having major problems with their marriage and would eventually divorce a few years later. Jenny was always supportive of me, knew I wanted to train one day and tended to be on my side. David spent plenty of time running his business but when he was in the office or the yard it was only natural that he wanted to be the boss. I tried to meet them both halfway and learned a lot about the art of diplomacy as the split in their marriage grew deeper.

I never quite knew which side of the fence to sit on. Sometimes it was a case of upsetting one or the other. Andy Hobbs and I were working hand in glove by then and quietly got on doing what we thought was best for the horses. We didn't change things dramatically but did do a fair bit more work with the horses each morning, with an extra canter here or there. They didn't have too many days off if we had our way.

Playschool, in particular, was a stuffy old boy, so Andy and I made sure he had plenty of graft. He also bucked all the time and was one of those clever horses that worked out how to unlatch his stable door with his teeth. I think he used to let himself out of his box just to annoy us. He was in fantastic form that winter, while I seemed to stumble from one injury crisis to another. A double at Hereford on 2 December was followed by a week on the sidelines after I aggravated my wrist injury when Grockle buried me at Bangor two days later. I came back earlier than I should have done because I didn't want anyone else to ride Playschool at Lingfield. I was a bit disappointed that he finished only third that day behind Rhyme 'n' Reason, but he was probably attempting the impossible in trying to give almost a stone and a half to a horse who went on to win the Grand National.

Two more falls at Ludlow on 22 December and another at Newton Abbot on Boxing Day left me in poor shape for my next appointment with Playschool, in the Coral Welsh National at Chepstow on 28 December. Ideally, I needed a few weeks off to allow my wrist to heal, but time was not on my side and I wasn't about to give up the ride in a race where everything seemed to be in his favour. A marathon trip, deep, testing ground, and a lightish weight, ten stone eleven pounds, which I could manage without cheating, all encouraged me that we had a great chance. So I kept the scale of my injury to myself, strapped up the wrist as best I could, took a few painkillers and listened to some sound advice from Jenny Barons. 'Remember that it is a long way home from the last bend,' she cautioned. 'So take your time and just sit on him for a while before making your move in the straight.'

A mile from home the race developed into a match between

Playschool and his old rival Rhyme 'n' Reason but this time the weights were in our favour. Although we were in front more than five fences from home I waited, as Jenny had suggested, before heaping on the coal approaching the final ditch, with Rhyme 'n' Reason snapping at our heels. The response from Playschool was astonishing on such tiring ground. That was the only time I rode him that I could physically feel him changing through the gears. He quickened up like a top-class horse and galloped willingly all the way to the final fence where I saw the longest stride I ever experienced in my time as a jockey. Even now I frighten myself thinking about it. If Playschool hadn't come up for me when I asked we'd have been rolling forever. But he did come up, like the brave horse he was, landed running and held on by a length.

It was a fantastic result after all the problems with my wrist. I was on a real high afterwards but came down to earth travelling home in the car with David Barons and the horse's owner, Ronnie Cottle, a lovely man who'd been in business in London for most of his life before retiring to Salcombe. I can still recall Ronnie's response when David offered him some chocolate. He said, 'I think I must have something wrong with me because I couldn't eat over Christmas and I can't eat anything now.' Tests revealed that Ronnie had stomach cancer and he was dead before the season was over. Sadly, he wasn't well enough to travel to Leopardstown for the Vincent O'Brien Gold Cup, which proved to be the highlight of Playschool's season.

I was horrified when I sat on the scales at the course to discover that I was eleven and a half stone with my riding kit on. Despite his fabulous form, Playschool wasn't even favourite that day. Forgive 'N' Forget, the 1985 Cheltenham Gold Cup hero, was sent off at 4–5 with Playschool next best at 2–1 in what was widely seen as a match. There was only one horse in it as we headed to the last fence with a decisive lead. One moment I was set for the finest win of my career, the next I nearly fell off. Photographs taken at the last fence show how close we came to disaster. Playschool jumped well until then but for some reason ignored the final fence, got in much too tight, and pitched so steeply on to his head that his nose was on the floor. Luck plays a part in these things. If a horse keeps straight you have a fair chance of survival unless the saddle hits you up the backside and fires you into orbit. But if he twists in midair it usually mean goodnight.

Playschool kept reasonably straight, found a leg and recovered his balance. I never felt as if I was going to fall off and he had enough left to canter home. We got a terrific reception as we made our way back to the winners' enclosure. Unfortunately Vincent O'Brien missed the race that bore his name, because he was suffering from flu, but I enjoyed chatting to his wife, Jacqueline, who I've met several times since. I flew back with the trophy and delivered it to Ronnie at his house in Salcombe. Twenty-one years later I carried the trophy home again for John Hales after the victory of Neptune Collonges in the same race. Playschool's famous triumph pitchforked him to the top of the ratings as Britain's leading steeplechaser. These were heady days for everyone involved with the horse as he was promoted to the head of the market for the Cheltenham Gold Cup.

Before then I found myself squaring up to David Nicholson, a trainer with a formidable reputation and a notoriously short fuse. It happened at Worcester after the horse I was riding clipped the heels of his runner Master Thomas, ridden by Richard Dunwoody. Danny's Luck was such a strong puller I couldn't hold one side of him as we sat behind Master Thomas coming past the stands first time. When Danny's Luck caught his heels I did my best to haul him back then overtook him with Dunwoody screaming and shouting at me.

Dunwoody was still having a pop at me after the race, even though I explained I hadn't done it on purpose. He wouldn't leave me alone so I thought, bollocks to you, walked away, stomped back into the weighing room and sat down. The next moment Nicholson came marching up in his trademark sheepskin coat, pointed his finger in a threatening manner and gave me a volley of abuse.

'What the hell do you think you were doing to my horse?' he bellowed, his face red with rage. 'After that performance I wouldn't give you a ride if you were the last jockey in the country. You are a disgrace,' he continued before adding a few more insults as he wound himself up into a fury. By this stage he was standing above me with his finger jabbing my shoulder. Trainers are not allowed into the inner sanctum of the weighing room; not even those, like Nicholson, who trampled over the rules when it suited them. I was knackered from doing light, steaming at his arrogant attitude and aware that twenty watching jockeys were waiting for my response. I had a fiery temper and didn't take long to explode.

As I rose to my feet like a fighter from his stool in the ring, someone beside me assumed the role of my corner man as he shouted out, 'Hit him. Just hit him. That will shut the bastard up.' When Nicholson saw the look in my eyes he withdrew his finger and started to back off. I flipped my lid, grabbed him by the scruff of his neck, told him I wouldn't ride for him if he was the last trainer on the planet, dragged him to the door and threw him out of the weighing room. He gave me a death stare as he retreated, then headed for the stewards' room to lodge a complaint against me. Later he turned his fire on David Barons.

The stewards, to their credit, didn't have me in because Nicholson was the aggressor and out of order in entering the weighing room. Frankly, he didn't have a leg to stand on. I showered, changed and headed for the car park in defiant mood. The next thing Nicholson appeared again beside me, grinning sheepishly, shook my hand and we both apologised. I think he was used to getting his own way and had more respect for those who stood up to him. Whatever the reason, from that moment on we were the best of friends. He'd telephone me regularly and was a constant supporter once I started training.

David Nicholson's lasting legacy to racing was a conveyor belt of talent he brought through as jockeys. Though I never worked for him I came to feel like one of his boys because he was always encouraging me to do better. Soon after I began training he pulled me aside and told me, 'I'm glad that you are doing it right.' Given how badly we started off at Worcester we became quite close and I was thrilled when he and his wife Dinah came to the party I threw in the summer of 2006 to celebrate my first championship. Tragically, he died three weeks later.

As a former jockey I think David would have approved of my quick thinking at Worcester that spring when I won a race which was in danger of turning into a farce. It happened when all five remaining runners in a novice chase were prevented by a loose horse from jumping the third fence. Some refused and a couple unseated their riders after being hampered by the runaway horse. No one seemed to know what to do next.

As I was on the favourite, Shropshire Lad, the last thing I wanted was to waste a winning opportunity, so I said, 'Right lads, let's sort ourselves out, go back a hundred yards and start again.' We waited until everyone was in the saddle before we all hacked back towards the previous fence, formed a line and set off again. Once we were racing two more came down before Shropshire Lad pulled clear to win by twenty lengths. I certainly earned my riding fee that day.

7

Gold Cup sensation

The defeat of Playschool in the 1988 Gold Cup was a sensation, partly because David Barons immediately voiced fears that the horse had been doped. Yet exhaustive tests by the Jockey Club's forensic team failed to discover traces of anything illegal in samples taken from Playschool after the race. Then, and in the years that followed, David continued to express his view that the horse, who started favourite, was got at.

As the trainer of Playschool, David was fully entitled to his opinion but I have to say I never believed it. The truth is that we experienced some ongoing problems with Playschool at home that season. He wasn't the soundest horse in the world, even before he started over fences, and there was probably a good reason why he tended to jump badly left-handed. We all had concerns about slight heat in one of Playschool's forelegs from time to time. It was never enough to put a full stop to his training, more a sign of the mileage he had clocked up over the years. It happens with lots of horses who race year after year. I know Andy spent time hosing his legs the evening before the Gold Cup, though you can be sure David and Jenny would not have let him run if they had the slightest doubt about his fitness.

I can remember feeling sorry for myself in the weighing room after the race when someone told me that David had just announced that Playschool had been doped. I couldn't believe he'd said it. My view then and later on, when things had calmed down, was that all Playschool's problems had finally caught up with him. Horses are not machines nor, unfortunately, can they talk. They have off days, just like human beings, but can't tell you if they are off-colour. I suspect that Playschool was feeling things. It just didn't happen for him on the day. He'd had problems like a footballer being injured and wasn't on top of his game. If an athlete or footballer isn't quite right, then he will underperform. At Cheltenham you have to be in peak physical condition. Playschool wasn't that day. End of story.

Perhaps David just couldn't accept that Playschool had problems. He was in a tricky situation because poor Ronnie Cottle, the horse's owner, had only a few weeks to live. David and Jenny obviously didn't want to upset Ronnie by expressing doubts about the horse that was his pride and joy so things might have been different if he had not been ill. The horse was favourite, he wasn't lame or anything, he hadn't missed any work and was fit to run for his life, but we were still struggling with him and it wasn't my place to make a fuss. One thing is for sure: despite the most extensive investigation no proof was found to indicate that he was doped. All the tests came up negative.

To this day I will not have any part of the suggestion that he was got at. Frankly, it's nonsense though in the weeks before the race David received threats to dope the horse in the form of large capital letters cut out from a newspaper and stuck on to a piece of paper. That preyed on his mind to the point where he convinced himself that Playschool was going to be doped. He persuaded his farm manager to sleep in a caravan parked outside the horse's box for the last three or four nights before the Gold Cup with his Alsatian, who used to bite the postman, tied to the caravan. The yard was secured so tightly that only a machine gun was missing. It all ensured that nobody could have got anywhere near Playschool but the downside was that, with so much activity outside his box, the horse wasn't able to relax for a minute in the countdown to the biggest race of his life. Playschool was quite a sparky character and I think all that activity in the yard fired him up too much. He might have left his race at home.

The furore in the days that followed the Gold Cup taught me two lessons which proved handy when I started training. If any of my horses has a problem, I try to make a statement in the press as soon as possible after speaking to the owner. That is what I did in September 2008 when I was worried about the condition of Denman. Being upfront with people makes sense when so much money is riding on the outcome of the big ante-post races. In addition, when I installed twenty-four-hour security at Ditcheat a few years ago in the run-up to the Cheltenham Festival I made sure it was done in a way that didn't affect the horses. Roving cameras, locked gates and regular patrols ensure that no one can enter the yard at any time without being spotted. We take every precaution but, crucially, the horses are un-aware that they are constantly under the spotlight. It is vital that their routine is not disturbed.

Playschool looked well enough in the paddock before the Gold Cup. There was nothing to suggest that he wasn't his usual lively self. No one got near him then or on the long walk out on to the course, but he felt so lethargic when he arrived at the start that I asked the starter to have a look at him. He couldn't see anything obviously wrong but did offer me the chance to withdraw him if I wasn't happy. That wasn't an option because David Barons would have cut off my balls if I'd taken the horse out at that stage.

Playschool didn't feel like a dead horse to me that day but nor did he feel right. He was never happy and always changing his legs. I wasn't totally surprised that he ran flat because, being so involved with his training, I half knew we were up against it. He was never galloping or jumping with any zest but he didn't run like a doped horse and just underperformed. We were beaten before halfway but, as it was the Gold Cup, I kept going to the top of the hill in the forlorn hope that he would finally spark into life. Then I pulled him up. For Playschool it was a sorry end to a fabulous season. He was never at the races, but at least he lived to fight another day.

Forgive 'N' Forget, winner of the race three years earlier, wasn't so lucky. Just as I was hacking back on Playschool I heard the sickening sound of a vet's gun going off as the horse was put out of his misery after shattering his off-hind pastern while still in with a chance. My despair at Playschool's dismal display was nothing compared to that experienced by his rider Mark Dwyer.

Playschool was badly dehydrated by the time he reached Woodleigh that evening after peeing several times on the way home. Andy Hobbs told me later that he was up half the night trying to persuade the horse to drink. I think Playschool was quite stressed by the whole experience but he recovered swiftly. A vet from New Zealand, who was staying with David and Jenny that week, suspected the horse had been doped, possibly with ACP, a quick-acting tranquilliser. A Jockey Club team visited the yard a few days later to carry out routine questioning of our stable staff but then and later they failed to uncover evidence of any skulduggery.

When Playschool returned to the track the following November at Cheltenham he broke down badly on his off foreleg. He gave me a great feel through the race but faltered a stride after the last fence. He was in front at the time, then began to drift to his left and, though he kept on gamely, he was pipped on the line by Golden Friend. That was the last time I rode him. I thought Playschool might be retired after that but David nursed him back to full fitness over the next twelve months.

He continued to race until he was thirteen but the fire that once set him apart had been extinguished. It still upsets me that Playschool is best remembered for the drama that followed his failure in the Gold Cup. He was a marvellous horse for me, the best I ever rode and came along at the right time. I achieved so much more with him than I could have imagined in my wildest dreams. He definitely helped put me on the map. Playschool spent most of his retirement at a farm a few miles from my home at Ditcheat and disgraced himself out hunting one day by kicking another rider. Even in his twenties he still wanted to be racing. I owe him so much.

8

The call that changed my life

My final season as a jockey was interrupted by a series of crunching falls that hastened the date of my retirement. One of the worst happened at Plumpton in October when Nicoghan reared over backwards and crushed me against an upright in the paddock. That was one injury I couldn't disguise. The pain was so bad it still gives me stick now though it took two weeks for the doctors to discover I had a hairline fracture of a vertebra.

My recovery was cheered by the sight of a horse called Olveston winning two bumper races in my mother's red and yellow colours. I was always on the lookout for suitable recruits among the New Zealand imports and picked out a useful gelding by Sea Anchor before passing him on to Mum and our family friend Alan Taylor. We named him Olveston after the village in which I'd been brought up. Following those early victories the two partners sold almost 50 per cent to Colin Lewis, who became one of my most loyal supporters once I started training.

Horses bred in New Zealand made quite an impact that winter. None was more promising than Seagram, a bonny little horse, not much bigger than a pony, who bounced back to form after missing a year with leg trouble that required an operation to put carbon-fibre implants in his tendons. Seagram won four races over fences that season. For such a tiny horse he jumped as if he was on springs, though there wasn't much in front of you when he landed over a fence. Most of all, I was impressed by his attitude because you could never get to the bottom of him. He was a tough little nut and stayed on so well in his races even then that I was thinking he might be one for the Grand National.

My role as Barons' stable jockey allowed me a useful input into running plans. Since we were both strong characters we'd sometimes clash about a horse's target in the future, though our biggest arguments tended to be about the fitness of our horses. It was a period when Martin Pipe's exploits were the talk of jump racing. From a modest start from his base near Taunton he quickly came to dominate the sport and by the late eighties he was breaking records with in excess of two hundred winners a season. Try as we might, we never seemed to beat his horses whenever we took them on in the West Country. I seemed to spend my time chasing the tails of Pipe's runners at Newton Abbot, Exeter, Wincanton and further afield. You didn't need to be Einstein to work out that his horses were fitter than everyone else's.

Most of Pipe's winners made the running in those days. If I tried to jump off handy and go with them, my horse would stop after a mile and a half and, if I dropped mine in and tried to creep into the race a mile from home, I never got there. Whenever I came back in afterwards and told David one of his had blown up or wasn't fit he'd reply, 'Don't be so stupid, boy', which made further discussion pointless.

David's horses tended to be big, raw-boned sorts compared to Pipe's, yet he just couldn't see that they needed more work. How do you tell a trainer that he is too set in his old-fashioned way of training? It was considered the norm by trainers of his era to give horses one or two runs to bring them to their peak. People had been doing the same thing for years. Then Pipe came along and turned the game on its head. His hardly ever improved for a run. They were lean and hard by the time they were sent to the races and from what I could gather all the work was done on a shortish, uphill, all-weather gallop.

Pipe's runners were flying compared to the rest. At the time people came up with all sorts of dark theories about his horses but I had no doubt it was simply a case of his being much fitter than the rest. Yet I could never really convince David, and other trainers, too, of the truth of it because they didn't really want to believe it. Andy Hobbs and I decided to take matters into our own hands. Since we were both positive and competitive we quietly upped the work schedule of the horses without the guv'nor knowing what we were doing. We'd canter a bit quicker than before on the all-weather gallop and generally do more with the horses without giving the game away. We took pride in what we were doing and wanted to get better results for everyone at the yard, including the trainer.

Yet winners were scarce that winter apart from a rare, purple patch when I enjoyed a rash of success over a period of five days. It began with a double at Bangor on 2 December. Next day at Worcester I achieved the only treble of my career on Just as Hopeful, Mister Christian and Yiragan. I then brought my total to six in four days with an easy triumph on Seagram at Leicester on 6 December.

For a few heady moments I had a glimpse of how it must feel to be a champion jockey enjoying success on a daily basis, but I was soon dumped on my backside once more and it would be months before I found myself back in the winners' enclosure. Part of the problem was that I was hardly getting chances from other yards. The days when trainers approached me to take spare rides had long gone. Agents were beginning to play a role in booking jockeys and I didn't appear to be on their lists, because I struggled to do less than eleven stone without a couple of days' warning.

On the odd occasion I let myself go on a Saturday night I'd spend a couple of hours at the New Inn at Moreleigh, not far from the yard. The attraction was the girl pulling pints behind the bar. Bridget Brackenbury worked for her parents, John and Becky, who owned the New Inn and kept a couple of horses behind the pub. John and Becky had two daughters. I eventually married Bridget and Mick Fitzgerald married her sister, Jane.

By that stage I was so heavy I couldn't have ridden every day of the week. By riding solely for David and Jenny Barons those last few years I probably extended my career by at least twelve months. If their horses were not running or, on occasions, out of form, then I was a redundant jockey. I didn't mind too much because I really enjoyed being involved with the training. Whenever I was out of action after a fall and unable to ride out I'd still go to the yard to help out one way or another.

Some jockeys fall athletically, like gymnasts. Others curl up in-stinctively into a ball to protect themselves from the impact of flying hooves. I used to fall like a sack of spuds tumbling from the back of a lorry. I was the wrong shape – tall and lean – and always seemed to get hurt when I hit the ground. My medical record book overflowed with entries in red ink, which prevented me from riding again until I was passed fit by a doctor. Concussion featured on every page because I tended to be knocked cold by the slightest bang on the head. I was so prone to concussion that Dr Allen warned me that he was considering standing me down permanently if I had many more head injuries. It wasn't what I wanted to hear.

My form as a jockey was so poor in the spring that my losing run extended to sixty-one consecutive rides. If they'd published a cold list back then I'd have been in the freezer. Things reached the lowest point when I had the most frightening fall of my career on Southover Lad at Worcester on 15 February. I was in agony, totally winded, and couldn't breathe for twenty minutes. When I was examined in the ambulance room they found two foot marks in the middle of my back protector. If I hadn't been wearing it I might not be here now. It was that bad. To this day I can't move my back as freely as I'd like.

My catalogue of injuries that time included three cracked vertebrae, a displaced collarbone, broken rib, cracked shoulder blade and bruised kidneys. You don't have to be mad to be a jump jockey, but we all have our moments of insanity. The following day I was aching all over with my arm in a sling but that didn't stop me announcing from my hospital bed that I expected to be back in action in a fortnight! It was, of course, a crazy deadline, partly because I put on so much weight over ten days that I was soon pushing the scales at approaching eleven and a half stone.

I made it back to the track in twenty-two days and sealed my return with a welcome success on Salcombe Harbour, though it was an enormous struggle to make the correct weight of eleven stone. At twenty-six I knew I couldn't sustain the deception much longer. I struggled on with a couple more winners but time was running out for me. I was always busy in the yard, riding four lots a day, and would then walk for up to three hours in the evening while Bridget was working in the pub. All this while I was starving myself. I didn't have an ounce of fat on me yet I was still piling on the pounds. Talk about self-abuse.

I sensed I was staring down the barrel of a gun when Dad and I set off on 16 May for Towcester's evening meeting for one ride. I was struggling with flu and felt even worse after giving Standard Rose no help at all as we finished in the rear in the handicap hurdle under the steadier of eleven stone ten pounds. Then, to my surprise, I was offered a spare ride that was due to carry eleven stone. I couldn't manage it, didn't feel like cheating and cried off, blaming the flu. It was a long journey back to Devon that night.

I briefly put my troubles behind me with a summer holiday in the Cayman Islands with Bridget and Andy Hobbs and his wife, Rosemary. We stayed in an apartment belonging to one of the yard's owners, Bruce Campbell, and had a great time, swimming every day, snorkelling and soaking up the sun. By the time I returned to work for David Barons early in July, my weight had shot up to almost twelve and a half stone. I barely shifted a pound in the following two weeks despite a regular diet and frequent sessions in the sauna. It was doing my head in because I was planning to ride again. How was I ever going to get down to a racing weight? The opening of the new season was less than a fortnight away when fate intervened.

I was leading the string on Topsham Bay walking and trotting on the roads that morning with Andy Hobbs at the back of the line of horses. Once we all turned round to trot up the long hill I was at the back and Andy at the front. Topsham Bay was a big brute of a thing and, as we set off, he decided to go from the back of the team to the front in three giant strides. He was bucking and squealing as he clattered up the lane, which inevitably set off some of the others. One of them, Purple Point, took exception as we shot past and let go with both hind legs.

I sensed them coming and tried to lift my left leg to protect myself but he was too quick for me and I heard an almighty crack as he caught me with both barrels four inches above my ankle. As the bone came straight through the skin all I could see was my foot swinging in the stirrup. Things got worse when Topsham Bay sped up the road out of control while I clung on grimly to his neck. I was screaming from the pain and about to fall off. Luckily for me, Topsham Bay slowed to a halt which allowed Andy to ride alongside, hand the reins to another lad and then lift me from the saddle and sit me down as gently as he could in the bank below the hedge. The pain was unbelievable by then, which was hardly surprising as X-rays later showed I'd broken my tibia and fibula.

I can remember thinking that at least I could have a few decent meals in hospital. As the ambulance taking me to Torbay Hospital had to pass the New Inn, I asked the driver to stop so that I could let Bridge know what had happened. She rushed out, full of concern, rounded up some clothes for me and followed on a bit later. By the time we reached hospital I was in so much pain that if someone had given me a gun I'd happily have used it to put myself out of my misery. Instead, I had to rely on gas, which brought some temporary relief. I waited in the hospital corridor for more than twelve miserable, pain-racked hours before I was seen by any doctors. Finally, it was my turn. I was just being prepared for an operation to pin the break when someone was rushed in on a trolley needing emergency surgery.

That left me in limbo for another two hours before I was taken to a ward for the night. The next day the doctors decided not to operate. Instead, they put my leg in plaster and sent me back to the ward for another week. I've never been a good patient and hated every moment of my stay in hospital. After being active for so many years I couldn't bear lying around for days on end unable to do anything but read or listen to the radio.

I'd become something of a medical expert by then and realised I was in big trouble. I was in agony as my leg blew up to twice its normal size, jammed tight inside the plaster cast. Eventually they listened to my pleas, cut off the plaster, put on another one and warned me that I wouldn't be riding again for at least six months. Then they sent me home. Four weeks later the doctors had another look at the damage and didn't like what they uncovered. Their solution was not for the faint-hearted. They gave me an anaesthetic, manipulated the broken bones into place and put me in plaster again. I knew exactly what they were doing, but luckily couldn't feel a thing because I was numb from the knee down. Then I just had to wait for the leg to heal, which took much longer than expected.

As I sat idly at home I knew deep down that I was finished as a jockey. Yet I spent much of the following year in denial by fending off all inquiries about my plans by insisting that I'd be riding again as soon as possible. Of course it was madness, though I half believed it at the time. I probably could have ridden a few with a decent weight if I worked at it but I was never going to earn a living again from race riding.

While I wondered what to do next, Jenny Barons suggested I should remain with them as an assistant trainer. That proved to be the final piece in the jigsaw. David was heavily involved in the farming business and Jenny, knowing I wanted to train, encouraged me to become more involved in the office side of things. David held the licence but Jenny was the one who was there every day with the horses, would often ask my view and was always 100 per cent supportive of me. I took some of the pressure off them, and tried to learn as much as I could from two vets, Peter Calver and Chris Cullen, who treated the horses in the yard. It was a team effort and we all had an input.

I relished my involvement in helping to train the horses. Between us all we got it right and had some great times. I wouldn't mind training there now. If David was elsewhere I'd represent him at the races, saddle the runners, look after the owners and talk to the racing press when we had winners. Being so closely involved with the training helped put me where I am now. Working in the office kept me sane because I was still on crutches at Christmas 1989, with my leg remaining uncomfortably swollen. The deadline for my comeback passed without any significant progress but, if anyone asked, I stubbornly maintained that I hoped to be back for the Cheltenham Festival in March. That was just me trying to be positive. A further setback in January ended any hope of me riding again that season.

As a jockey I liked to think ahead by trying to plan a horse's campaign through the season. Being in the office gave me the chance to spend hours leafing through the programme book, looking for opportunities. Checking on race conditions at different tracks day after day might sound boring but I've always found it a rewarding exercise. I recall suggesting to David that we should enter Topsham Bay and Royal Battery in the four-mile NH Chase for amateur riders at Cheltenham. Topsham Bay was slow and still a maiden but he was always running on at the finish and I thought the race was made for him. At first David laughed at my idea of entering the pair but I persuaded him to change his mind and there were no complaints when Topsham Bay, ridden by my old housemate Paul Hacking, led home Royal Battery in a notable one-two for the stable.

I spent my spare time that winter revving up a couple of point-to-pointers stabled in the Brackenburys' yard behind the New Inn. I concentrated on Nicol John, formerly with Barons, and Its Nearly Time, who, I soon realised, was a fair tool capable of winning decent races. I used to argue with John and Becky because they were not

doing nearly enough with their horses before I got involved. I immediately increased the work rate using fields, banks and hills up on
Dartmoor and also began winging them up David Barons' gallops on a
regular basis.

Nicol John showed we were on the right lines by winning a local
point-to-point early in February 1990 at 6–4. His success encouraged
me to go for a punt in a maiden hunter chase with Its Nearly Time
who had plenty of speed and showed bags of promise ridden by
Bridget in a ladies race. The horse wasn't wound up that day and
made the running until dropping out in the last couple of furlongs.
I made sure he was spot-on next time. The newspapers had Bridget
down to ride Its Nearly Time at Ludlow, but those were the days
before overnight declaration of jockeys so we were able to substitute
the leading amateur, Philip Scholfield, at the last minute. We went for
a right touch and backed the horse all morning.

So much for the best-laid plans. Its Nearly Time lost twenty lengths
at the start when another horse whipped round and dumped his rider.
Philip made up the ground steadily and cruised round before easing
into the lead on Its Nearly Time, running away going to the last fence.
Watching with mounting excitement in the stands I remember thinking I'd be able to afford a holiday in Barbados for the first time in my
life. Then Its Nearly Time ruined the script by falling. In due course
he'd win over hurdles and fences but that was the day that counted.

My broken leg gave me plenty of grief that spring and summer. A
year after the accident I was still unable to run even a few steps, so
nobody can have been surprised when I announced my retirement
from the saddle on 1 August 1990. The decision was taken out of my
hands after Dr Allen expressed concern that one more fall on the leg
could lead to major complications. There was no way he was going to
let me take the risk. I wasn't too disheartened because it had been
coming for a long time. The first thing to go was the sauna, where I'd
spent so much of the previous few years. I hated the smell of it so
much I'd be physically sick if I looked at a sauna now and I swear on
my life I've not jumped on a set of scales since I retired from riding. I'd
already done enough sweating for a lifetime.

In the months that followed, Bridget helped me come to terms with
being an ex-jockey. We were pretty much an item by then, shared an
interest in the horses at her parents' pub and were married at Newton

Abbot Register Office late in January 1991, followed by a reception at the Glazebrook Hotel in South Brent. Since we were at the height of the racing season we put back our honeymoon to the summer though it would be two more years before we managed to get away for a sunshine break. So, after barely thirty-six hours as a newly married man, I was back at work early on Monday morning.

Nigel Hawke was the man chosen by David Barons to ride most of his horses. He'd been at Josh Gifford's as an amateur, followed me down to Devon, was the right shape and could do ten stone comfortably on a decent saddle. Lucky man. We were the best of friends. However, the stable's claimer, Rodi Greene, initially rode Seagram at the start of the new season without much success. Things improved when Nigel took over on him on New Year's Day 1991 in a four-mile handicap chase at Cheltenham, a distance I felt sure would play to his strengths.

Seagram led at halfway and kept on strongly to beat Bonanza Boy. I told David afterwards that he could win the Grand National if we played him right. He wasn't so sure because he doubted the horse's stamina and felt he was too small to jump round Aintree. Once I have an idea about a particular target for a horse I don't let go. To me the National was the obvious race for Seagram and, having won on him five times, I was confident that he'd cope with the big fences. Yet still David hesitated.

Matters came to a head in the office one day late in January when I asked David if he was going to enter Seagram in the Grand National. He repeated his reservations but my perseverance must have paid off because the next thing I heard him on the phone telling the horse's owner, Sir Eric Parker, that he was keen to have a crack at Aintree. Seagram justified the decision by romping to victory in the Ritz Club National Chase at Cheltenham. He was thriving on the hard work we gave him and clearly ahead of the handicapper.

Most of the pre-race publicity at Aintree concentrated on the attempt by Garrison Savannah to match the unique achievement of Golden Miller who, in 1934, became the only horse ever to win the Gold Cup and the National in the same season. We were becoming increasingly confident that Seagram could spoil the party. He was in sparkling form after Cheltenham, had a perfect racing weight of ten stone six pounds and a bit of ease in the ground that brought out the best in him.

I was hoping to be at Liverpool to cheer him on but for some reason David didn't want me to go, so I settled down in front of the television at home knowing that I was going to watch Seagram win. I was so confident by then that I couldn't see him being beaten. You have these feelings about horses and they don't always come off. Not this time: I'd convinced myself that only bad luck could prevent Seagram pulling it off. David gave Nigel his orders on the big day but, as it was his first ride in the National, I'd already talked it through with him a dozen times and told him to try to switch the horse off and take his time because four and a half miles is a hell of a long way to be racing.

Watching Seagram win the National was one of the proudest moments of my life. David Barons was the trainer, yet we both knew I'd played my part and even when Garrison Savannah started up the long run-in with a healthy lead, I always felt our little fellow would catch him. He had to make up five or six lengths from the last fence but I could see he was flying towards the centre of the course. It was going to be tight but Seagram showed bags of character as he closed with a steady rhythm before sweeping to the front one hundred yards from the post. It was a magical sight, but the feeling didn't last long because a falling out with David led to my leaving shortly afterwards.

The writing was on the wall the day after the Grand National when I was expected to man the phones in the office before the celebrations got going, while locals came from miles around to welcome the horse home and the place was swarming with reporters and TV crews. Maybe David wanted to keep me out of the way so that I couldn't take any of the credit, which was a shame as Andy and I had a big input in the planning and preparation of Seagram's famous triumph. He was a horse that required a huge amount of work and we made sure he got it in the weeks leading up to Aintree.

It was frustrating that David seemed to be pretending that I didn't exist. He wasn't the easiest person in the world to get on with and I've never been slow to stand up for myself. Relations between us became increasingly strained that last season when we had a few unpleasant rows. I realised that I had to move on. It was just a question of when.

The moment arrived two weeks later when we argued once more. I think it was obvious to both of us that my time with him was up. I'm sure David was delighted to see the back of me, but at least I left with the warm wishes of Jenny, who, with typical generosity, invited me to remain in the cottage where Bridget and I lived until I sorted something out.

It was all so sudden that I didn't have a clue what to do. I was twenty-nine, hooked on training and prepared to do anything to take the first step on the ladder. I had nothing planned when I left and hardly any money, just a few thousand pounds in savings, and a new wife who was happy to support me in whatever I chose to do.

In those first uncertain weeks I can remember half-heartedly looking at a pub with the view of taking on the tenancy. The main bar of The Ring O'Bells, on the moor at Drewsteignton, was like an old-fashioned sitting room with the toilets outside in the garden. It might have seemed a good idea the night before but driving away from the place I knew beyond doubt that I couldn't face the prospect of running a pub. That would be living a lie, a never-ending nightmare. It was time to stop fannying about and take the plunge to set up as a trainer. I've always been decisive and couldn't see any purpose in delaying the inevitable. It was what I had been working towards for so long.

Fate has a way of shaping your life. Seagram winning the National was the thing that triggered a startling change of direction. Yet if I hadn't broken my leg two years earlier I might have bumbled on trying to keep going as a jockey and the chance to start training might have passed me by. I phoned friends, contacts and anyone I thought might have a horse with me, told them of my plans and, within a few days, had the promise of half a dozen, including Olveston, who was the ante-post favourite for the Schweppes Gold Trophy at Newbury until snow caused the meeting to be called off.

I told the Jockey Club about my plans and began searching urgently for a suitable place to train. As I didn't have the finance I put a few irons in the fire, half hoping to find someone to back me. Richard Barber, a friend from my point-to-pointing days, mentioned that his brother Paul had a place that might become available later in the year, but the timing was uncertain.

Gerry Reynolds, a Torquay businessman, whose wife Franny was keen on horses, discussed buying a yard and leasing it to me. One of the places we looked at was owned by Neil Kernick, near the old racecourse at Buckfastleigh with a seven-furlong gallop and a yard with scope for expansion set in sixty-three acres. Gerry had it valued at between £150,000 and £170,000 and made an offer, but it was miles below the asking price of £300,000 so our plans came to nothing. It is a point-to-point yard now. I also looked at stables bought on the moor by one of David Barons' owners, Norman Lake. Almost as soon as I got out of the car I knew it wasn't going to work because it had only a handful of boxes and no gallops of any note. If I was going to train I needed better facilities.

Time was passing and with horses ready to come to me I was beginning to panic early in June when my dad rang to tip me off about a yard with twenty boxes in Somerset he'd seen advertised in the *Racing Post*. Best of all, the owner promised to have a couple of horses with the successful applicant. I was on the phone like a shot with the call that would transform my life.

9

A glimpse of seventh heaven

Paul Barber seemed to have been waiting for my call. The moment I introduced myself, he asked, 'What kept you?' Maybe his brother, Richard, had marked his card about me. Paul explained that he was looking for someone to replace Jim Old, who was moving to a new base near Swindon, then invited me to have a look at the yard the next day. I hardly slept that night before setting off with Bridget in the morning.

As we approached the village of Ditcheat, just off the A37 near Shepton Mallet, my spirits lifted at the sight of field after field of lush green grass and hundreds of cows. I've always believed horses and cows go together. This was clearly proper dairy country and all the better for it as I'd already made up my mind that I wouldn't train anywhere close to farms that grew oil seed rape. My time with David Barons had taught me that rape, particularly in flower, is hopeless for racehorses. It makes them all sick.

Just before we drove into the village I spotted an all-weather gallop snaking steeply uphill towards the skyline. Things were getting better by the minute. The hill brought back memories of happy days with Dick Baimbridge, who could get horses fitter than anyone else I'd worked for. That hill could be the key to training winners at Ditcheat.

Paul Barber turned out to be a brisk, no-nonsense type of farmer. He talked about his great friend, the late John Thorne, who trained for him with notable success with horses like Artifice, said how much he still missed him and showed me round the neat little stable yard which he'd converted, at the suggestion of his wife Marianne, from the old dairy at the bottom of his garden. As a youngster, Paul milked cows in the barn that is now the home of my assistant, Dan Skelton.

Today Paul's farming interests extend to 2,000 acres in Somerset, another 1,000 acres in Dorset with several dairy herds, pig units and a factory in the village which produces around 45 tonnes of cheese a day. All along his passion has been jump racing. He told me that his ambition was to milk 1,000 cows and own the winner of the Cheltenham Gold Cup. I couldn't do anything about the first one but, given half a chance, I'd try to deliver the second; if, of course, he chose me.

Paul learned the hard way as an owner. As a teenager he started with some slow point-to-pointers, bought his first horse, Crazy Slave, in instalments and was acutely embarrassed when Justatic, his first runner with Thorne, was described by the commentator as 'the aptly named Just Static' as he trailed the field at Exeter! In the early days he had plenty of ordinary horses, but that never put him off. Then and now his motto has always been that owning racehorses should be fun.

The rent Paul was asking for a three-year lease wasn't over the top but on my tight budget it was going to stretch me to the limit. I told him I had hardly any money, just my savings of £10,000, that I was fiercely ambitious and would work night and day to succeed. I could bring half a dozen horses with me, maybe more, if he gave me the nod, and promised to fill all twenty-eight boxes in the yard within twelve months. Britain was in the depths of an economic recession at the time, with people cutting back everywhere, but I told Paul that didn't bother me one bit. I was determined to make it as a trainer, however tough things might be.

Paul had other candidates to see and gave no indication of how he was thinking. Feeling the interview had gone well, I headed back to Devon in a state of nervous apprehension. Paul seemed a great guy. With him, the hill and cows as far as you could see I thought, wow, this is everything I want. I'd had a glimpse of seventh heaven, but would I be given the keys?

That night I wrote a four-page letter to Paul outlining my plans and dreams and explaining that, throughout my riding career I had been more interested in the training side of things. I added that I was dedicated to the business of producing winners but obviously needed a bit of luck and help to get me on my way. Though I was a jumping man I hinted that, to keep the operation going twelve months of the year, I'd like to take out a flat licence as well. Little did I know then that Paul wouldn't step across the road to watch a flat race! Nor is he interested in summer jumping.

I ended by suggesting that we might be able to help each other as he was obviously keen for his yard to develop into a successful operation and my ambition was to make my mark as quickly as possible. Paul called a week later to say he'd chosen me, promised to buy me two horses at the next Doncaster Sales, and added that he'd delay my first payment of rent for six months. It was an amazingly generous gesture from a man I hardly knew and it set the tone of our relationship for the years to come.

I felt as if I'd just won the pools as I put down the phone. Which, in a sense, I had. Paul asked to meet up again the next day when he sounded every bit as ambitious as me. He had big plans for his new trainer, no question, and was eager to set it all in motion. That was one of the best days of my life. I was elated beyond words, scarcely believing what was happening, but driving home afterwards I had a severe attack of nerves for five minutes before I got a grip of myself and realised I had to make it work. I couldn't wait to get started. Looking back now, it would have been a life-changing body blow if Paul had picked someone else. Much later he admitted that he was swayed by my enthusiasm even though he thought I was a cocky little bugger.

The next few months passed in a whirlwind of activity. There was so much to arrange but our plans were complicated by delays to the date that Jim Old could move out. When Jim first showed me round the yard he was full of gloom and doom, convinced the place had a virus that affected his horses. It wasn't what I wanted to hear and put me off for a minute, but by then I had nowhere else to go and had given my word to Paul. It was too late to change tack. Waiting eagerly on the sidelines, I kept some of the horses behind the New Inn at Moreleigh and sent others to a friend, Martin Saunders, who had a livery yard nearby. Sometimes I took the horses for a blow out on Neil Kernick's gallop near Buckfastleigh. I was itching to get cracking at Ditcheat and didn't enjoy marking time in Devon.

In the early days a lot of people assumed that I was a salaried trainer employed by Paul Barber but that was never the case. From the start I paid him a rent and he paid me training fees for his horses; it has been that way ever since. I knew beyond doubt that I had to be my own boss. I could never have worked for anyone else again because my temper wouldn't allow it. I wanted to paddle my own canoe. Paul and

I set off on the right foot with a strictly business arrangement, though he soon became a friend, too, and has supported me in so many ways down the years.

A lot of people warned me that Paul was a tough man and so fiery that he was bound to make life difficult for me if things didn't work out. That hasn't been my experience. I've never seen that side of him, perhaps because he realised I was so totally driven I always put the horses first. From day one we got on brilliantly with barely a cross word and on the few occasions we have disagreed the argument was forgotten within minutes. He has never interfered and soon realised I wouldn't take any notice anyway. We both know where the boundary is and whenever we get close to it we beg to differ. I'm sure it helps that in many ways we are quite similar. We are both positive, ambitious, go-ahead people who can't stand dilly-dallying or defeatism. Paul took me under his wing and treated me like one of his sons in some ways. I've always seen him as something of a father figure. He wanted me to get ahead and his enthusiasm matched mine.

In August, Paul and I drove together to the Doncaster Sales, which was a novel experience for me as I knew nothing about buying horses and didn't have a clue about the location of the sales ring. In the next two days we bought two likely youngsters, paying 21,000 guineas for a bumper winner, See More Indians, from Gerry Blum and a bit less for Pere Bazille. On a hunch I also forked out 8,000 guineas for Head or Harp and passed him on within twenty-four hours to Des Nichols, who quickly became a good pal.

See More Indians, a great big scopey sort, was the first horse I bought at public auction. Paul and I had both him ticked off as an obvious one, so he said get on and buy him. He was a bit plain, didn't have the greatest confirmation and couldn't trot at all, but he was a good walker and obviously had an engine. The most gorgeous, good-looking horses with classy pedigrees don't always make the best racehorses. Dick Baimbridge had often told me that you want a racehorse, not a show horse. I've always followed that.

Aware that I could do with some timely publicity, Paul made sure that both horses were knocked down to me. They then joined my modest team assembled in Devon behind the New Inn. I was encouraged by almost daily phone calls from Paul keeping me up to date on the situation at Ditcheat. He knew I was bursting with impatience to move in.

These days, would-be trainers have to go through a series of courses at Newmarket before gaining a licence. For me, after years already working at the sharp end, that would have been a nightmare and I'm not sure I could have handled it. I'd had a pretty good grounding in what was required though some guidance in running a business would have been handy. That was the hardest part, so having Paul around whenever I needed advice was a big plus. Wise beyond his years, he taught me a fair bit about running a business, especially in the early days. His benchmark has always been pay and be paid. That was just about the best tip he ever gave me. I hate owing anyone and expect people to pay me. Paul also suggested that any decision is better than none at all and warned me about the pitfalls of owning horses myself. 'Hoteliers don't fill their rooms with their own families. They need paying customers,' he'd say.

By late autumn I had pretty much run through my savings on new tack, sheets, rugs, office equipment and a hundred and one other things you need when you set up on your own. Once I'd put in my last penny it was 'shit or bust'. If it didn't work out then I was on the road to financial ruin, simple as that, so it was up to me to make things happen. My granddad Frank weighed in with a wonderful gesture by lending me £8,000 to buy a second-hand lorry.

Bridget and I kept our own living costs to a minimum. As we couldn't afford expensive cars or foreign holidays, our honeymoon was put on hold indefinitely. We didn't expect to make any money for a long time. Every last penny would go back into the business. In those days I did just about every job going, including feeding, mucking out and riding up to half a dozen, driving the lorry, unloading the hay and shavings and sweeping the yard and all the paperwork in the office. I gave myself five years to make a go of things. If it didn't work out then I'd move on and try something else.

Getting my licence was the least of my worries because I thought it would be a formality. I had a business plan which I showed to the Jockey Club, and the licensing panel already knew who I was and that I had a good set-up at Ditcheat. Jenny Barons played her part by providing the authorities with a glowing testimonial. One way and another, I owe her so much. The moment I tracked her down on holiday in Portugal she rang the Jockey Club telling them they might as well try to stop the River Avon flowing as prevent me from training racehorses!

I was determined to keep costs reasonable for my owners and not leave them in the dark about anything. I've always preferred to keep things straightforward and above board. If a horse has a problem, its owner should be the first to know. Finding people to support me was quite hard. I didn't have much to spend and was scratching around to sell bits and pieces of horses. Colin Lewis promised his support from the start and has been with me ever since. Mike Disney let me have Vomero and, more importantly, helped me get Thatcher Rock. A guy called John Gainsford, a long-time owner of Barons, kindly sent me Mister Christian. Sid Williams, who was involved with Paul in See More Indians and Pere Bazille, played his part by letting me have Musical Monarch. Des Nichols also had a major interest in Mystic Palace. One of his co-owners in the horse was Gary Walker, a police-man I'd met on honeymoon with Tarnya a few years earlier. You can imagine my shock when I heard that Gary was jailed for life in 2004 for murdering his pregnant partner.

Several of these horses had been with Barons, which inevitably led to more aggravation. I had reached the point of not caring by then because I had worked my balls off for David for six years, and done well for him without so much as a thank you. As my first head lad I took on Graham Piper, who had looked after Seagram and was only twenty-three. It suited me to have a younger man who was not set in his ways. It takes a lot of crumbs to make a cake and I wanted to put together those crumbs my way, which was pretty much Dick Baimbridge's way.

I managed to round up eight or nine horses, either at the New Inn or with Martin Saunders, but told anyone who asked me that I had double that number. It was a white lie but one I felt was justified because, when you are starting out, you don't want to sound as if you are struggling for horses. By late September I was all dressed up with nowhere to go. We were due to start at Manor Farm Stables on 1 October, but there was no sign of Jim moving out. Exasperated by the situation, Paul travelled with him to his new yard and gave the builders the hurry-up in his own unique way.

When Paul and his wife Marianne flew off on holiday at the start of October they invited Bridget and me to stay in their house. We jumped at the chance and moved lock, stock and barrel with our horses, two dogs and a bucketful of dreams. I knew from day one that the set-up and the environment were right for me, but until you deliver the results you can't be too cocky. For the next three weeks Jim and I trained our teams side by side from the same yard. That was a bit of an eye-opener as he kept a couple of goats, too. I think we were both relieved when he finally departed. Bridget and I then moved into the trainer's house, a converted dairy in the middle of the yard.

All new trainers try to start with a flourish. I certainly had high hopes for Southover Lad, my first runner in a handicap hurdle at Chepstow on 2 November. Definitely fit enough to win, he was pulled up before halfway after breaking down badly. Talk about a rude awakening. Fitness was the key, then and now. Even a blind man could spot that Martin Pipe was winning everything because his horses were fit. I've never seen the point of giving a horse a run or two for the sake of it, so I was doing more at home with them in a day than some trainers do in a week. It was all short, sharp exercise and the horses loved it. I was determined to have mine primed to win first time, yet still have room for improvement.

That was the grand plan but, over the next two months, I began to wonder if I'd ever train a winner. The horses seemed well at home and often showed up prominently in their races without getting their heads in front. Approaching Christmas I'd racked up half a dozen seconds and was in danger of getting a complex about being a runner-up in life. Bumbles Folly was typical of my luck when he was caught and passed at the last fence at Hereford on 20 December after leading most of the way.

Half an hour later I finally had my moment in the sun when Olveston won for the first time over fences. As his part-owner, Mum was there with Dad to enjoy the moment. They had done everything possible to support me down the years and I was thrilled that they played their part in a little bit of family history. Olveston had become frustrating by then and had fallen last time at Newbury. To give him confidence I probably schooled him over more fences at home than the great grey Desert Orchid jumped in public. Yet he was still prone to alarmingly erratic jumping and nearly spoiled the script at Hereford by trying to demolish the fourth fence.

Christmas arrived a day late for me at Newton Abbot when I enjoyed a double in the space of half an hour with Musical Monarch and Mister Christian, both ridden by Hywel Davies. After the frustrations of the previous two months it felt brilliant to be on a bit of a roll, though the reaction in the racing press the next day was way over the top. 'NICHOLLS DOUBLE PUTS PIPE IN THE SHADE' shouted a headline in the *Sporting Life*. Fat chance of that!

See More Indians was my big white hope for the season but he unseated his rider at the last flight at Cheltenham and then came back with a leg problem after finishing second to Hawthorn Blaze at Newbury, which put him out of action for eighteen months. It was a big blow for everyone in the yard. Paul took it all like a true sportsman, unlike one or two owners I've had who react to news of an injury as if you've deliberately kicked their horse in the leg. A week later, Paul had some consolation when Lucky Crisis whizzed home on his debut at Southwell. Our delight didn't last long. Within a month he developed a heart problem and was eventually put down. No wonder old sages tell you this game tames lions.

After a lean spell in mid-season, caused, I suspected, by a batch of dodgy feed, my horses hit form with a vengeance in the second half of March with five wins in fourteen days, but it was a point-to-pointer that really put me on the map with a bold effort in the Grand National at 50–1. Just So, a dour stayer who jumped for fun, couldn't quite get his head in front that winter but he was always running on at the finish so I had Liverpool in mind for him from an early stage. He was known in the yard as Just Slow. What he really wanted was a marathon trip, bottomless ground and a following wind.

Just So finished second four times and booked his ticket for the National when he was beaten only half a length in the Eider Chase at Newcastle. It didn't bother me that he was seventeen pounds out of the handicap on the big day at Liverpool. I was just pleased to be having a runner in the world's greatest steeplechase in my first season. It was unbelievable, really. Although the horse was a 100–1 chance a week before the race, I expected a big show, even if it was probably asking too much to match Seagram's victory.

Unfortunately, Just So lost vital ground when he was hampered early on but he finished like an express train in sixth place behind Party Politics on going that was not nearly soft enough for him. Two years later, on ground that was virtually unraceable after torrential rain, Just So failed by just over a length to overhaul Miinnehoma in the National with the rest miles behind. By then he was trained by his owner-breeder Henry Cole at his farm near Taunton. I ended my first season with ten winners and set about doubling my team for the autumn.

I was still a total greenhorn at finding horses at the sales, had to learn the whole tricky business from the start and made some bad calls early on. You've got a chance picking out store horses that have never run, as that's something of a numbers game, but it is much harder at the horses-in-training sales. I soon discovered which trainers to buy from, and, more importantly, which ones not to buy from. You are a young fellow looking for bargains, don't know many of the vendors, believe what people say, buy something on their recommendation, bring it home and find it has a problem. Some sellers definitely saw me coming, put a horse into me and never thought twice about stitching me up. That's life.

I found the whole process a bit of a minefield and my lack of experience let me down badly at first. Realising that two heads are better than one when you go shopping, I began to lean on the advice of Richard Barber, who is a great judge of horse flesh, a brilliant stockman and has been breeding horses for years as well as training point-to-pointers. I relied heavily on his judgement in those early years.

Richard took over the training of See More Indians in his second season at the suggestion of Paul Barber. After surgery on his tendons he would be back too late to start over fences with me so it made sense for him to gain useful experience in the less demanding arena of point-to-points. It meant he'd still be a novice when he came back to me. That's a system we have used frequently since then. It's been the making of so many of our horses.

In the spring of 1993 See More Indians won all three points including, memorably for Paul, the Blackmore Vale and Sparkford Hunt race at Kingweston in April, named after his greatest friend, John Farthing, who died at the age of fifty-seven. See More Indians was ridden by

John's son, Justin. Lifting that trophy meant the world to Paul and I was thrilled to win the same race in 2008 with my own horse, Goblet of Fire.

Winners arrived in a variety of guises in my second season. The strangest of all was Its Nearly Time at Warwick three weeks after he was found running loose on the M5 after the horsebox he was travelling in was destroyed in a serious accident which left Bridget's mum, Becky, in hospital needing surgery and her dad, John, nursing a broken arm. In the chaos Its Nearly Time escaped but he didn't get too far before he was caught by a friend of theirs, Ollie Bush, driving another horsebox.

John and Becky transferred Its Nearly Time to Ditcheat and booked Mick Fitzgerald, who'd already ridden winners for me and was going out with Bridget's sister, Jane. At the time Mick was running away with the conditional jockeys' title. He rode with tremendous confidence and I used him whenever I could, even though I gave him the bollocking of a lifetime two days earlier after he left Thatcher Rock too much to do when they finished third at Taunton. I lost the plot in full view of everyone, which made Mick look small. He wasn't best pleased but, as he was only a conditional, he just had to stand there and take the abuse.

Once I'd calmed down I realised I was totally out of order. That evening I rang Mick and apologised. I used to take defeat so badly; still do, if I'm being honest. After another reverse at Hereford I sulked all the way home without saying a word to Bridget in the car. I wasn't prepared to compromise even when she told me I had to change my attitude. Sulking, I suggested, was marginally better than ranting and raving at my jockeys.

In my early years as a trainer I found it so hard to watch someone else riding my horses because it was beyond my control. I used to wear my heart on my sleeve and tended to have a go at my jockeys without thinking. They were the ones who usually got a piece of my mind when things went wrong because they were the easiest targets for my frustration.

At times I was the one who felt the victim. There I was working my balls off, putting everything into training winners, only for things to be ruined in a few seconds by jockeys who didn't listen to my instructions. I found it impossible to cope when things didn't work out. I tried to learn from the incident with Mick by shutting up, counting to ten and not saying too much until I got home. Sometimes, though, despite the best intentions, I couldn't stop myself launching into my jockeys. I think, and hope, I am a lot better now.

10

The worst day of my life

See More Indians was my first really good horse. Even at that early stage I felt that with luck he could go to the top, because he had everything you look for in a classy staying chaser. In one eventful, uplifting season he more than lived up to my lofty ambition. Then the sky fell in.

When he returned to me in July 1993 he had grown and strengthened. Because he was such an exciting prospect I didn't want to rush things, so I started him off over fences at Worcester. The man we chose to ride him was Graham Bradley, a jockey with something of a reputation for sailing close to the wind. Perhaps that is why he called his autobiography *The Wayward Lad*! Brad had won the Cheltenham Gold Cup on Bregawn for Michael Dickinson and later moved south to revive his career. With a bigger team of horses than before, I felt we needed more continuity in the saddle and chose him at the suggestion of Paul Barber. One of my biggest headaches in the early days was the hassle of finding jockeys who suited my owners. Often I'd be pulling out my hair, stressed about riding arrangements. Because I wasn't sufficiently established to attract the big names on a regular basis, I used to chop and change a fair bit. It made life difficult for me and didn't please some of the jockeys. Often I had to settle for the best available rider on the day, which didn't suit some of my owners.

By signing up Brad as stable jockey I hoped that uncertainty would be a thing of the past. We knew we were taking a bit of a gamble and it wasn't ideal that we had to share him with the Lambourn trainer Charlie Brooks, but Brad was keen to come aboard and it was handy to have a top-class rider on call. See More Indians made his debut over fences at Worcester over two and a half miles on 23 October. The plan was to settle him and get him jumping and he came through the test with flying colours as he pulled clear to win with plenty in hand. He was even more impressive at Worcester a fortnight later in a more competitive race. Again he cruised home, this time by thirty lengths, and was full of running at the end. Paul, Brad and I completed a good day by landing a decent novice hurdle with Rampoldi, on his first outing for two years. Dick Baimbridge would have been proud of that one.

Next stop for See More Indians was Cheltenham, where he beat the future Grand National winner Earth Summit with something to spare. As he was on a roll and improving at a rate of knots, we raised our sights again and sent him to Kempton on Boxing Day for the Feltham Chase, a race that invariably attracts some of the best young staying chasers. Others were preferred in the market but See More Indians extended his winning sequence to four, despite ploughing through the last fence.

It was my first Grade One, the biggest prize I'd won by far. Soon we were on the warpath for bigger scalps. The race I had in mind for him was the Sun Alliance Chase at the Festival and I was also tempted to enter him for the Gold Cup just in case the field cut up. Brad and I both felt he'd be a stone better horse back racing left-handed. I gave him a short break in the New Year then started the countdown to Cheltenham by running him at Wincanton in the Jim Ford Cup, a traditional Gold Cup trial. Although he was probably only 90 per cent fit, that was enough for him to see off Another Coral by two lengths, but I've often wondered if the hard race he had that day took the edge off him at Cheltenham.

See More Indians was a savage to the point that his lad, Michael Prosser, took his life into his hands every time he stepped into the box at evening stables. The horse was a menace even when he managed to tie him up. Michael still has the scars to prove it but the experience can't have done him any harm because he is now director of racing at Newmarket.

I couldn't have been happier with the condition of See More Indians going to Cheltenham. He was tough and reliable and looked a picture. I was desperate for a winner at the Festival and knew this was my best chance by far, but he ran no race at all. It led to an acrimonious parting with Graham Bradley. He was supposed to have See More Indians handy the moment they jumped off, because he was an out-and-out stayer who didn't do things too quickly. So the writing was on the wall when Brad missed a beat at the start and found himself much too far back going to the first fence. Though I hoped he could work his way into the race, I knew in my heart that his chance had already gone. See More Indians did make some ground on the leaders in the final mile, but a mistake three out was the final straw and he did well to plug on to finish fifth.

We were all devastated as we tried to work out what had happened. Paul Barber was furious, almost spitting blood, and immediately blamed Brad for a poor tactical ride. I was gutted, too, though until that day I never doubted our jockey. It certainly wasn't his finest hour because he should have been much more positive from the outset. I had a shortish fuse back then and left him in no doubt about my feelings. Up to that point our partnership had shown signs of flourishing. Now, suddenly, it was in the balance.

Paul wouldn't let the matter drop. After watching the race a few times on video in the following week and talking at length to his brother, Richard, he came to the conclusion that Brad had to go. There was no room for compromise. Over a drink one night he gave me instructions to sack Bradley and book Richard Dunwoody for See More Indians on his final run of the season at Ayr.

This was one debate in which I had no input. The decision was taken for me. Paul and his friends loaded the gun and I fired it. Telling Brad the bad news was hard for me. It got me the reputation of being a shit, when I was acting under orders. I got the slagging though I was only doing what I was told. Brad was really bitter and had a right go at me. Perhaps if I'd been more established I could have handled it all better, but once Paul makes up his mind there is no going back. At least See More Indians set the record straight by ending a fantastic first season over fences at Ayr by winning in style. As Dunwoody was mad keen to retain the ride, we moved quickly to retain him whenever he wasn't required by Martin Pipe.

See More Indians started his summer break with several others in the cider orchard beside Paul's farmhouse. A month later they were joined in the field among the neat lines of three hundred apple trees by a couple of youngsters we purchased at Doncaster. We checked them over once or twice a day and waited impatiently for the coming season when See More Indians would be aimed at the Gold Cup, the ultimate challenge in jump racing.

I will never forget the Monday morning in July when I found See More Indians in the orchard lame on one of his front legs. A week later he'd have been safely back in his box after his summer holiday. Instead, he was standing awkwardly with his foot barely touching the ground. I thought at first he might have a bit of poison in his foot or maybe he had bruised it, but once I brought him in I suspected it might be more serious, called in our vet and put Paul in the picture.

The point of the injury turned out to be much higher than the foot. There was just a little scratch on his elbow which the vets initially believed was bruising from a kick, but within forty-eight hours it became clear that the damage was life-threatening. Numerous X-rays revealed that his elbow was fractured in three places, almost certainly from a kick by another horse. It was the diagnosis I had been dreading. Somehow, anyhow, I was clinging to the hope that we could save him even if he never raced again. But our two vets, and a third we called in for a further opinion, all advised that he should be put down as swiftly as possible on humane grounds.

That was the worst day of my life. Paul came down to the yard, insisted on leading See More Indians out of his box and stood there beside him close to tears as they put him out of his misery. It was a horrific experience for both of us. The previous Sunday, over a drink, we'd been discussing the chances of the horse delivering his dream in the Gold Cup. Now the poor animal's life was over.

Telling Paul that See More Indians had to be put down was one of the hardest things I've ever had to do. I knew he was upset, as much for me as for himself, but he did insure his horses then and within a few weeks, as the gloom finally started to lift, he began looking in Ireland for a replacement. At first he was thinking of buying another novice but eventually he found a pot of gold at the end of the rainbow called Deep Bramble, who'd already run with great promise. I liked the fact that he would be able to run in the same sort of races we'd mapped out for See More Indians. Yet deep down we both felt our chance of winning the Gold Cup had gone forever because we were unlikely to find another as good as him.

It didn't take me long to identify the culprit who injured See More Indians. As soon as the horses started coming back in one of our newcomers, Call Equiname, spent his time out on the roads trying to kick everyone and everything within range of his hind legs. He was lethal. Paul and two friends, Mick Coburn and Colin Lewis, had paid 54,000 guineas for the horse at Doncaster in May after he won two bumpers in the north. His aggressive behaviour out with the string soon convinced me that he was the one who had delivered the fatal kick to See More Indians. In time he would repay us by winning the Queen Mother Champion Chase, but I made sure he was never let loose in a field again with more than one other horse. His sole companion at grass for several summers was See More Business, another so and so who was more than capable of looking after himself. Together they were pals and weren't going to kick each other.

Turning horses out in Paul's orchard used to terrify me because I felt it was only a matter of time before one of them wrapped himself round an apple tree. Paul tried to play down my fears. He's a farmer, after all, and the trees provided a decent crop of apples each autumn. Eventually he changed his tune after an incident involving one of his team in the orchard. One day the trees were there. The next they were gone after a culling operation carried out with military precision. I slept easier in my bed after that.

See More Business slipped through the net that summer. Paul and a friend, John Keighley, had picked him out from the catalogue at the Doncaster Sales in May, partly, of course, because he shared the same sire, Seymour Hicks, as See More Indians. So they instructed Paul's brother, Richard, to buy him. He was knocked down to Richard for 5,600 guineas but he was small, only 15.3 hands, and didn't really have the stamp of a chaser at that stage. In addition, he was a bit of a scratchy mover with a scar on one of his joints. Paul prefers horses with a bit of size and wasn't too keen once he'd seen See More Business, so Richard passed him on to another of his owners, Richard Williams.

Soon Paul began hearing stories of a newcomer burning up the gallops at Richard Barber's yard. Sure enough, it turned out to be See More Business. Richard told me in November that he was one of the best he'd ever had. The news galvanised Paul Barber. Six months earlier he had turned his nose up at See More Business. Now he was desperate to have him. It was eventually agreed that Paul and John could have first refusal if Richard Williams decided to sell him at the end of the pointing season. A deal was done and would pay huge dividends for Paul and John in the years ahead.

At that stage plenty of my horses were doing their winning at the lowest level. Baroness Orkzy was a fruitcake and had been pulled up six times on the trot for other trainers. At home she was such a madam she had to go out on her own every day. We got her fit to run for her life first time out before she landed quite a touch from 14–1 to 10–1 in a selling chase at Newton Abbot. I felt that, if I could train her to win a race, I could win with anything.

Va Lute had much more talent but was compromised by legs of glass. One of the many benefits of the hill at Ditcheat is that it is very good for horses with problems, because it tends to keep the weight off their front legs. We didn't gallop Va Lute much, just sent him up the hill three times every morning. When we managed to get him to the races in one piece he usually ran well or won. Sometimes, though, he'd break down again in the process, so we'd give him a break, patch him up and do it all again.

Va Lute was sent to me in my first season after winning a claiming race at Wincanton. I then managed to pick up a handicap with him at Fakenham. It was touch and go whether I got him on the track the next season before he won his only race that winter, a claimer at Lingfield in February 1993. He then broke down so badly that we were close to having him put down. As he was a smashing little pro, we took a chance, had him fired and gave him a year off before bringing him back once more, aged ten. The race I had in mind for him was a claimer for lady riders at Stratford in October 1994. Ridden by Sophie Mitchell, he hacked up but there was a sting in the tail when he was claimed afterwards for £4,000. It was a bit of a shock to lose Va Lute as he'd become something of a family pet to his owners.

Deep Bramble proved to be a terrific flag bearer for the yard in my fourth season at Ditcheat. We needed all the help we could get after the horses suddenly lost their form following a bright start that saw us register ten wins in double-quick time. They caught a bug of some kind, no question, though loads of tests failed to pinpoint the problem. Deep Bramble definitely performed below par when he finished legless in eighth place in the Hennessy Gold Cup at Newbury. He was one of those horses who stayed longer than your mother-in-law but was so idle at home that he was very hard to judge, particularly when so many of mine were wrong.

I hoped the worst was over when I found the ideal race for him at Sandown in January over three miles, five and a half furlongs. It was a valuable prize and a useful stepping stone to Cheltenham. Deep Bramble needed every yard of the trip and was all out to fend off Riverside Boy, with others snapping at their heels. Less than three lengths covered the first five home, with Deep Bramble strongest on the final hill. I was already looking ahead towards the Grand National. First, though, I brought him back to Sandown a month later to land the Agfa Diamond Chase. I've never known a horse eat like Deep Bramble. He was so full of himself that evening he was kicking down the door of his box at home at ten o'clock, demanding another meal. I knew how he felt: he was just like me in my riding days after a hard day in the saddle!

We couldn't resist the challenge of the Cheltenham Gold Cup with Deep Bramble, who was pulled up by Chris Maude long before the end. As he wasn't quite right after the race, we bypassed Aintree and foolishly brought him back to Sandown for the Whitbread Gold Cup where the going was quicker than ideal. After walking the course, Paul and I were in two minds about letting Deep Bramble take part. I wish we hadn't because he ran no sort of race, came back with a leg injury and was never the same afterwards. Paul still says we were idiots for running him. I hold up my hands for talking him into having a go. It was an expensive lesson for both of us. Owners get plenty of stick for not running horses on fast ground but, if people saw for themselves how many break down, they wouldn't be so critical. We patched Deep Bramble up and brought him back for a crack at the National the following year. He was still going well, too, when he broke down badly with two fences to jump and didn't run again.

The first four years at Ditcheat were unbelievably tough. I was having winners and starting to get some welcome publicity, but the business wasn't making any money. Financially, we were barely treading water. Each autumn Paul built a few more boxes to accommodate the increase in numbers in training. By that stage I'd worked out that by putting my own money into the yard I was investing in my future.

I couldn't expect Paul and his family to bankroll me forever so we reached an agreement that I'd pay for any new boxes in future and for other improvements. That way, I felt, I'd make money out of them once they were occupied. Frankly, I'd have done it even if it left me almost skint because I was determined to have the yard full to over-flowing. The more guns you possess, the more shots you can fire.

People were starting to ring up asking to look round. Aware that first impressions count, I've always kept the place as smart and tidy as possible with flower baskets strategically placed around the boxes. Given the time I've always enjoyed a bit of gardening and did all the baskets myself back then. I've never regretted ploughing every last penny back into the business. If the flowers brought in one new owner they more than paid for themselves.

As I started to progress as a trainer I had the odd falling out with people along the way. I wouldn't say I'm ruthless but if you are successful and positive you tend to become a bit bolshie, too, and I'm not slow to stand up for myself when necessary. Jealousy doesn't bother me. You just have to ignore it when people snipe at you. I had plenty of supporters, too, top trainers like Tim Forster and David Nicholson, who usually offered an encouraging word at the races. I was pleased to be clocking up a few winners and getting a bit of a reputation. Even so, I'd have given anything for a Cheltenham success to take me to the next level.

11

Prospecting for gold

As the numbers continued to increase at Ditcheat I found myself heading for the toughest decision I'd faced so far as a trainer. Sending horses up the hill each morning was fine up to a point, but after four years I knew with absolute certainty that I needed a second gallop to sharpen them up with faster work. You can only do so much with the hill. By sticking to steady stamina work you can almost train horses to become slow.

In a lot of ways that hill is the best gallop in the world because I've trained well over 1,700 winners on it. Yet on its own it was not enough. Exercising horses is all about hearts and lungs. You need to be able to sprint them as well. For barely a month in the late autumn we used to wing them across a grass field before it became too soft. It did the job well and helped prepare them to win first time, but normally we could only use it for a few weeks so I couldn't rely on it.

With the help of a second all-weather gallop I was sure the horses could be made fitter and faster. Without it I was in danger of throwing away the springboard I'd built for myself over the past four years. Paul Barber had already proved to be the best landlord imaginable, but would he agree to give up more of his land on another part of the farm to help me out?

There was only one way to find the answer to that question. And, if Paul didn't approve, then I was fully prepared to move elsewhere to find what I wanted. Luckily, it never got the point where I had to say to Paul: if you don't do this, I am going to have to leave. The moment I approached him he was as keen as me. I remember he said, 'Come on, boy, let's go and see if we can find somewhere to put this gallop.' We jumped into his farm vehicle and set off like two small boys prospecting for gold.

Paul chose a site in a flat, level field just below his cheese factory. A gallop alongside a hedge could run for four and a half furlongs with a collecting circle at each end. Paul gave up quite a bit of ground to make sure the job was done properly, brought in diggers to remove the earth, laid a tarmac base, added loads of stone, then topped it off with a foot of Wexford sand. As a canny farmer who doesn't like wasting land, Paul suggested planting some trees as well that might hold a fox one day, which is a great attitude. The project cost £35,000.

The grey chaser Sunley Bay, owned by Paul's wife, Marianne, opened the new gallop in the summer of 1995. He led the string as they breezed down to the end, where they pulled up, turned round and came back a fair bit faster than they could possibly manage on the hill. It was a wonderful sight, which swiftly produced the results I'd been hoping for and was a key turning point in my career. I felt it was the final piece of the jigsaw.

What a time we enjoyed that winter! See More Business and Call Equiname gave a glimpse of what was to come with a series of impressive victories over hurdles and General Crack delivered my 100th winner as a trainer at Chepstow on 4 November. Des Nichols marked the occasion by giving me a china figurine of a newsboy delivering the *Daily Mail* with the front-page headline reading 'NICHOLLS HITS TON'. It was a lovely gesture, one I treasure to this day.

Tony McCoy, the champion conditional, was a significant addition to the team. Such was his impact in the early months of his first season as a full professional that he was making a bold bid to win the jockeys' title. He was already a brilliant rider, aggressive, fearless and unbelievably competitive. In those days he wanted to win so badly that sometimes, when he got beaten, he was inconsolable and nothing I could say could lift him. It meant that much to him. I'd spotted his potential soon after he arrived from Ireland, thought he was a bit special and used him for the first time on Warfield in a boys' race at Sandown early in 1995. They didn't win, but I was impressed by his style and attitude. Already AP was in a different league to me as a jockey. He would do for me any time.

As AP was still based with Toby Balding at the time, the three of us reached a gentleman's agreement in August 1995 that he would ride the majority of my horses. When I appointed him stable jockey, some people couldn't wait to tell me that he couldn't ride over fences. Yet, when he schooled at Ditcheat it was just like watching Richard Dunwoody at work. I was thrilled to have a jockey with his will to win and I imagine he was happy enough, too, because we provided more ammunition for him that season than any other trainer.

We shared a hatful of winners, including a treble at Newton Abbot in November. A sound judge for someone so young, AP was bowled over by the raw power of See More Business who joined me with a big reputation after winning his first two point-to-points with ridiculous ease before falling at the last when he was a fence in front at Chaddesley Corbett, where he'd dropped Polly Curling before the start and ran loose for a circuit.

He had a peculiar way of jumping back then. I was at Larkhill the day he won his maiden and remember that he jumped eighteen fences in eighteen different ways, yet was so strong at the end that Polly couldn't pull him up. Given the choice, See More Business would have done another lap. Nor was his technique much better the next time at Larkhill. He was still quite small back then yet surprisingly strong and had a tremendous engine, though he tended to suffer from sore shins.

Seemore, as we called him, also had a nasty temper and was really tricky to ride each autumn, a nightmare when he first came into training until we got the freshness out of him. We had to dope him before clipping him or he'd try to kill you, but he was born to race. However, he kicked just about every hurdle out of the ground when he won on his debut at Chepstow in October 1995 before rattling up a quick hat-trick. His third victory, in a valuable novice event at Sandown, was hugely impressive. AP couldn't disguise his excitement in the winners' enclosure and declared he was by far the best he'd ridden in England and Ireland.

We all hoped he would be the one to break our duck at the Cheltenham Festival until we found a bit of heat in one of his front legs shortly after Sandown. It was quite a minor problem, really, not enough to require firing, but with a horse of his quality you take no chances. We let him down, took him out of training and gave him a nice long break in the belief that he would be fine the following season.

AP's other favourite was Call Equiname, a classy grey with bags of speed whose previous campaign with us had been bedevilled by chronic sore shins, often the sign of immaturity in young horses. The problem was so persistent that we pin-fired his shins in April 1995. Call Equiname won four times over hurdles the following season but his shins continued to trouble him. He could hardly walk in his box on the Saturday night after a battling success at Ascot shortly before Christmas, yet after treatment he usually recovered within days.

We were helped that season by the arrival of half a dozen horses that had been given time to mature and develop at Richard Barber's yard near Beaminster by hunting and point-to-pointing. It made good sense to introduce some of our younger, more backward prospects in the calmer waters of pointing rather than starting them off in com- petitive novice hurdles where they can learn bad habits. The system worked well. See More Business was by far the best-known graduate from Richard's academy. Others to shine for us included Cherrynut and Straight Talk, who won a string of races for Richard.

Thanks to our new gallop I ended my fifth season in ninth place in the trainer's table with fifty-two winners. I felt I'd finally left base camp but from my position in the foothills it looked a hell of a long way up the mountain to the summit. Sunley Bay, the horse who opened the gallop, played his part by winning the Mandarin Chase at Newbury.

When I first started training I spent every waking hour in the yard. There are always jobs to be done in a busy racing stable and I wanted them done properly. I wasn't so good at delegating then and at times I'd rather do the last feed at ten at night and check their rugs than go out for the evening. Sad but true. I had several head lads in those early years but often ended up sharing some of their jobs. In some ways I was my own head lad, but as we continued to expand I knew that couldn't continue because there were not enough hours in the day. I can remember Paul Barber telling me more than once: 'Delegate my boy, delegate.' It was excellent advice.

Then, out of the blue, I heard that David Nicholson's head lad, Clifford Baker, was looking to move on. Apparently he wanted a change of scenery and, best of all, his parents lived nearby at Bruton. I got a message to him to ring me if he was interested in joining us. When we met it was clear straightaway that Clifford fitted the bill. He had bags of experience after coming through racing's school of hard knocks, had been in charge of a yard much bigger than ours and was definitely up for a new challenge.

It helped that we were the same age and had both been in racing all our lives. Clifford joined the Duke straight from school at sixteen on £2 a week and had ridden a winner for Jenny Pitman before he took the view that race riding wasn't for him. He'd been head lad for the Duke for the best eight years the stable had enjoyed. I knew within five minutes that Clifford was the man for me and had no hesitation in signing him up. It was one of the best decisions I've ever made. I badly needed someone like him to take some of the day-to-day responsibility from my shoulders.

I told him how I wanted things done, made sure he had a good wage and a decent home in a cottage opposite the yard and left the rest to him. Clifford is in the yard every morning by six, feeds round on his own, usually rides out one or two lots, takes a keen interest in the schooling, has a short break at lunchtime and is then back early in the afternoon.

As he was now the senior man in the yard I let him sort out the ones he wanted to ride in the mornings but he had a nasty shock when he tangled with See More Business on the day he started work for me. Moments after he legged Ross Darke on to the horse's back, all three ended up in a crumpled heap against the door of his box forty yards away as Seemore shot across the yard at a million miles an hour with my new head lad hanging on for dear life. The horse's feet didn't touch the ground and neither did Clifford's! When they adjourned to a nearby paddock, Ross was promptly dropped four times. It didn't put off Clifford riding Seemore every morning for the next few years.

With Clifford at the helm in the yard, AP riding most of the horses and all fifty-two boxes full, I was keener than ever to get cracking. But a dry autumn that year left me struggling to use the schooling area because I wasn't prepared to risk the horses on firm ground. Paul Barber came to the rescue with a fleet of tankers that poured 8,000 gallons of water on to the ground where we put the horses through their paces over hurdles and fences.

Paul was the dominant figure in a short, intense board meeting we held that autumn with John Keighley on the immediate future of See More Business. While I wanted him to stay over hurdles for another season Paul was adamant that he should go straight over fences. John wavered briefly before siding with his fellow owner. The die was cast. At the end of the season I thought I was right but a year later Paul was certain he was right!

Seemore was the opposite of a natural when we popped him over hurdles for the first time the previous year. He was horrendous and had no idea, perhaps because he'd been in first gear in point-to-points under heavy restraint and so never jumped with any fluency. I was relieved to see he was much better when we schooled him over fences. AP was happy enough, too, after he hacked up in his first novice chase at Chepstow, which is a tricky course for a novice. He jumped very well once he warmed up.

As we all thought he was the business, we took him to Ireland next, which was a novel experience for me. The new Irish star, Dorans Pride, was a warm favourite in the Drinmore Chase over two and a half miles. Mistakes cost Seemore ground at a couple of fences but he was only beaten a length by Dorans Pride. I wasn't always having as much influence on the riding tactics as I'd have liked in those days because other opinions were being thrown into the pot. We got done for toe that day, basically, and I remember thinking that as our horse stayed three miles well AP should have been more aggressive on him.

I was mightily relieved to win a big pot with Belmont King on his debut for me at Chepstow early in December. I'd bought him in May 1995 for a new owner, Mrs Billie Bond, who was in her seventies, lived in Cornwall, had £100,000 to spend and was looking for a horse that she could watch running on Saturdays on TV and which might develop into a Grand National candidate. The introduction came from my old friend John Dufosee, who put me through the wing at Hackwood Park all those years ago and now breaks in horses that I've bought at the sales and also has several for me for pre-training. No one does the job better.

John did me a huge favour by pointing Mrs Bond in my direction. She said she wanted the best and the day I found Belmont King in Ireland I felt that she might just have achieved her aim. He was a huge horse, 17.2 hands, strong and athletic. I used to ride him when he first came in and didn't look particularly big on him. At home in the early days I thought he was the best I had until we found a bit of heat in one of his forelegs that forced us to put him on the sidelines for twelve months.

Back in training, Belmont King was giving me all the right signals late in 1996 and, ridden by AP McCoy, brought a smile to Mrs Bond's lips by landing the valuable Rehearsal Chase at Chepstow's Saturday meeting in December on BBC TV. I felt I'd delivered the first part of the bargain and thought he was a natural for the Grand National.

AP didn't want to be at Chepstow that day. If he'd had his way he'd have gone to Sandown to ride the favourite, Teinein, in the William Hill Hurdle. We managed to persuade him to come to Chepstow where he rode four winners, including two for Martin Pipe who had started using him whenever possible once his stable jockey, David Bridgwater, walked out on the job in September, just as Richard Dunwoody had done seventeen months earlier.

It was a sign of the times and, for me, an alarming development because I knew that, if it came to a tug of war, I couldn't begin to match the firepower of Pipe. Tony McCoy was becoming the top hired gun in jump racing. He was already champion, fearless, committed and inspired, and at twenty-three, barring injury, had a glittering career ahead of him. Pipe had been quietly trying to poach him for many weeks and finally got his man in January. It was a sensation at the time, fuelled by forthright comments from Paul Barber, who didn't pull his punches as he told several pressmen exactly what he thought of Pipe and AP. Paul is a man of his word and felt totally let down by the way AP broke his agreement with us.

The horse that caused the falling out between us was Flaked Oats, owned by one of Paul's friends, Eddie Swaffield. AP had won on him at Fontwell and told us on Sunday 19 January that he would ride him again the following day at Newton Abbot. He rang later to say he'd changed his mind and would be switching to Pipe's Cyborgo. It was the news I'd been dreading. At first I hoped we could work round the problem, but Paul was having none of it. We were both steaming at the way AP had deserted the camp and in no mood for compromise. Once the press got wind of the story there was no going back.

I told the *Racing Post* I wasn't going to be messed around any more. I'm usually pretty flexible but my owners were giving me grief because AP had broken a gentleman's agreement to ride my horses. For the moment at least he was out and I'd be using other jockeys, including Philip Hide. Secretly, I hoped it would all blow over and I could start putting up AP again on most of the horses but Paul wasn't for turning and didn't even speak to him for the best part of two years. To Paul a man's word is his bond and he took a long time to forgive AP for the way he turned his back on our agreement. When the shit hit the fan, Paul said that AP would never ride for him again. Never is a long time and I'm pleased to say they eventually made up.

What made it worse was that Pipe kept denying that he had offered AP the job as his stable jockey. Who was he kidding? He'd been pursuing him for months and there was nothing I could do about it. It would have been much better if he'd had the good manners to ring one of us up and explain what he was trying to do. You learn from these disputes. When I chose Sam Thomas as back-up for Ruby Walsh in 2006 I rang his boss, Venetia Williams, to explain my decision. I don't blame her for being upset at losing first claim on Sam but at least she heard it direct from me.

In a perfect world I would have liked AP to ride for me full-time, from the point of our split right up to the present day. I'd used Graham Bradley and Richard Dunwoody but they also had commitments to other trainers. I thought I was finally getting somewhere when AP joined us because it felt as though he was mine. Unfortunately it all happened ten years too early because, back then, I couldn't muster the firepower of Pipe. I still think that in some ways we both lost out when AP left. We suited each other so well because we have the same competitive edge and the same ambitions. Neither of us lets anything get in the way of the business of winning races. I'm sure AP would still have been champion through all those years if he'd stayed with me and I might possibly have been champion a bit sooner, too.

Cyborgo rubbed salt in the wound by winning at Newton Abbot on the Monday, with Flaked Oats and his new jockey, Philip Hide, on the floor at the last fence when they looked booked for second place. In the years ahead Pipe would be a constant thorn in my side and Cyborgo, the horse at the heart of my split with AP, would return to haunt me at Cheltenham.

With AP strictly off-limits we asked David Bridgwater to ride Belmont King in the Hennessy Gold Cup at Leopardstown in February. The horse wanted ground so heavy it was almost unraceable but walking round beforehand I'd have called it good or, at worst, good to soft. Belmont King was badly outpaced before being pulled up, but the visit was memorable for my first meeting with a nineteen-year-old amateur rider with dark hair already starting to turn grey. Ruby Walsh, who had a ride in the hunter chase, was walking the course with his dad Ted, a famous amateur who is now an outstanding broadcaster.

Paul Barber and John Keighley moved quickly to sign up Richard Dunwoody for See More Business but they didn't get off to the greatest of starts. The new partnership was well beaten by Dorans Pride at Leopardstown on 2 February when I again felt we should have made more use of his stamina. The next time Seemore ran he gave Richard one of the worst falls of his life in the Racing Post Chase. It looked so bad it could have finished both of them. Seemore galloped off unhurt but Richard wasn't so lucky and ended up in intensive care for the first time in years with a broken sternum, which many assumed would force him out of the Cheltenham Festival. Not a chance. Richard was pretty much indestructible and, despite the pain, was back riding out ten days after he left Kempton in an ambulance.

Seemore's jumping was becoming a huge concern. He fell at home when we popped him over some fences after Kempton and fell again with Richard Johnson when we took him to Wincanton for a schooling session five days before Cheltenham. We were worried that he was beginning to go the wrong way but at least he put in a clear round when my young amateur, Joe Tizzard, took him round two circuits of a local point-to-point course. He was far from a natural and frustratingly slow to learn, maybe because he wasn't overly big. We might have sorted out his problems earlier if I'd had my outdoor school and the other facilities which are in place now. Part of the trouble was that he was still suffering from sore shins. And, as Jenny Barons once warned me, they can turn a Derby winner into a selling plater.

We started the season with such high hopes for See More Business, who seemed a natural for the Sun Alliance Chase, but he wasn't jumping well enough to take him to Cheltenham, so we called a halt and turned him out. Call Equiname, too, failed to make it to the biggest meeting of the season. He began brightly over fences with stylish victories at Chepstow and Worcester, jumped well and had bags of speed. Unfortunately his wheels were always a cause of concern and he was quite badly jarred up after his second success. I was never really happy with him after that and opted to take him out of training for six months.

Another Cheltenham Festival passed without a sniff of a winner. It was great to be there to see my friends celebrating, though I admit to a twinge of envy as Ron Hodges and Richard Barber stepped up to receive their trophies. Ron was over the moon after landing the Sun Alliance Chase with Hanakham. Next day it was Richard's turn as he won the Foxhunters with Fantus. They were having winners at the greatest meeting in the world and I didn't even look like cracking it. My long drought was getting to me a fair bit by then. As I raised a glass to them I wondered if my luck at the meeting would ever change.

I can't tell you how bad I used to feel going home from Cheltenham. It wasn't so much depression as a feeling of anger because I wanted success so much and couldn't see where it was coming from. That's me all over. I'm usually in a bit of a hurry and back then was always madly jealous of everyone who had winners at the Festival. Looking back now I wonder what on earth I was doing running some of the horses I took to Cheltenham early on. I tended to squeeze the lemon dry beforehand by winning what I could along the way. There wasn't much left by the time we got to the Festival. I was still learning and too hungry at times.

Aintree was no better. I didn't manage a runner on the first two days and my hopes for Belmont King in the Grand National came to an abrupt end when the race was called off after a bomb scare. I was just about to tack up my two runners in the saddling boxes when all hell let loose. The chaos was indescribable as everyone was made to leave the course. At least the horses were safe back in the racecourse stables. Initially, we assumed the delay was caused by a silly hoax and that the National would still go ahead a couple of hours later, so we all hung on for ages hoping that the show would get back on the road. Robert Blackburn and I gave someone £40 to buy fish and chips for our party. The fish was already sold out but at least he came back with a huge cardboard box stuffed full of chips. We ate them standing in the drizzle outside the main entrance.

For several hours tens of thousands of racegoers were milling around on the streets and pavements outside the course. As darkness fell the confusion was made much worse by the decision of the police to prevent any cars leaving the course. Thousands walked back into Liverpool. Others consoled themselves in hundreds of pubs around Aintree. Many jockeys still in their riding gear ended up at the Adelphi Hotel in Liverpool with a dozen bunking down in David Walsh's room. Apparently it was a hell of a party.

Sanity eventually prevailed when someone in the chain of command agreed to our requests to let the horseboxes leave the parking area behind the racecourse stables. Then it was a case of rounding up the troops and trying to get home as best we could. We loaded up our National runners, Belmont King and Straight Talk, and scooped up various refugees eager to hitch a lift back to Somerset and all points south. Some, including BBC commentator Jim McGrath and John de Moraville, then of the *Daily Express*, just wanted to escape from the racecourse in the hope of finding a taxi a couple of miles away. Others, like Robert and Claire Blackburn and Joe Tizzard, with his parents Colin and Pauline, were ready for the long haul home.

We pulled out of the car park with at least seventeen passengers, most of them standing in the spare stalls at the back of the horsebox, with a few lucky ones in the area behind the cab used for hay and straw. We dropped off McGrath, de Moraville and several others at a roundabout near their hotel and by the time we'd made several more stops it was past midnight before we reached Ditcheat.

I fully supported the decision to run the 1997 Grand National on the Monday because you can't be seen to give in to threats. Unfortunately Belmont King wasn't fit to return to Liverpool as he became quite stressed during all the drama, lost a lot of weight from the long hours of travelling and looked like a horse that had already run his race. As the ground at Aintree had also dried up markedly I was happy to keep him back for the Scottish Grand National twelve days later. Even so, he had a nightmare trip to Ayr because of some bomb scares on the motorways which meant that our box took almost eleven hours to reach the racecourse.

I made up with Tony McCoy in time for him to ride Belmont King. I snapped him up once Richard Dunwoody preferred Sister Stephanie, the favourite. AP was the obvious choice. He was available, had won on the horse back in December and was even hungrier for winners than usual after missing three weeks, including Liverpool, with a mandatory suspension to recover from concussion. We spoke in the

A badly broken leg in 1989
ended my days as a jockey. It was
enough to drive me to drink!

Olveston (Hywel Davies) delivers
my first victory as a trainer at
Hereford in December 1991.

The proud trainer in the
winners' enclosure with
part-owner my dad Brian
and stable girl Sarah Inglis.

See More Indians and Graham Bradley survive a terrible blunder at Kempton on their way to giving me my first Grade 1 success as a trainer.

100 Up. General Crack completes my first century at Chepstow in November, 1995.

Belmont King and Tony McCoy on the way to victory in the 1997 Scottish Grand National.

In command... Flagship Uberalles (Joe Tizzard) gives me my first Cheltenham Festival winner in the 1999 Arkle Chase.

Stress. What stress? I love every part of my job.

A day later Call Equiname (Mick Fitzgerald) pips Edredon Bleu (Tony McCoy) in an epic finish to the Queen Mother Champion Chase.

Paul Barber and John Keighley proudly lead in See More Business after the King George VI Chase at Kempton in 1997.

See More Business (Mick Fitzgerald) completes an amazing three days for me at Cheltenham by winning the 1999 Gold Cup.

Left See More Business returns in triumph.

See More Business (Andrew Thornton) after his third triumph in the Rehearsal Chase at Chepstow in December 2002.

My head lad Clifford Baker gets the chance to shine on See More Business as they canter past the packed stands at Wincanton.

See More was a right old bruiser who took me to all the best places.

Poetry in motion... Evergreen See More Business (Ruby Walsh) wings a fence on the way to his final success at Wincanton in February 2003.

Calling Wild (Joe Tizzard) lands the Paddy Power Chase at Leopardstown on 27 December 1998. It was my first success in Ireland.

Another big prize safely landed.

Auditioning for a summer job with Earthmover's owner Roger Penny.

Ad Hoc (Ruby Walsh) claims his first win in the 2001 Attheraces Gold Cup.

Cenkos (Barry Geraghty) lands the Celebration Chase at Sandown in April 2002.

Safely over the last... Azertyuiop and Ruby in the 2003 Arkle Chase.

Happy days. The winning team flanked by Lisa and John Hales.

In charge. Azertyuiop romps home in the 2004 Queen Mother Champion Chase at Cheltenham.

Building a Better Bournemouth

Winton Library
Wimborne Road
Winton BH9 2EN
Tel 01202 528139

Borrowed Items 13/01/2017 14:48
XXXXX7405

em Title	Due Date
Lucky break : the tobiography	03/02/2017

ndicates items borrowed today

ollow us on Twitter @Bmthlibs
ww.bournemouth.gov.uk/libraries

paddock as if we'd never had a problem between us. Life moves on and this was not the time for recriminations. What had happened in the past was water under the bridge because the three months we'd been apart taught me for sure that I'd much rather have AP riding for me than against me. There was hardly any need for orders since he had confidence in the horse, knew he'd stay and appreciated that mine are always fit.

I was happy with his plan to make plenty of use of Belmont King and was thrilled to see them lead all the way. It was a brilliantly aggressive ride from the front and showed exactly what I'd been missing in the saddle since January. Belmont King was my 50th winner of the season. AP definitely made the difference that day, but I couldn't count on him in the future and knew I had to bring another jockey on board.

I enjoyed another trip to Scotland that April. Barry Simpson, racing manager to one of the country's leading owners, Sir Robert Ogden, rang one day asking Joe Tizzard to ride Grosvenor in an amateur's race at Perth. I was all for him going provided he was paid his travelling expenses. Joe booked his flight and on the spur of the moment I decided to fly up with him. I waltzed into the paddock at Perth, introduced myself to Sir Robert, had a long chat with him and later wrote to him saying I'd love to train for him. Some time later he sent me Grosvenor and since then we've had a lot of success together. My first success for Sir Robert with Grosvenor came on a day of high emotion for everyone connected with the yard when we buried my blacksmith, Gary Hooper, who was killed in a motorcycle accident ten days after See More Business won the Gold Cup.

12

The race panned out like a dream

It's fair to say that Timmy Murphy is one of the most frustrating jockeys I've ever employed. I've hired him twice and parted with him twice and he still has the odd ride for me today as the retained rider for one of my owners, David Johnson. Timmy has talent to burn, is a wonderful horseman and has travelled far from unpromising beginnings in Ireland. But he isn't the easiest to get on with and the darker currents in his nature sometimes let him down with irrational behaviour which badly hampered the early part of his career.

Most of the top lads were already committed for the new season in the autumn of 1997 and, though I'd long hoped to snap up Mick Fitzgerald, he quickly made it clear he'd be staying with Nicky Henderson. I had lots of confidence in my teenage amateur, Joe Tizzard, but he lacked experience and it was much too soon to be pitching him in at the top level.

Timmy was young, keen, on the up and available. I knew I was taking a bit of a gamble when I chose him to be my stable jockey as he'd already lost one decent job with Kim Bailey because he wasn't great at getting out of bed in the morning. That didn't put me off because I was more interested in how he performed in the afternoons. What I didn't know was that he already had a drink problem which would eventually tip him over the edge.

I gave Timmy his big break after he'd ridden a couple of winners for me in the West Country. I liked what I saw and, crucially, he wasn't tied up with any of the big yards. I hoped we could develop a long-term relationship that would benefit the pair of us. Timmy never said much when he rode out. Sometimes all I'd get out of him was a grunt of satisfaction after he'd schooled a nice youngster over fences; on another day it was as if I was his best mate. I was prepared to back him all the way and we enjoyed immediate success with horses like Mutual Agreement, Galatasori Jane, Strong Tarquin, Dines and, best of all, Call Equiname in the Shogun Chase at Cheltenham in mid-November 1997.

Joe Tizzard was shaping up well, too, and made his own little bit of history when he won over the Grand National fences at the age of seventeen on With Impunity in the Sefton Chase. He was six months younger than Bruce Hobbs when he won the 1938 National on Battleship. I was immensely proud of him.

Although Timmy quickly grew into the job, I didn't like the way he gave some of my horses an unnecessarily hard time with the whip once they were beaten, and neither did some of their owners. I hate the sight of horses getting a hiding at any time and particularly when they are not involved in the finish. It is horrible to watch and sours them quicker than anything. Timmy had a major problem when he lost his temper and got stuck into Bramblehill Buck, owned by Paul Barber, as they finished a distant third at Newton Abbot on 18 November. Paul and I were fuming because it looked as though he'd hit the horse seventeen times.

The stewards sent the case on to the Jockey Club's disciplinary panel at Portman Square after deciding that Timmy had used his whip with excessive force and when out of contention on a horse showing no response. Probably the worst crime was that he had also injured Bramblehill Buck by hitting him in the wrong place. With three whip offences already on his file that year, Timmy probably got what he deserved when he was suspended for thirty days at a hearing in London.

So, less than a month into our deal I was without a jockey during one of the busiest periods of the season. As Timmy was able to continue for another few days before the long ban kicked in, he was free to ride See More Business to a stylish victory under top weight in the Rehearsal Chase at Chepstow. At Haydock the previous time we made a mistake in riding him for speed. He didn't jump with much confidence but, despite a bad blunder at the thirteenth, he was doing all his best work in the last half-mile as he took third place behind Suny Bay. It was a highly encouraging return after all his problems in the spring.

At Chepstow, Timmy was even more reserved than usual in the

paddock but afterwards he couldn't disguise his delight at the way See More Business saw off some of the best chasers around with plenty to spare. Soft ground clearly suited him well and the way he finished again suggested he had bags of stamina. His jumping was better, too, so it was time to raise our sights. Some bookies introduced Seemore in the betting for the King George VI Chase on Boxing Day. Although it was an option, I was worried that a sharp three miles round Kempton on decent ground would be a bit too quick for him, so I was thinking of other options. His jumping was also a concern. Once that improved we could ride him up with the pace to make the best use of his stamina. It was difficult to make plans but I was hoping it rained for a fortnight so I couldn't resist a crack at the King George.

A timely wet spell saw us heading for Kempton on Boxing Day. Timmy Murphy played his part by coming down to school Seemore on the Tuesday and again on Christmas Eve and I was happy with my choice of Andrew Thornton, a long-legged horseman, to replace him. I was even happier after walking the course with Paul Barber and John Keighley. We all felt the ground was genuinely soft, which was definitely in our favour and not ideal for One Man, a prolific winner who sometimes tied up badly at the end of his races.

The race panned out like a dream. See More Business jumped well, apart from one mistake, and took a narrow lead at the fourth last. He was immediately challenged turning for home by Suny Bay and One Man. Once they both weakened in the straight I began to shout and roar my horse home from my position between the last two fences. Then Tony McCoy appeared on Challenger du Luc to spoil the party. The pair of them arrived at the last fence running away, but AP's horse had a heart as big as a pea and, once again, when it came to a battle he was found wanting.

One moment Challenger du Luc was cantering on our heels. The next I was in wonderland as Seemore refused to let him past and battled on grimly to win the biggest prize of my career so far in an incredibly tense finish. It felt even better to do it for Paul Barber, who'd backed me to the hilt from day one. Most of the pubs near Ditcheat were shut that evening so we all ended up at Paul's viewing endless replays with Marianne producing heaps of sandwiches to go with the champagne.

The more we watched See More Business winning the more I

thought it was a brilliant performance by a horse on only his seventh race over fences. We'd always known he was exceptional. Now that his jumping was more reliable he was living up to all our expectations, though I never felt Kempton was his ideal track. As the Cheltenham Gold Cup was definitely on the cards I took the opportunity to give See More Business some practice over the course in the Pillar Chase with Timmy Murphy back in the saddle. I'd left a bit to work on and the going was faster than I'd have liked but you can't have everything.

The chief priority was a clear round, which nearly didn't happen when he was almost on the floor after clouting the fourth last fence. It was a blunder that cost him priceless lengths at a key stage of the race and by the time he recovered Tony McCoy had shot eight lengths clear on Cyborgo. I thought it was all over yet he made up the lost ground easily, swept past the leader on the final bend and sprinted clear up the hill. Seemore showed an incredible change of gear that day. It was a proper Gold Cup trial and an amazing display of resilience and stamina which left us all believing he could win the real thing in March, though he wouldn't even be lining up for the Gold Cup if the ground came up good to firm.

Suddenly, I was flavour of the month. In the lead-up to the Gold Cup no end of journalists and TV crews wanted to watch Seemore on the gallops and talk to all the people connected with him. I made them all welcome because we don't have any secrets and the publicity could only be good news for us. The horses were in top form and people were already starting to take notice before we notched up our 50th winner of the season at Taunton. For one glorious month horses from our yard plundered the feature race on four successive Saturdays.

They always go flat out from start to finish in the Gold Cup, which was definitely in our favour, and I didn't disguise my confidence as the big day approached. You could see the change in See More Business after Kempton. Until then he had been a boy. That day he became a man. Going about his work that spring he really did believe he was king of the castle. He'd always had a Rolls-Royce engine and his enthusiasm at home and for racing had definitely increased. For a streetfighter he was cute, too. Of all the horses I've trained he's the only one we didn't put on the automatic horse walker after exercise for the good reason that he wouldn't play ball. As soon as you attached him to the walker he dug in his toes and refused to move.

Seemore left for Cheltenham in the pink of condition. He was much more relaxed than his trainer, who was getting pretty wound up, as usual, after two more blank days at the Festival. In the weeks leading up to the Gold Cup I'd run the race a hundred times in my mind. I was prepared for just about anything until Paul Barber, who is not normally a pessimist, told me the night before the race about his fears that See More Business could be carried out by a loose horse. It was eerily clear to me that he had a bad feeling about the next day. At the time I thought he was talking nonsense.

13

War in the West

I watched the 1998 Gold Cup through a red mist. Even now, more than ten years on, I still get angry thinking about what happened. I wasn't overconfident that day, partly because the ground had dried out quicker than we wanted for See More Business, who was always at his best when the mud was flying. But I still felt he was the one with the best chance by far of ending my drought at the Festival. In the paddock, as Georgie Bown led him round, he looked like a flower ready to bloom. Timmy and I decided that he should be prepared to go wide, if necessary, so that the horse could have plenty of daylight at his fences. Better that, we agreed, than the hassle of jumping almost blind in the middle of the pack in such a big field. I legged Timmy into the saddle and made my way with Robert Blackburn down to the lawn and out on to the course close to the last fence.

I don't like distractions or idle chatter when I'm watching one of my horses running and prefer to be on my own whenever possible. As a long-time friend who often used to drive me to the races, Robert was an ideal companion because he seemed to know instinctively when to speak and when to keep quiet. Dorans Pride was a warm favourite with See More Business clear second best at 11–2. The way he looked I couldn't see him being out of the first three. One I didn't fear was AP's mount, Cyborgo. We'd beaten him decisively last time and the girls in our yard had been hearing from Pipe's stable staff that he'd had problems since then and might not even run. Racing chat like that is normally right. People don't make up these stories.

We soon knew our fate, though in the confusion it took a few seconds to work out exactly what happened. One moment Seemore was cruising along handily placed towards the outside. The next he was one of three horses out of the race after a melee at the seventh fence. I've never been the greatest at watching my own horses. I tend to listen, rather than watch closely, and I just heard this big groan from the crowd when the commentator said that Cyborgo had run out and taken two others with him, including See More Business.

The blood drained from my face as I heard his words. I was stunned beyond belief, totally shell-shocked, my hopes and dreams shattered in an instant. I'd had so many disasters at Cheltenham already and this was the worst of all. It felt as if someone had written a horror story and I was the victim. What the hell had happened? All around me people were asking the same question. In the distance I could see Timmy cantering slowly back on See More Business. At least they were OK.

When I realised the identity of the horse that had caused all the trouble my disbelief quickly turned to fury and then full-blown rage. Robert says I went ballistic. As I stumbled back towards the walkway with him I was like a volcano about to erupt and I had a fair idea about the first person to suffer the fallout. I'd had so many issues with Martin Pipe and Tony McCoy, and now Cyborgo, the wretched horse that first caused the trouble between us, had come back to haunt me again.

Apparently the moment AP felt Cyborgo falter under him, he pulled him sharply to the right to miss the fence looming up in front of them, badly hampering his stable companion, Indian Tracker. As the pair of them veered sharply off the course they gathered up See More Business and carried him out of the race with them. There was no blame attached to Timmy Murphy. Jockeys react in split seconds, but this all happened so fast there was nothing he could have done to avoid being forced out.

I know AP well enough to appreciate that he'd never have taken us or anyone else out deliberately. His horse was injured and he didn't want to risk causing further harm by allowing him to jump another fence. Later, I understood that; but in the heat of the moment, when things go spectacularly wrong, you don't always think rationally. Sometimes common sense goes out of the window and my first reaction was that we'd been the victim of a conspiracy, which I fully accept now was a crazy idea. The thought of what happened ate away at me for ages.

I'd set my heart on Seemore winning and couldn't take the pain when it all went spectacularly wrong. Maybe I wouldn't have felt so bad if another horse had caused the damage. But Cyborgo was trained by my arch enemy who had stolen my jockey from me. I knew there was no way they would have taken out See More Business deliberately. But that didn't stop me blaming them at the time.

As I headed along the chute where the horses come back in I spotted Martin Pipe scuttling towards me. Just the sight of his foxy face set me off. He looked at me for a second, all embarrassed, and smiled but didn't say bad luck or anything like that. In fact he didn't say a word. I kept going for a stride and that's when I lost it.

I turned back, caught him up, and was all set to grab the lapels of his coat and lift him off the ground as I told him, 'I'll wipe that fucking smile off your face one day if it's the last thing I do.'

Pipe looked like a startled rabbit caught in headlights. He was frightened to death that I was going to hit him and I might well have done but for Robert Blackburn calling out, 'For Christ's sake, Paul, don't do it. You can't do it. Let him go. Leave him, leave him.' Thirty yards away Paul Barber was shouting much the same but I was in such a state by then that I didn't take any notice.

Frankly, I was in the mood for violence and part of me still wishes I'd clocked Pipe. It wouldn't have done me any good in the long run though it sure as hell would have made me feel better at the time. Robert was at my side by then and I'll never forget his words as he intervened like a referee in a title fight. 'If you must hit anyone, hit me, not him,' he hissed, gripping me firmly by the back of my collar and dragging me off the victim of my onslaught. At least I'd had the satisfaction of confronting Pipe before Robert pulled me away. Paul Barber was totally crushed, every bit as livid as me, and for a long time blamed AP for what happened to Seemore. His fears the night before about the Gold Cup had proved horribly correct and even now he maintains he was much more upset about AP's part in the Cyborgo shambles than his decision to turn his back on us fourteen months earlier.

Timmy Murphy was going mad when I caught up with him. He felt AP could at least have shouted a warning as he realised Cyborgo had gone wrong behind, though that is not always easy in the heat of the moment. My dad, more than anyone else, realised I was spitting blood and looking for revenge. Seeing the look in my eye that he knew so well, he told Robert to take me right out of the way before I did some serious damage.

Robert proved to be a brilliant minder by ushering me from the track before I did something I'd regret. 'Come on, we are going home,' he told me and apparently I followed him as if I was in shock, with Bridget and Claire close behind. Less than half an hour after the Gold Cup I was heading through Cheltenham towards the M5 beside Robert at the wheel of his new Range Rover. The rest of the afternoon passed in a blur until I heard on the radio that Pipe and AP had landed a treble in the final three races. That was rubbing salt into my wounds.

We nearly had a punch-up at a roundabout in Bristol when someone tried to drive into us. I was halfway out of the door, looking to have a go, but the other driver shot off when he saw me coming. My mood didn't improve when a report on the radio suggested that See More Business had run out in the Gold Cup. I whacked the radio and, if it hadn't been Robert's vehicle, I'd probably have ripped it out and thrown it out of the window.

I was inconsolable by the time we reached Ditcheat and hardly spoke to anyone for two days. Watching the tape of the incident again and again only made me feel worse. Bridget gave me a good talking to and said it was about time I learned to cope with defeat. That set me off again because I've never minded getting beat fair and square; but what happened to See More Business was different.

Part of the problem was knowing that the Gold Cup had been won by the outsider Cool Dawn from Strong Promise, who was pretty much a non-stayer. I'm still convinced that See More Business would have beaten them both with a clear round. On all known form he was the better horse, but Cool Dawn's was the name on the trophy and I raise my hat to Robert Alner for a brilliant piece of training. In her own sensible way Bridget got it right when she told the *Racing Post*, 'We have studied the video and come to our own conclusions and it's up to everyone else to do the same. Whatever we say, it isn't going to make any difference to the result.'

Most of the papers missed my spat with Pipe. Peter Scudamore had a sniff of the truth when he hinted in the *Daily Mail* that I'd taken Pipe to task at Cheltenham. Pipe, he suggested, was left reeling by my verbal onslaught and upset by my attitude. Poor man. If only I'd told him what I really thought! Monty Court then wound up the temperature in his column in the *Sporting Life* under the headline 'WAR IN THE WEST'.

It provided lively entertainment for the media, yet such clashes happen all the time between Premier League managers. The tabloids feed on these feuds with the fourth official often struggling to keep them apart in the technical area in the full glare of the TV cameras. Hardly a weekend goes by without one manager gesticulating and snarling at another over some incident on the pitch.

Who can possibly forget Kevin Keegan's astonishing outburst against Sir Alex Ferguson? More recently, in January 2009, Newcastle's then manager Joe Kinnear and Phil Brown of Hull had a major bust-up on the touchline that ended with both men being sent to the stands by referee Phil Dowd. Next it was the turn of Liverpool's boss Rafael Benitez to launch into Sir Alex Ferguson at his regular press confer-ence. That one has rumbled on for months. It's part and parcel of sport at the highest level where the difference between winning and losing can be life-changing. Compared to football managers, race-horse trainers are definitely tame. I am sure we are all guilty of being nice to everyone at the races, then sticking the knife in behind their backs.

You don't have to like all your rivals. As it happens, I get on really well with most of them, but Martin Pipe was the exception. He always made me feel I was in opposition to him – although I got on very well with his father, David, who died a couple of years ago. I have plenty of respect for Martin because of what he has achieved, but that is as far as it goes. His son, David, who took over the licence in 2006, is a completely different character, much more approachable, and even won a point-to-point at Larkhill on my hunter, Granville Guest, a few years ago. We get on fine and text and ring each other over running plans.

I took a fair bit of flak for getting so upset at Cheltenham. That's the way I am. It was a hell of a kick in the teeth because I knew the horse was better than he had ever been. To see the race snatched away in that manner was hard to take. No wonder I was cross. See More Business is an intelligent horse and couldn't understand what had happened either. He was in a right strop for days, just like his trainer.

I wasn't alone in my reaction. It's just that others close to the horse were a little more restrained in their comments. John Keighley spoke of his devastation, while Paul Barber suggested that people should look at the tape of the incident and reach their own conclusions. Deep down, Paul was absolutely gutted. We both felt our chance of winning a Gold Cup had gone forever in the most controversial circumstances. The pair of us got so upset talking about it that we kept out of each other's way for a bit.

There was an unpleasant postscript to the 1998 Gold Cup when a parcel with a Taunton postmark arrived in the post a week later containing a T-shirt with a slogan on it reading GO WIDE MURPHY, FOLLOW McCOY. Some nice bastard had gone to the trouble of having it made and delivered to my office. I just binned it.

Liverpool was another desperate meeting for us. I was well overdue a change of luck in the Grand National, but it didn't come. Belmont King was ruled out of the race with a last-minute injury and the three we ran all failed to complete. I ended the season in fourth place in the trainers' list with eighty-two winners, yet it was the one that got away that I remember the most.

The highlight of the year by far came on 3 July with the birth of my daughter Megan. It was wonderful to be there at Yeovil Hospital, though I found it all a bit scary. You feel guilty about the pain your wife is going through but luckily Megan's was a fairly quick birth. I've never been one for other people's children but, when you have a child of your own, it is a massively uplifting experience. Megan is the light of my life.

Bridget, clever girl, planned things so accurately that she gave birth at the quietest time of the year for us. A couple of weeks later the horses started coming back in and Bridget made such a quick recovery that she was soon back in the yard every bit as involved with the training as before, which was a bit of a surprise to me. She'd always had a big input in things and clearly that wasn't going to change. Mum and Dad, together with Geoff and Julie, all played their part in looking after Megan in those early years when Bridget was often away racing. Life was a lot easier once we employed a full-time nanny, Sarah Munns, who later married our head lad, Clifford Baker. Megan was a bundle of fun from the start, is now twelve and heavily into sport, including ponies and racing. She is bound to break a lot of hearts in the years ahead.

One way and another Timmy Murphy missed fifty-two days through suspension that first season with me. It was a ridiculous amount of time for any sportsman to be out of action and left me with a regular headache ringing round looking for substitute jockeys. By the end of April I'd just about had enough of his quirky behaviour. I'd bent over backwards to give him every chance. When he was on song, he was right up there with the best of them, but I never knew which Timmy Murphy was going to turn up. My owners wanted continuity and they were not getting it.

One day that season he rode three for me like a bungling novice. All three might as well have stayed in their boxes. I couldn't believe what I was seeing and remember having a long conversation about it with Paul on the way home. Perhaps Timmy had a terrible hangover. That was the obvious conclusion when his drink problem became public a couple of years later. He is very honest about it in his autobiography. A lot of things became clear when I read that book and I admire him enormously for sorting himself out and giving himself a second chance as a jockey. Unfortunately I didn't have a clue about his drinking during that first season with me. I never knew what to expect when he walked into the paddock and that's a hopeless basis for a working relationship.

In the early days Timmy was a loose cannon with a whip in his hand. Sometimes his habit of hitting horses came out of a misguided sense of frustration that they were not trying as hard as he was. In addition, he had an ugly habit of tapping them down the neck with his stick on the roads, on the gallops and walking round at the start before a race. I tried to stop him doing it but sometimes I might as well have been talking to a brick wall. Racehorses are not household pets. They need discipline and guidance and are creatures of habit but they also want to enjoy their work and I hate anyone riding for me niggling them with a whip. That can sour them quicker than anything.

The fact that Timmy was such a hard fellow to get on with made me wonder how long we could work together. Luckily, I had a ready made replacement nearer to home. Joe Tizzard worked as hard as anyone in the yard, lived near Sherborne and had come up through the pony club, hunting and showjumping before starting in point-to-points at sixteen. I asked him to join my team after watching him win a hunter chase on The Jogger at Wincanton. Though Joe was still inexperienced, some of my owners liked him and he rode with plenty of dash. At eighteen he was on the young side, but age hadn't stopped Michael Owen from becoming one of the world's most feared strikers after he'd scored that wonder goal against Argentina in the World Cup in 1998, and he was only a day younger than Joe, who had packed a lot into the last two years and really looked the part when he won on Mutual Agreement for me at Fontwell at the end of May that same year.

On the way home I told Joe he was wasting his time as an amateur, persuaded him to turn professional and promised that I'd back him 100 per cent. I knew I'd have more horses the following winter and needed a reliable back-up to Timmy Murphy. Five months later Joe stepped into the hot seat when I took the decision to loosen my ties with Timmy, who was getting stressed with the horses. He was generally stroppy and uncommunicative and not helping himself. Perhaps if he'd come clean about his drinking problems we might have worked something out, but my owners were becoming frustrated with him and it was time for a change.

Things came to a head at the end of October when he was cautioned at Fontwell for his use of the whip on Qualitair Memory, trained, ironically, by Joe's father, Colin Tizzard. Joe finished third on one of mine called Distant Echo. Some way behind Timmy was knocking lumps out of Qualitair Memory. It was horrible to watch and made up my mind for me. I didn't want this man to continue as my stable jockey, but as he knew lots of our horses it made sense to continue to use him from time to time and, despite everything, I couldn't help liking him.

Joe Tizzard was keen, uncomplicated, mature for his age and down to earth. It was a big ask for someone so young but he suited me, was already retained by John Keighley for his horses and I hoped would grow into the job and be part of our team for many years. A lot of people thought I was mad to take on an eighteen-year-old but I had a lot of confidence in Joe and horses jumped for him. You can't please everyone all the time and some of my bigger owners were soon asking to use the best jockeys available on the day. It was a sign of things to come.

All three of us made the headlines on 7 November when I sent out seven winners and three seconds from ten runners. I'd never experienced anything like it and would have settled for a couple of winners at the start of the day. I hardly ever have a bet and never thought of putting them all together in a multiple punt. More's the pity, though I was tempted to have a few bob on my nap, Court Melody, because I knew I had him spot-on. It was a brilliant day. Joe led the way with a treble at Chepstow on Calling Wild, Irbee and Nearly An Eye, while Timmy did his bit at Sandown on Laredo, Court Melody and Mr Strong Gale. My seventh success came with Derrymore Mist at Wincanton.

Joe continued the good work on Green Green Desert the following week. I've had some classy flat horses through my hands but he is the only one to have headed the ante-post market for the 2,000 Guineas after an easy success at two for Sir Michael Stoute. He didn't fulfil his potential on the flat and had a reputation as a bit of a monkey until he won four times for Oliver Sherwood the previous season.

Though one of mine, Mrs Em, had beaten Green Green Desert at Worcester in September, I thought there were races to be won with him over fences. I fancied trying to revive his interest and bought him privately from his owner, Darren Mercer, then worked the balls off him up our hill, morning and afternoon, until he was super fit. Green Green Desert wasn't that quick at home so to give him confidence I let him work with something slower so that he was always running away. He paid me back at Cheltenham on 13 November, won twice more that season and ended up finishing fourth in the Champion Chase, which was quite something for a handicapper with a question mark over his attitude.

Joe didn't make a winning start on See More Business but I wasn't expecting fireworks in their first race together at Haydock. The horse was over his optimum racing weight, I'd left something to work on and was more than happy when he finished fourth after blowing up in the last couple of furlongs. That put him spot-on for Chepstow where he won the Rehearsal Chase for the second time. He was still making the odd mistake but his class usually got him out of trouble.

We headed to Kempton with high hopes of a second King George on seriously testing ground, which seemed to suit him so well. He ran a stinker, didn't jump with any fluency and was miles behind the winner, Teeton Mill, when Joe pulled him up. I was stunned at the time and couldn't believe he could run so badly. It was a desperate display, a rare blemish on a brilliant career. I scratched my head over that one for a long time and eventually came to the conclusion that he'd reached the stage where he didn't really want the ground as deep as it was on Boxing Day.

Our hearts were in our boots leaving Kempton. Twenty-four hours later Joe and Calling Wild provided the perfect pick-me-up as they squelched through the mud to land the Paddy Power Chase at Leopardstown. It was an amazing result because the horse had been coughing his head off for two weeks after winning at Wincanton late in November and was still giving the odd bark. He lived in the next box to See More Business, which gave another possible explanation for his poor show at Kempton.

Calling Wild was one of our finest graduates from Richard Barber's yard. Owned by John Keighley, he was a decent pointer, but taking on twenty-five others in a madcap Irish handicap worth IR100,000 was something else. While all the tests on him were clear after his spell of coughing I was looking for an excuse not to take him to Ireland right up until the last minute. But run he did and fortune favoured the bold as he gave me my first success in Ireland.

One horse above all others was exciting me in his homework that winter. Call Equiname's frailties had driven me round the bend over the past two or three years. He had so much ability it was frightening, but you always feared the worst when you stepped into his box and felt his front legs, which were like delicate pieces of porcelain. I'd given him a long time off when he'd broken down in November 1997 and brought him back steadily before upping his work rate in December. For four years I thought he was good enough to win the Champion Chase but unfortunately it took me four years to get him there.

Call Equiname gave me more sleepless nights than anything else in the yard because he had it all – class, courage and blinding speed if I could keep him sound. The root cause of the problem was chronic sore shins, which led to several more niggling issues. Maybe now with better quality gallops in place he'd have been easier to train. Back then our woodchip all-weather surface probably didn't help his cause. I wouldn't have too many shots with him and settled for one run before Cheltenham in the Victor Chandler Chase at Ascot in January.

Mid-winter is a maddening time for trainers, jockeys and owners.

You make your plans months in advance then find yourself forced to rethink by the weather though heavy rain worked in my favour after Call Equiname picked up a little cut on his hind leg at the start of the week. I thanked my lucky stars that Ascot was waterlogged. The wound cleared up so quickly we were back in the frame when the race was rescheduled six days later for Ascot, where Joe was set to ride him. This time fog caused the card to be lost.

I had a difficult decision to make when the big chase was switched yet again to Kempton the following day. Joe was already down for several of mine at Haydock, including Calling Wild, so I booked Robert Thornton to replace him. Robert proved a terrific substitute as he brought Call Equiname home a neck in front of Get Real. Given the horse's catalogue of setbacks and that he was little more than a novice on his fourth start over fences on ground much softer than he liked, I think that was one of my best training performances.

We had further cause for celebration at Kempton when Flagship Uberalles continued his impressive progress with a runaway victory in the novice chase. He was one of a team of horses sent to me from Ireland out of the blue the previous summer by Austin Brady, who turned out to be a serious punter. After we shared a double at Worcester in July with Lord Esker and Flagship Uberalles, Austin told me he won so much money he left the course with a carrier bag stuffed with cash. I won a stack of races for him that season, including six with Flagship Therese.

The best of his by far was Viking Flagship's half-brother, Flagship Uberalles, a huge, strong animal who was only just beaten in the champion four-year-old hurdle at Punchestown in April before he joined me. I was thrilled to have him though he wasn't the soundest horse in the world and was always scratchy in the morning. The fact that he was a poor mover at the trot didn't bother me because he was such a good walker; he reminded me of one of those loose-limbed West Indian fast bowlers striding purposefully back to their mark. In addition to all this, he was a wind sucker. We used to spend plenty of time warming him up and then let him kick on. What he needed was a serious amount of graft.

Flagship Uberalles was so big I thought he was wasting his time over hurdles. If ever a four-year-old was made for steeplechasing this was the one, and he proved to be the pathfinder for all the four-year-olds I have run over fences since then. He was precocious, well forward and more than ready for the switch to the bigger obstacles. His schooling was awesome before I took him to Exeter in December, where he won his first novice chase with his head in his chest. Although he was beaten next time he was back on track at Kempton, where he couldn't have been more impressive.

I thought Flagship was a natural for the Arkle Chase at Cheltenham, where he'd get a handy weight allowance for being a five-year-old and was a bit surprised when Austin Brady told me that he was prepared to sell the horse at the right price. Austin was struggling for funds at the time, told me he wanted £160,000 and wouldn't take a penny less. As I felt the horse was a machine I offered him to Paul Barber and then Graham Roach, who enjoyed so much success with Viking Flagship. Aware of his problems, Paul wasn't interested and Graham, being a canny Cornishman, was tempted but wanted a deal involving a discount. Graham was still in the frame when Flagship Uberalles turned over the odds-on favourite, Tresor De Mai, at Warwick on 20 February.

Austin Brady wasn't there that day. As I had a runner to saddle in the next race I invited two of my owners, Michael Krysztofiak and his partner Liz Gutner, to collect the trophy on his behalf. Afterwards, over a drink, I told them the horse was for sale and that I rated him as a major player at Cheltenham. Liz was a lovely woman, pleasant and enthusiastic, but Michael was hard work. He'd once been employed as a head waiter in Stow-on-the-Wold and didn't seem to enjoy it when one or two people reminded him of his old nickname, Manuel.

Looking back now, I wish I'd never mentioned the horse was on the market but the damage was done and a few days later Michael rang from their home in Arizona to say they were interested in buying. The deal was done and they paid £160,000 direct to Austin. Subsequent events would prove that Michael and Liz had a terrific bargain, but to this day one of my biggest regrets is that I failed to persuade Graham to buy the horse. Things would have been so different if he had owned Flagship.

14

See more gold

I've never been a punter and don't begin to understand how heavy-weight gamblers like Harry Findlay can risk hundreds of thousands of pounds on the result of a horse race when so many things can go wrong. My nerves couldn't stand that kind of stress, but I don't mind an occasional bet if the odds are long enough. Given my dismal record at the Festival and the disaster in the previous year's Gold Cup, I was hardly expecting to conquer the meeting this time. Knowing that top trainers like David Nicholson and Josh Gifford had both taken forever to open their account there was enough to temper my natural confidence. But as the horses were in form I linked my runners in the three championship races in a series of doubles and trebles at big prices. I thought it was about five million to one against all three winning, which is probably why I promised to buy Bridget a new Mercedes if the miracle happened.

My nap of the week was Flagship Uberalles, running in the star-spangled colours of Liz Gutner and Michael Krysztofiak in the Arkle Chase on the opening day. Although he was an 11–1 shot I thought he had the ideal blend of strength, power and speed and couldn't see him finishing out of the first three. The pressure was on me more than Joe, who had broken his Festival duck the previous year on Earthmover in the Foxhunters.

Flagship looked like a battleship in the paddock. He was so mature for his age it seemed ridiculous that older horses had to give him eight pounds. The furious early pace helped Joe settle him behind the leaders and long before the end it was clear he'd win bar a fall. He led at the second last and galloped on up the hill to give me my first winner at the Festival. My sense of relief at finally getting the monkey off my back was overwhelming and it was a huge bonus to do it in the second race on the opening day. I was thrilled with the horse and the jockey, who had more than justified my faith in him on the biggest stage.

The rest of the day passed in a blur but keen-eyed observers will have noted that I used a young Irish jockey for the first time in the William Hill Chase. Ruby Walsh had taken advantage of a cold snap to fly over and ride out for me on a couple of days in February. It wasn't the first time he'd been to Ditcheat. Ruby's parents, Ted and Helen, had been friends of the Barbers for years and a photograph in Paul's kitchen shows a baby-faced Ruby in short trousers in the back of the farm pickup with the rest of his family. Ruby had no luck on Earth-mover that day but more than made up for it in the years ahead.

I felt Call Equiname was my most exciting runner of the week in the Queen Mother Champion Chase because he had so much quality, but finding the right jockey for him wasn't so straightforward. His owners, Paul Barber, Mick Coburn and Colin Lewis, preferred an experienced man who would hold him up as late as possible before making his move. It was the biggest day of the horse's life and they wanted the best available, which rather ruled out Joe mostly because he had never ridden Call Equiname. As Joe had already won twice on Green Green Desert, my other runner in the race, it made sense for him to continue the partnership. My brother-in-law, Mick Fitzgerald, was the obvious choice for Call Equiname but he'd already given his word to Charlie Mann that he'd ride Celibate.

I warned Mick that he was making a mistake in sticking with Celibate, though he didn't need a lot of persuading to change his plans. He then got an earful of abuse when he told Charlie Mann he was switching to mine. We had the right jockey, the drying ground was definitely in our favour and Mick Coburn, for one, wouldn't hear of defeat. When he met the Queen Mother at Sandown the previous Friday, after Court Melody won the Grand Military Gold Cup, he assured her that she'd be handing over her own trophy to him at Cheltenham.

Call Equiname travelled and jumped like a dream some way behind the leader, Edredon Bleu, then eased into the race going down the hill so that he was barely a length down at the last fence. I could hardly believe my eyes as Mick sat hard on the bridle waiting to pounce like a winged assassin. All they needed was one more fluent jump but they didn't get it, lost momentum and suddenly had a fight on their hands as Direct Route came through to join the party. It was touch and go for a moment as Edredon Bleu rallied but Call Equiname was equal to the challenge and edged ahead for the first time with a hundred yards to run and held on bravely by one and a quarter lengths. It was a stunning performance by a horse who had overcome so many problems and his three owners later collected a hefty bonus from Victor Chandler for completing the big race double.

With Robert Blackburn at the wheel as usual, we stopped off for fish and chips near Bristol on the way home for the second night running before heading down to the Manor Inn for a few drinks later in the evening, but we wouldn't have been quite so cheerful if we'd known that Call Equiname would never win another race. Unfortunately he was never the same again.

I woke up feeling like death on the morning of the Gold Cup and nearly didn't make it to Cheltenham. I struggled with a stomach bug all week and the stress of the previous two days at the Festival only made things worse. Early nights were out of the question after the excitement of the first two days, so getting stuck into the champagne on Tuesday and Wednesday probably didn't improve my condition. I like to help the press if I can and achieved a first for me that morning by doing an interview with Cornelius Lysaght on BBC radio while sitting on the loo in the dark next to my office to prevent the noise of the fan drowning our conversation.

My condition had improved to critical by the time we planned to leave for the races. I was in no fit state to travel but how could I stay away from Cheltenham on jumping's biggest day of the year? This time I had two big shots at the Gold Cup, Double Thriller, ridden by Joe Tizzard, and See More Business, who'd rather lost his way since his disastrous exit a year earlier. Joe was full of hope on the 9–1 shot Double Thriller, a big old-fashioned ex hunter who'd won both of his prep races by a mile since joining me.

See More Business was dismissed in the betting at 16–1 after a couple of below par efforts. When he was soundly beaten again at Cheltenham at the end of January I began to think he might be pulling the wool over my eyes. I decided to put blinkers on him in the Gold Cup but kept it to myself at that stage. When the time came I had the devil of a job to persuade his owners, Paul Barber and John

Keighley, to go along with it. John, in particular, was totally against the idea.

Determined to have my way, I arranged a demonstration, with the help of Mick Fitzgerald, on the schooling grounds in front of Paul and John a fortnight before the Festival. First time up without blinkers See More Business couldn't have cared less as he fiddled his way awkwardly over the first two fences before winging the ditch in style. That was him, maddeningly inconsistent when it came to jumping. He'd become so lazy he couldn't be bothered.

Five minutes later, equipped with blinkers for the first time in his life, Seemore was a revelation. Given a crack of the whip by Mick to wake him up, he set off like a two-year-old out of the stalls, keen as you like, and attacked the fences with real zest. When we asked him to do it again he was every bit as good. It was like watching two different horses and Mick came back purring like a cat that had got the cream. Next morning I put the blinkers on See More Business again for his daily breeze up the hill. He took off with Clifford, whoosh, pulled his arms out the whole way, didn't want to stop at the end and nearly charged into the big hedge on the other side of the road at the end of the gallop.

Paul was beginning to come round to the idea of blinkers, but John wasn't for turning even when Seemore, in his new headgear, worked as well as he'd ever done at Wincanton a week before the Gold Cup. Several of my owners watching the gallop hurried quickly from the stands to snap up the 33–1 for Cheltenham on offer with our local bookie, Andy Smith.

Although John was still totally against using blinkers I took the law into my own hands and declared them anyway. Running the horse without them would have been a waste of time. Using blinkers for the first time, I felt, could well be our trump card. If he improved as much on the course as he'd done at home, then we were definitely in with a shout. We were further encouraged as the ground dried up in the final few days before the Gold Cup. Joe knew Double Thriller well by then and planned to make use of his jumping by being up there the whole way. As Mick had not ridden See More Business before, I drummed into his head that the horse had so much stamina he'd stay all day. I urged him to be positive because he wouldn't be stopping at the end.

Standing on my own, I watched the race on the big screen with my dad a few yards away. This time it wasn't a stressful experience. Double Thriller was in charge for a long way and still led at the top of the hill as the race came to the boil. Go Ballistic, a 66–1 shot, then took over but behind him I could see Mick moving with stealthy intent on See More Business beside Florida Pearl. Mercifully there was no sign of the jumping errors that had held him back in the past.

Down the hill and into the straight I was already calling him the winner because, bar a calamity at the last fence, I knew he'd outrun Go Ballistic on the flat. Two hours earlier I was so weak and light-headed I couldn't have raised a whimper. Now, as See More Business joined battle with Go Ballistic on the flat, I began to ride the strongest finish of my life. I shouted and hollered and cheered like mad while Dad was leaping up and down like a lunatic.

The job still wasn't quite done, though once Seemore edged ahead he was never going to be beaten. He wanted to win every bit as much as I did and held on grimly by a length from Go Ballistic with Florida Pearl in a different county back in third. Talk about poetic justice! All the horrors of twelve months ago were swept away by an electrifying charge of emotion that I had finally won the Gold Cup. The way I felt right then in the winners' enclosure that was the best day of my life. No question.

There is no feeling in the world to match the thrill of entering the winners' enclosure at Cheltenham and I was doing it for the third time in three days. No wonder I was on another planet. The Gold Cup was a massive result for us, and even better for Paul Barber because it had always been his dream to win it. John Keighley had put so much into racing, too.

Sticking the blinkers on See More Business made a massive differ-ence. I've never known them have such a dramatic effect on a horse's jumping. It was amazing. When he came to me I was surprised at his lack of scope, but he developed and thickened in time and always had a serious engine. Mick Fitzgerald was astonished how small he was when he sat on him for the first time. He described him unkindly in his book as a horrible little thing, small and narrow, but I didn't hear any complaints when he rode back in triumph after the Gold Cup.

Fish and chips were off the menu that night. Instead, we headed for home, watched the video of the Gold Cup over and over again before ending up with a night of celebration at the Manor Inn. The next day we paraded all three of our winners through Ditcheat. The sun shone and a large crowd turned out as we led the trio past the pub where the party continued from the previous night. You could almost reach out and touch the pride in Paul's face as he stood holding See More Business in one hand and the Gold Cup in the other. Megan, who was twenty months at the time, got a great cheer when she posed cheekily on Seemore's back.

My big race treble at Cheltenham delivered the largest winning dividend of my life. I'd taken 33–1 about See More Business, and 25–1 Call Equiname in doubles and trebles with Flagship Uberalles, who started at 11–1. When I did my sums I was thrilled to discover that I'd won around £36,000. The following week I bought the Mercedes for Bridget. That was the whole lot gone in one hit!

That week was a huge turning point in my career. In the space of three unforgettable days I'd gone from being an OK trainer to sitting at the top table. My three Festival winners pitchforked me to the head of the trainers' list. Going into the meeting I hadn't thought about the championship because I was too far behind Martin Pipe. Then, suddenly, I had a handy lead of almost £46,000 over him. It was a challenge I couldn't resist because I might never get another chance. I still had sixty-five to run if the ground didn't dry out too much and was determined to do all I could to stay in front.

The previous autumn I'd have given anything to head Pipe for one day. Now I was in the driving seat I was hardly going to let it slip. If we had to claim one or two out of selling races to help out, we would. If it meant going to Hexham late in May, we'd be there. My horses didn't know they had even started; they could all have a long holiday when it was over. It was always going to be an uphill task to stay at the top of the table because, back then, the season didn't end until the start of June and Pipe always seemed to have a fruitful month in May. Flagship Uberalles did his bit by landing the Grade 1 Novice Chase at Aintree but my hopes of a big dividend in the Grand National came to nothing when Double Thriller, the 7–1 favourite, crumpled on landing at the first fence.

A week later I reached my first century of winners in a season with a treble at Ayr highlighted by Fadalko just beating Pipe's Potentate in the Scottish Champion Hurdle. I managed to stretch the lead to almost £100,000 at one stage but drew a blank at the Whitbread meeting at Sandown and had less than twenty top-of-the-ground horses left to run as April turned to May. Already I was feeling a bit like a horse that had been out in front too long. I wanted to keep going until I reached the finishing line but kept glancing over my shoulder, knowing that my only rival, with much more firepower, was closing relentlessly.

I was still around £30,000 ahead with three weeks to go and getting a huge amount of support from my friends, owners and others in racing. Charlie Mann, for instance, rang to say that if I needed a few extra horses to make the difference, he would let me have as many of his as I wanted to run in my name. It was an extraordinarily generous gesture, but one I couldn't accept.

For a while the bookies couldn't split the two of us but eventually Pipe was installed as favourite to retain his crown. Our stamina-sapping head-to-head duel caught the imagination of the public, but all the fun went out of it for me when Estate Agent was killed in a fall at Bangor in May on his first attempt over fences. I felt guilty at what happened because normally he wouldn't have been running at that stage of the season. He was a smashing horse, had won three for me already over hurdles and his owner, Terry Curry, generously encouraged me to have a crack with him over fences to help my push for the title. He schooled brilliantly, went to Bangor and was killed. I lost another one the same way. It wasn't worth it.

I should have called a halt then, but I was too competitive to see the sense of it. Even though I was struggling to hang on I wasn't prepared to concede defeat. How could I give up when I was still in front? I didn't usually get involved with summer jumping but I couldn't just shut up shop and walk away with my first title tantalisingly close. Deep down, though, I could see the championship slipping from my grasp because our battle was rapidly turning into a numbers game and I was running out of ammunition. Pipe seemed to be entering anything in his yard with four legs. I couldn't compete with that. On the last Saturday in May, two days before the end of the season, I had a total of two entries at the three jumps meetings while Pipe entered forty-seven. It was that one-sided. No wonder Pipe was a 1–4 favourite by then.

That was when I finally conceded defeat. I hadn't enjoyed the last few weeks and realised that the whole thing had descended into farce when Pipe entered twenty-two horses in one race. On 31 May, the last Bank Holiday Monday of the season, I conjured up three runners. Pipe's scattergun policy of twenty-five runners at six meetings on the same day yielded eight winners and sealed my fate.

I was desperately disappointed to lose out but at least I'd given it my best shot. I hoped I'd have another chance but wasn't convinced it would come. Pipe had so many more runners that season than me. He ran nine hundred. We managed four hundred. I ended my best season with 110 winners and prize money of £1,192,566. It wasn't enough.

It was heartening and flattering that just about everyone wanted us to win but unfortunately we came up short. Because I got totally caught up in the race for the title I'd run horses that should have been at home in their boxes or already out to grass. I made decisions that I knew were wrong. That was unlike me because I don't normally do things I'm not happy to do. Next time I wouldn't put myself under so much pressure. Never again.

15

Married to racing

The dawn of the new millennium was a time for celebration around the world but I didn't feel like joining in the fun because my marriage to Bridget was as good as over. Though things hadn't been right for a while we'd soldiered on hoping we could patch things up. Our last Christmas together in 1999 was a miserable one and showed there was no chance of making it work.

I was mostly to blame because I've always had tunnel vision when it comes to training the horses and have never allowed anything to get in the way of my ambition to get to the top. If my marriage was breaking down around me I didn't realise it because I continued to bury myself in my work. I was like a horse in blinkers: I couldn't see what's going on around me. I was married to racing.

That can't have been easy for Bridget, who wanted to be a trainer every bit as much as I did. She'd been heavily involved with the horses since we arrived at Ditcheat and loved riding work and going off to the races. When Megan was born I hoped she'd take a back seat and spend more time at home. No chance: she didn't want to be a house-wife and preferred to be making decisions and helping in the yard. It reached the stage where I was calling myself the trainer's husband! That was unacceptable since you can only have one boss. As she wanted to be doing everything and running the office as well, we clashed too much about the way she'd become involved with the training. It got to the point where I resented her input, which was a bit unfair because she definitely played a big part in the early days.

Living in the house in the middle of the yard put an added strain on our marriage. The pair of us felt as if we were conducting our lives in a goldfish bowl. With no privacy at all, I felt on call twenty-four hours a day. Since different people would turn up at all times I used to lie on the floor of the lounge to make sure no one could see I was there!

As Bridget and I were going through a sticky patch I thought that moving out of the yard might give us a new start, and shortly after See More Business won the Gold Cup I managed to buy a house, ten acres and a few run-down buildings a mile from Ditcheat. At £460,000, Highbridge was just about the best investment I've ever made. I felt it had bags of scope for development and would give us some much needed privacy when we moved there in September 1999. Maybe the cracks in our marriage were too wide by then.

We were together for almost ten years with plenty of good times, but most men go off to work first thing in the morning and don't see their wives again until they come home for supper. I think it is so hard to eat, sleep, drink and work together 24/7. It might suit some couples but, sadly, I found it very stressful. With all the ups and downs in racing I'm probably impossibly hard to live with.

Maybe I should have tried a bit harder but, with close on a hundred horses to train, I had to be out of the door by seven in the morning and never found enough time to try to put things right or give thought to personal issues. Towards the end I was more interested in the horses than saving my marriage. With me, racing always comes first. It might sound wrong and selfish, but that's the way I am. There is no room for compromise. I couldn't have survived if I'd had to change lots of things to please Bridget. That wouldn't have been me.

Eventually, I told Bridget there was nothing in our marriage for either of us. Not for the first time I was putting my career before my personal life. Bridget wasn't ready to walk away at once after helping to build up the business so she stayed in the house for six months while I got on with my life and she got on with hers. It was a difficult time for both of us but we managed to keep the peace for the sake of Megan, who was too young to realise what was happening. Most people would probably have gone away for a month to try to sort things out. That wasn't possible for us in the middle of another hectic season. Despite moving to Highbridge, we didn't really have the luxury of dealing with it behind closed doors.

The decision to go our separate ways came on the run-up to a fabulous Millennium and Gold Cup party thrown by Paul and Marianne Barber in a large marquee on their lawn to mark Paul's

57th birthday. It was an emotional night for so many reasons, not least because See More Business had won his second King George VI Chase a few days earlier, but for once I couldn't get wrapped up in the celebrations.

No one at the party knew of the turmoil I was going through but they did the next day when I told my owners of the situation before issuing a press statement saying that our marriage was over. The previous season had been our best ever, but it came at a price. My sister Julie always says I've made a lot of sacrifices to be so successful. One of the biggest was my marriage to Bridget. It would have suited me so much better if Bridget had been a homemaker who wanted more children, but you can't change the way people are. Towards the end she was almost as competitive as I was when it came to training winners.

I didn't feel like facing the world when news broke that our marriage had ended. The papers were full of it and I was scared of the reaction I'd receive at the races. Heading for Uttoxeter on 2 January, I was worried that everyone at the track would be dreadful to me. Maybe it was a sense of guilt; I don't know. Perhaps I'm too sensitive because it really wasn't anyone else's business.

At times like that you need a little bit of help and, luckily, I had the support of Paul Barber and Graham Roach, who came with me to Uttoxeter. But for them beside me I doubt I'd have managed to walk into the course without turning round and heading back to the car. I half expected people to be pointing the finger at me. That prospect really frightened me but, as it turned out, everyone I met couldn't have been nicer. I felt a mixture of relief and gratitude for all their support. Shotgun Willy and Young Devereaux did their bit by providing me with a timely double. Two winners were never more welcome than that day.

For six months Bridget and I lived separate lives at Highbridge. She occupied one end of the house and I camped in the other before she moved to Faringdon as an assistant trainer to Henrietta Knight. Bridget had set her heart on training and eventually rented a yard ten miles away, at Charlton Mackrell. That was great for me because it meant I saw a lot more of Megan. I helped Bridget in a number of ways, put a horse in training with her and encouraged others to do the same; but she didn't enjoy much success even when she married my assistant, Jeremy Young.

I parted company with Jeremy when I discovered that he was going to her yard at lunchtime and spending most afternoons there. I told him there were a million women out there while he was working for me and he had to choose my ex-wife. That was crazy. These days Bridget and Jeremy work for Charlie Mann at Lambourn and for the last four years Megan has lived with me, which is fantastic.

Initially, I was determined to live on my own for the next four or five years because I didn't want to allow anyone to get that close to me. I enjoy female company, have had some lovely girlfriends over the years and remain close to quite a few of them. I've also ended up with a lot of personal heartache, mostly because I'm selfish and single-minded to the point of obsession. Like it or not, the girls have to accept that my first priorities at all times are the horses, the owners and all things racing. That's how it has always been.

I was badly in need of a pick-me-up during the dark days of January and got it when Flagship Uberalles ran his heart out under top weight in a spellbinding finish to the Victor Chandler Chase at Ascot. He looked like winning as he edged ahead two fences out but couldn't quite shake off Nordance Prince, who, in receipt of twenty-four pounds, got up on the line under a power-packed finish from Tony McCoy. I thought my Flagship was greater in defeat that day than in some of his victories.

He'd already won two major prizes that season, the Haldon Gold Cup at Exeter and then the Tingle Creek at Sandown. His owners, Elizabeth Gutner and Michael Krysztofiak, used to fly over from their home in Arizona, watch him land another big pot, then return home forty-eight hours later. Flagship Uberalles was a stuffy horse who needed plenty of racing and normal service was resumed next time in mid-February when he hacked round Newbury to beat two opponents in the Game Spirit Chase. He wouldn't have blown a candle out afterwards.

Flagship Uberalles did his work all season over five furlongs upsides See More Business, who had a new owner when he ran at Newbury the same day. I was a bit surprised when John Keighley sold his half-share in the horse soon after his second success in the King George, though I fully understood his reasons as he needed to cut back on his team at the time. Seemore was magnificent at Kempton, jumped soundly the whole way, led three out and galloped home seventeen lengths ahead of his old rival Go Ballistic. It was a superb performance but the champagne had to remain on ice in the bar when the racecourse was evacuated twenty-five minutes later following a bomb scare.

Sir Robert Ogden was the man who bought John's half-share at a figure close to £250,000 and he must have been pleased when the horse ran in his colours for the first time at Newbury. Seemore was relentless and still fresh at the finish after pulling miles clear of Macgeorge in the Aon Chase. As he was five kilos heavier than at Kempton I was sure he'd come on a lot for the race.

I'd started that season determined not to become involved in another duel with Martin Pipe for the trainers' championship. We never had more than sixty-three horses in full training at the same time during the previous campaign and I couldn't see how the addition of twelve more boxes was going to change things. With a capacity of seventy-five at Ditcheat and thirty others tucked away elsewhere, I thought I had the strongest team ever but still couldn't begin to match the firepower of Pipe. Anything with an injury would be moved out of Manor Farm stables and allowed to recover under specialist care at other yards. Fresh horses replaced them.

We've never had the same type of jumpers as Pipe, who tended to rack up a huge lead in the summer while mine didn't begin to move into gear until well into October. I'm much too competitive, though, to concede defeat before a ball has been bowled and privately felt a change in the rules gave me a sniff of a chance if I was still in touch with him after Cheltenham. In 1999–2000, for the first time, the season finished at the end of April on Whitbread Gold Cup day.

You always feel you are walking on eggshells in the run-up to Cheltenham because so many things can go wrong when high-mettled racehorses are in hard training. One false step or careless jump during schooling and months of planning are blown away. Two of my best horses failed to make it to the Festival. Double Thriller needed an operation to sort out his breathing and Young Devereaux, a lively contender for the Arkle, had yet another setback.

At least my two aces were in sparkling form, though Seemore had to defy the lessons of history since no horse had won back-to-back Gold

Cups since L'Escargot in 1970 and 1971. During a series of Festival previews I couldn't disguise my confidence in both of them, but my hopes for another fruitful festival were sunk by unseasonably fast ground. Try as he might, Paul Barber, the best weather guru in the West Country, couldn't find a spot of rain at Cheltenham in the week ahead to ease the conditions. The official description of good on the opening Tuesday seemed hopelessly misleading after four course records were broken, some by wide margins.

More records were shattered on Wednesday, which was like a day borrowed from early summer. Walking the course that morning I knew the drying ground was against Flagship Uberalles because he was such a big, heavy horse. That didn't stop punters sending him off favourite at 11–10. He travelled well enough through the race as Tony McCoy set a scorching pace on Edredon Bleu but he wasn't fluent three out and then made a crucial mistake at the next fence. From that point Flagship was never going to win and did well to claim third place, some way behind Edredon Bleu who just pipped Direct Route in a tight finish.

The moment the horse was beaten that day I knew it was the beginning of the end, although it was clear to me the ground was too quick for Flagship. Obviously the mistake two out didn't help and he hadn't come down the hill too well. Joe felt they were going a bit too fast for the horse on the ground. Flagship had one or two niggling issues with his feet at the time, which wouldn't have mattered if there had been some ease in the going.

Krysztofiak saw it differently. For him anything bar a win was going to be a disaster, yet in jump racing you cannot guarantee success. So many things can go wrong and when they do you discover the true nature of the people involved. Some of my owners, like Paul Barber, are terrific in defeat. He has had some terrible days on and off the course, yet on the darkest days, when the game doesn't seem worth the candle, he takes it on the chin and always tries to look forward. Krysztofiak, however, couldn't cope when the dice rolled against him. He was so confident at Cheltenham that day he wouldn't hear of defeat. After Joe had gone to weigh in I remember Michael saying to me, 'Well, he'll win the Gold Cup next year.' I replied that he wouldn't be winning the Gold Cup if I was still training him because he wouldn't be running in it. I read somewhere that Krysztofiak had already backed him for the 2001 Gold Cup but that was the end of the debate as far as I was concerned. Why go further? It was nonsense. He wouldn't stay the trip in an aeroplane!

The lightning-fast ground also found out See More Business, but there was no question of him leaving me. He ran his usual honest race and led briefly at halfway, but they were always going a stride too quickly for him though he stayed on to finish fourth around six lengths behind the winner, Looks Like Trouble, who set yet another course record. I think he was cute enough by then to look after himself a bit if things weren't right.

Mick told me See More Business felt like a cat on a hot tin roof. Sure enough, the next day his shins were so sore you could hardly touch them. He looked so incredibly uncomfortable in his box that, if you didn't know better, you'd have said he was finished. However, he'd recovered from a similar problem several times before and showed his toughness of spirit by bouncing back at Aintree to land the Martell Cup.

That was the only bright spot at the meeting where all four of my Grand National contenders failed to finish and Flagship Uberalles, the 11–8 favourite for the Mumm Melling Chase, was pulled up by Joe Tizzard after dropping out of contention five from home. We had difficulty getting on one of his shoes that day and something wasn't quite right afterwards. I decided to finish Flagship for the season, but he seemed so full of beans that I took him to Ayr eight days later, hoping he could go out on a winning note. In hindsight, I shouldn't have done that because the ground was faster than I expected. He didn't travel with his usual fluency and was lame when Joe pulled him up approaching the second last fence. It turned out he was again suffering from a foot problem.

That was the last time Flagship ran for me. I turned him out in a field at home for the summer and can't say I was surprised when his owners took him away in June and sent him to Noel Chance, who had him for barely a year before he was moved yet again to Philip Hobbs. It had been on the cards ever since he was beaten at Cheltenham. I was desperately sorry to lose the horse who was a star for me from day one. But I can't say I was unhappy about seeing the back of Michael Krysztofiak.

I think I did extremely well with Flagship, who was far from easy to train, was a habitual wind sucker and trotted so badly to the point of being lame. A lot of people would have struggled to get him to the races, let alone collect a string of big prizes. He won all the races I promised, but for Michael that didn't seem enough. I helped him buy the horse and he wouldn't have enjoyed his time in the limelight if it wasn't for that. If I'd made a pig's ear of training Flagship I might have understood Michael's displeasure.

The following March I didn't pull any punches at a Cheltenham Preview evening when I was asked by someone in the audience for my opinion of Flagship Uberalles. 'Nice horse, shame about the owner,' I replied without thinking. It wasn't the most diplomatic comment of my career but I felt better for saying it.

16

A first for Ruby

Telling Joe Tizzard he was no longer stable jockey was one of the hardest things I've had to do in my life. I dreaded giving him the bad news and put off the moment as long as I could. Joe ended his first season as champion conditional jockey with ninety-one winners, which trumped AP's previous record of seventy-four. It was a tremendous start, though we had an understanding that he didn't ride everything in the yard. That's how Mick Fitzgerald came to be on some of the better horses, including Call Equiname. We had a good team at the time I appointed Joe and improved the quality of our horses quicker than anyone could have imagined, to the point where some of my bigger owners started to give me grief about him. John Hales, in particular, was furious when he was beaten on one of his at Ludlow. Others soon followed John's lead.

Joe was young, keen, suited me and learned fast, but not quick enough for some of my owners. Suddenly the job was bigger than either of us had anticipated. It was a bit like having a decent player in the Championship who takes time to adjust when his team is promoted. If horses are beaten unexpectedly, the jockey is usually the first to get the blame and I used to take a lot of flak intended for Joe. He was tall and not the tidiest in a finish, but very effective.

Jockey-related problems have given me more headaches than anything else since I started training. I stood up for Joe for as long as I could, but eventually some of the owners made it clear they didn't want him on their horses. Successful businessmen who become multi-millionaires are used to getting their own way. They invest a lot in racing, demand the best available and they weren't prepared to give Joe any more chances. You wouldn't believe the hassle I was having from people complaining that Joe wasn't experienced enough at the time.

That was the last thing I wanted to hear because we'd had a marvellous season together and I thought the world of Joe. I wasn't so powerful in those days and couldn't make a stand by telling them to take their horses elsewhere if they didn't want Joe. I could probably do it now, but not then, so I was forced to play the role of executioner.

I hated calling Joe down to my house and telling him he was no longer stable jockey because we worked so well together. He was still at school when he first came to the yard on his 50cc moped to ride out three mornings a week. Everyone likes Joe because he is such a lovely lad. That made my decision all the more difficult and the look on his face as I spoke left me in bits. It wasn't my proudest moment as a trainer, but I had no choice. I said I'd help him as much as I could and eased the blow by promising that he'd still have plenty of rides for me. I'm pleased to say that's exactly what happened. Joe has ridden hundreds of winners for me though he's busy with his dad's horses these days. He will make a very good trainer when the time comes.

A welcome new addition to the team that winter was my dad Brian, who retired from Avon & Somerset Police after forty years on 1 September, took a month's holiday then started with me on four mornings a week. It was his suggestion, really, because he always wanted to come and help. Mum and Julie were a bit surprised by the arrangement. Knowing we are both strong characters, they forecast that Dad's new role wouldn't last five minutes! It's fair to say that we did have one or two arguments in the first few weeks. It was hard for Dad, who was used to being in charge and had to adjust to the realisation that I was now the boss. He quickly learned not to cross the boundary and has proved a brilliant member of the team, full of enthusiasm and common sense.

Dad loves being involved, will turn his hand to anything, saddles horses for me at the races, gets on famously with my owners and is a useful sounding board when I want a second opinion. He'd be up long before dawn at Olveston near the Severn Bridge, would drive the short distance to Tockington to help out with the ponies belonging to Julie's children, Harry and Amy, then head down to Ditcheat in time for first lot. He found all that driving a bit tiring and things have been a lot easier since he and Mum moved into a house close to mine at

Highbridge in 2008. Dad's main role is harrowing the gallops after each lot. He hates being idle and says he couldn't possibly retire. My parents supported my ambition to be a trainer from the very beginning and it is great that I am able to repay them in a few small ways now that they are living on the spot at Highbridge.

It felt a bit strange to find myself in opposition to Flagship Uberalles in December in the Tingle Creek Chase transferred to Cheltenham when Sandown was waterlogged. I booked Tony McCoy for Fadalko at the request of his owner, Sir Robert Ogden, and thought our best chance of winning was to try to steal a decisive lead at the top of the hill. It looked like working until Flagship came tanking past on his favoured soft ground.

An hour earlier, Mister Banjo, ridden by Mick Fitzgerald, showed immense promise in beating Run For Paddy in the Relkeel Hurdle. It was a definite improvement on his first run for me in France when he looked like taking a part in the finish of a valuable race at Auteuil until unseating Adrian Maguire at the second last. Mister Banjo briefly held the title of Britain's most expensive jumper with John Hales paying a record price of 240,000 guineas for him at Doncaster. We were really marking time until we put him over fences.

Seemore was his usual impossible self when he came back into training. The fire in his belly was as strong as ever as he took his earnings past £500,000 by winning the Charlie Hall Chase at Wetherby for the second year running. Mick Fitzgerald was purring afterwards as he suggested there wasn't a horse in the country to trouble him when the ground was soft.

We headed for Kempton with high hopes that he could join the select band to have won the King George VI Chase three times, but it wasn't to be. They seemed to go a bit too fast for him that day and he was already beaten as they turned for home before plugging on to be fifth. Even though he won the big race at Kempton twice, I'm still not convinced the course really suited him. Above all it is a sharp track for speed horses and Seemore's greatest asset has always been stamina.

It was a different story back at Cheltenham a month later where he showed his true colours by storming home unchallenged in the Pillar Chase, despite two serious blunders that would have stopped lesser horses. He was never the best jumper in the world but had his own way of getting from one side of a fence to the other and, though he was eleven by then, you wouldn't have known it from his work. He was a bit like a proud old prizefighter who could still land a knock-out punch on his day and I felt he was the one they all had to worry about in the Gold Cup in March. Shotgun Willy's defeat of the King George winner First Gold at Newbury suggested he was a Gold Cup horse, too. It was tempting to go for the big one but, as he'd run only four times over fences at that stage, I aimed him instead at the Sun Alliance Chase.

My banker for Cheltenham was an exciting four-year-old, Azertyuiop, who arrived from France with a massive reputation after landing four races on the bounce the previous autumn, including three on the flat. He had the make and shape of a chaser and already jumped like a cat. The sky really did seem the limit for him when he showed his class with a stylish winning debut for me in the Kingwell Hurdle at Wincanton. He looked tailor-made for the Triumph Hurdle.

The countdown to Cheltenham in 2001 was even more tense than usual. We were on tenterhooks for weeks after an outbreak of foot and mouth disease paralysed movement of livestock in parts of the country. It was a terrible time for farmers as hundreds of thousands of sheep and cattle were destroyed before their carcasses were burned in huge funeral pyres that scarred the countryside for weeks on end. Racing was soon swept up in the crisis with meetings cancelled at courses close to areas where foot and mouth had been detected.

Cheltenham continued to issue positive bulletins but it wasn't a good omen when racing was called off for ten days at the end of February, and the announcement we were all dreading came on 7 March, once it was discovered that sheep had been grazing close to the racecourse. That was the end of the 2001 Festival, though they were going to stage it a month later until that plan went up in smoke, too, after another case of the disease was found inside the restriction zone.

It was a body blow for everyone in the sport because there is nothing in jump racing to match the splendour of Cheltenham. However much we moaned at the loss of our showpiece, things were ten times worse for farmers forced to slaughter their herds of healthy cattle and sheep to prevent the disease spreading. They were the ones in need of sympathy. While the racing industry would recover, many farmers faced ruin.

As racing stumbled on intermittently through late March, I took advantage of the crisis to establish a satellite yard with Richard Barber at Seaborough. Richard had long been a key player in our team by bringing on young horses like See More Business and Calling Wild. With point-to-points at a standstill, it made sense to race some of his horses under National Hunt rules. We spoke to the Jockey Club, who readily agreed to his setting up an additional yard for me. The horses would remain with Richard but race in my name. The system works really well for both of us with up to twenty-five of my horses in his care. We've helped improve his gallop and, if some of my horses can't handle the hill, or need a change, I send them to him.

After the mind-numbing loss of Cheltenham it felt great to be racing at Aintree but for me the meeting was pretty much a washout because the ground was so deep. The conditions definitely counted against Azertyuiop, who struggled on gamely through the mud to finish second to Bilboa in the Glenlivet Hurdle. After torrential rain on Saturday, it was touch and go whether the Grand National would take place. Forty horses set out, but only four finished. My interest in the race ended when Earthmover fell at the fourth fence.

The one bright spot of the meeting was the triumph of Fadalko in the Mumm Melling Chase. That was the first of countless important winners ridden for me by Ruby Walsh, the man I badly wanted to join us on a permanent basis. It took me much longer than I expected to bring him aboard, but it was worth the wait.

I ended that season with a purple patch that took me tantalisingly close to my first trainers' championship. With a week to go, Martin Pipe had such a big lead I thought I didn't have a prayer. Doubles at Perth and Fontwell on Thursday set the tone for a frantic final two days, but I was never going to catch him. On Friday I notched up five winners at my local meeting, Wincanton, and also landed the feature race at Perth with Norski Lad. Percolator, the first of the quintet, took our horses' earnings past £1 million for the season but the win I enjoyed the most was that of Satshoon in the race named after one of my most loyal supporters, Alan Taylor. He backed me all the way as a youngster, owned shares in several of the point-to-pointers that I rode and never needed an excuse to nip away from his paper shop and come racing with me when I was riding.

Ruby Walsh showed just why I was so keen to sign him up with two sensational rides for me on the final day of the season at Sandown. Although he earned the plaudits for his victory on Ad Hoc in the Whitbread Gold Cup, he was even better in defeat on Fadalko in a barnstorming finish to the Championship Chase against Tony McCoy on Edredon Bleu. The sight of the two greatest jockeys of their generation at the limit going head-to-head set the packed stands alight.

As the horses crossed the line locked together no one could be sure who had won. Although AP feared he was beaten, he got the verdict by the shortest of short heads. The Sandown stewards then rubbed salt in the wound by banning Ruby for one day for his use of the whip.

Compensation arrived forty minutes later when Ruby romped home on Ad Hoc by fourteen lengths in the Whitbread. The winner had rather lost his way with his jumping after falling twice and it took a while for him to regain his confidence. Ruby is brilliant on horses like that. He's such a gifted horseman, sits quietly and soon gets them into a rhythm over a fence. He'd never ridden Ad Hoc before but you wouldn't have known it as he smuggled the horse round in midfield without a semblance of a mistake before making his move after the Pond fence. Ad Hoc's victory sealed a first owners' championship for Sir Robert Ogden, which had seemed unlikely when he trailed Norman Mason by over £130,000 two days earlier.

There was no such luck for me. For the third year running I had to settle for the runners-up spot behind Martin Pipe. This time I wasn't complaining.

17

Drama at 30,000 feet

Timmy Murphy was back in the fold for the new season in the summer of 2001. I think it was a bit of a surprise to him and to me. This time it would end in tears after a nightmare journey halfway round the world which made the headlines for all the wrong reasons.

Timmy wasn't our first choice, or the ideal choice, but with Joe Tizzard settled into the role as second jockey my owners wanted first call on a top-class rider and Timmy fitted the bill. He was the best available, had done really well since we'd parted company three years earlier, was riding with bags of confidence and appeared to have put behind him the worst excesses with his whip.

We turned to Timmy when it became clear we couldn't tempt Ruby Walsh to come over from Ireland on a full-time basis. Back in January a group of my owners tried to sign him up with a retainer of £30,000 for the period between 1 October 2001 and 1 June 2002. A clause left the door open for him to nominate two Irish-trained horses, which he could choose to ride over any of ours. Crucially, though, we wanted Ruby to live in the area. Paul Barber and I felt it was the right time for him to make the move but he was still quite young, only twenty-two, and had lots of good horses to ride in Ireland for his father and Willie Mullins. At least he left the door ajar by assuring us that he would ride for us when he wasn't needed at home.

With Ruby unwilling to come to England and Mick Fitzgerald firmly tied up with Nicky Henderson, we switched our attention to Timmy Murphy in May. I rang his agent, Chris Broad, explained the situation and a few days later Timmy accepted my offer to be our stable jockey for the second time.

Early in May a horse called Cenkos won on his debut for me at Warwick for a new owner, Andy Stewart. Ten weeks earlier one of mine, Desert Mountain, had beaten Cenkos into third place in a decent race at Kempton. That night Paul Barber told me, 'I've met a guy called Andy Stewart. Don't be surprised if he has a horse with you in a minute.'

I'd forgotten all about it when I had a call from Andy. He was a bit upset because Cenkos hadn't been entered for the end-of-season Championship Chase at Sandown and asked me to pick the horse up from Oliver Sherwood's yard in Lambourn. He then won at Warwick less than two weeks later. It was the start of a tremendous partnership with Andy and his family, who now have around twenty-five horses with me. You couldn't ask for a more enthusiastic or generous owner. Andy is a big player in the City, named his own company Cenkos and racing provides much needed relaxation for him. He's not much older than me and proud of the fact that he made a fortune after being expelled from school. Andy quickly became a mate, someone I could talk to about my problems, and we often speak three times a day. I'm pleased to say I've trained nearly a hundred winners for him and his family.

Another influential owner came on board that summer. I'd never heard of Harry Findlay at the time but he has since gained a reputation as a fearless punter on all sports and as the joint owner of Denman with Paul Barber. Harry became involved after meeting Paul by chance in the bar at the Doncaster Sales where I had an order from a well-known showbusiness figure. We paid 175,000 guineas for Garruth, a runaway winner for Tim Easterby at Aintree, but within an hour the purchaser got cold feet and changed his mind. We were wondering what to do next when Harry bravely stepped in and said he'd have the horse but unfortunately we must have left the keys to him at the Easterbys in Yorkshire!

I thought Garruth would make a cracking chaser on soft ground but he turned out to be gutless, hated jumping fences and let us all down badly. He was so slow the first time he cantered up our hill I could have run faster. He did manage to win a couple of poor novice chases before ending up performing badly in point-to-points.

Garruth made us all look like chumps and left me wary of doing business again with the Easterbys. It was embarrassing to have bought a high-profile horse at an inflated price, but it happens from time to time and is one of the reasons I now do most of my shopping privately in France, where you are not in competition with four or five others. Garruth was a shocking introduction to Ditcheat for Harry Findlay but he took it on the chin and has had plenty of good times since.

Kadarann offered the other side of the coin after I bought him for 15,000 guineas at Doncaster out of Nicky Henderson's yard that summer and immediately had his breathing done. He won five times for us that first season when I put him over fences, earning a bucketful of prize money in the process and continued the good work the following year.

Once we sorted out his wind, Kadarann earned over £120,000 for his owners, but, like so many consistent horses, he became a victim of his own success and was hit hard by the handicapper. We should have sold him then because you reach a point where you can hang on to horses too long. To stay ahead at this game you sometimes need to sell. His team of owners could then have reinvested in another horse but the moment passed and Kadarann was so badly handicapped he became impossible to place.

It is dangerous for owners to fall in love with their horses because it can hurt when things go wrong. That's why I try to dissuade mine from becoming too emotionally attached to their horses. You mustn't do it. Sometimes there is a time to sell. That might sound hard and unfeeling but it is true. I feel a bit like a football manager with a big squad of players. Sir Alex Ferguson can't afford to stand still and retain the same personnel year after year at Manchester United and neither can I. To stay at the top, Sir Alex knows he has to let some older players go at the end of each season and reinvest in bright young talent. It's exactly the same for me.

One that slipped through the net was Rooster Booster, who won the Champion Hurdle in 2003. I had the chance to buy him as a youngster when his breeder, Richard Mitchell, put him on the market at £60,000. I didn't take much notice of him when he was offered to me, probably because I didn't have an order at the time.

Timmy Murphy had matured a great deal since our previous uneasy partnership and rode a stack of winners for me that season. He had talent to spare, was clearly keen to do better second time round and was much more professional in every way. Although we were never going to be close friends, we shared a better understanding. I was pleased to have him on my side. Shortly after we shared a four-timer at Chepstow we enjoyed a big race treble at Wincanton, capped by the stylish success of Azertyuiop in the Elite Hurdle. He was a huge horse, too big for hurdles really, and was marking time until I could run him over fences.

Timmy never had much luck on See More Business and endured a shocking experience on him at Chepstow when they fell heavily at the second last fence in the Rehearsal Chase in December. It was the worst type of fall because Seemore was flat out trying hard to see off the persistent challenge of Arctic Camper. A less generous horse would have accepted defeat and coasted home in second place. Not Seemore. He was compulsively competitive and refused to give in even though he was exhausted. Watching on television from Sandown, I was horrified to see him lying motionless on the ground as dark green screens were erected at the scene.

Poor old Seemore was down for fully five minutes and I remember hoping against hope that he was only winded and would clamber to his feet. Paul Barber, my assistant Jeremy Young and Georgie Bown were all there with him. That was a terrible few minutes for everyone though Paul told me that night he knew the horse would be OK when he opened one of his eyes and looked at him!

It was the best feeling in the world when I had a call from Jeremy telling me that Seemore eventually scrambled to his feet and was led back up the course to sustained applause from the stands. That was the best result of the year. Paul admitted later that he was in tears fearing the worst, yet Seemore was so tough that he was bouncing again at home within days so we took him back to Chepstow for the Coral Welsh National. That was probably a mistake but at least he finished in one piece before winning the Jim Ford Chase at Wincanton in February and then, remarkably, finishing third to Best Mate in the Gold Cup at the age of twelve. What a star.

Cenkos ran his heart out to be third in the Champion Chase. He briefly looked like winning when he was left in front by the fall of Latalomne at the second last fence until my old warrior Flagship Uberalles came steaming past on the flat. I had other plans for Cenkos, who was best suited to a flat track and didn't seem to appreciate the hill at Cheltenham. The lure of £1 million in prize money was enough to tempt me to take him to Japan the following month for the Grand Jump over two miles, five furlongs at Nakayama.

First, though, I had to negotiate the most frustrating Grand National of my career. Time and time again I'd arrived at Aintree bursting with expectation, only to retreat to Somerset with my tail between my legs. This year I was determined to end my drought in the race. Torduff Express, ridden by Polly Gundry, gave us the perfect start by winning the Foxhunters with eye-catching ease and Timmy played his part with a stylish victory on Armaturk in the Grade 1 Novice Chase just over an hour before the National.

My hopes were focused on Ad Hoc, who had been primed all year for this one challenge. He was fit, stayed well, had a reasonable racing weight of eleven stone one pound and was ridden for the first time by Paul Carberry, who had already won a National on Bobbyjo. He was the right man for the job once Joe Tizzard was ruled out with a serious back injury.

Ad Hoc wasn't the best jumper in the world but, given a clear round, I thought he couldn't be out of the first four. Paul is famed for switching his mounts off towards the rear and conserving their energy before creeping quietly into a race in the closing stages. That's what I asked him to do on Ad Hoc. I also ran Murt's Man, a 66–1 shot ridden by Andrew Thornton, as Timmy Murphy asked me to release him to partner David's Lad, the horse he'd partnered to victory in the previous year's Irish Grand National. David's Lad and Ad Hoc started joint second favourites at 10–1.

I watched the race with mounting excitement, which was a novel experience for me as usually I'm helping to round up my loose horses after a circuit. I could see Ad Hoc moving with a steady rhythm, closer to the leaders than I expected, jumping safely enough and handily placed as they set off into the country for the second time. I kept thinking, 'I'm not used to this. Ad Hoc is still there.'

This time, for once, everything seemed to be going to plan as I spotted Paul's turquoise cap bobbing along just behind the leading bunch on the run down to Becher's Brook. Ad Hoc jumped that fine, survived a mistake at the next fence, Foinavon, and another at Valentine's, the 25th. With four fences to jump, Ad Hoc was in the perfect position, cruising along close to the inside rail tracking Timmy Murphy on David's Lad two or three lengths behind Bindaree. He couldn't have been better placed if I'd given Paul a slide rule and a calculator but you can never count your chickens in the National.

One minute Ad Hoc was running away looking all over the winner. The next he was on the ground after David's Lad fell directly in front of him and brought him down. It was a heartbreaking way to be taken out of the race at such a late stage but that's the Grand National for you. Each year it has so many unexpected twists and turns. I didn't need to speak to Paul Carberry to discover what happened and I've never really discussed that incident with him. After watching the replay several times I've no doubt Ad Hoc would have won if he hadn't been brought down, but what might have been doesn't pay the bills. I'd had so many reverses in the National. This one topped the lot.

Four days later, I was on my way to Japan travelling first class with Timmy Murphy on a Virgin Airways flight thanks to the generosity of Andy Stewart. Just behind, separated from us by a curtain, were Martin Pipe and Rodi Greene, trainer and rider of Exit Swinger, and Venetia Williams and Norman Williamson, responsible for Banker Count. Timmy immediately abused Andy's hospitality by getting stuck into the free booze at the bar. At first I wasn't fully aware of what was going on. I was so naïve then I remember saying to Andy, 'Don't worry. He is only drinking tonic.'

As the flight continued I became increasingly embarrassed because Timmy was helping himself to more and more drinks at the bar, getting merrier and merrier. By then I realised he was on something stronger than tonic water. When we arrived at Narita airport in Japan and reached customs, Timmy was in such a state that he left his passport on the plane, which held us all up for an hour.

You can imagine how Andy felt at seeing his jockey straight on the booze almost before the plane had left the runway. At the hotel I told Timmy he'd been out of order, asked him to be sensible for the rest of the trip and hinted that unless he kept off the drink he wouldn't be riding for us in the big race.

Cenkos did us proud in finishing fifth against horses accustomed to flicking through the brush at the top of the fences rather than jumping them big and clean, as they do here. That cost Cenkos a little bit of ground but he was the best of the European contingent on going that was much faster than he liked over a distance that stretched his stamina to the limit. The race was started from stalls, which was something of a novelty in itself. It was all a new ballgame to him, but, nonetheless, he earned £41,942 for his efforts with the winner, St Steven, collecting a massive purse of £419,000. I was thrilled with Cenkos and the ride Timmy gave him.

Andy Stewart was pleased, too. We had a lively dinner back at the hotel before ending up with a few drinks at the bar but there was no sign of Timmy who slipped the leash for a night out in Tokyo. That was a relief for Anthony Bromley who'd bought Cenkos for Andy a couple of years earlier and had flown out on his own for the race. He was sharing a room with Timmy because the hotel was full. It had only one large bed but Timmy assured him, 'Don't worry. I will not be sleeping in it tonight.'

Apparently Timmy was flying by the time he returned to the hotel in the early hours. He teamed up with a few others at the bar and, when he got back to his room, he woke up Anthony by banging on the door then drove him mad by insisting that they share the contents of the minibar. Anthony was all for getting a bit of shuteye but that proved impossible.

Timmy then decided he was hungry and started giving room service some grief on the phone. At the same time he began jabbing at Anthony repeatedly with a sharp pencil, asking, 'Do French bastards bleed?' This was a reference to the fact that Anthony buys so many horses in France.

Sensing a chance to escape, Anthony suggested that Timmy should head down to the lobby to find some food. The moment he left the room Anthony packed his bag and rang the handicapper, Phil Smith, on the floor below looking for sanctuary. He was heading for the door when Timmy returned, making no sense at all. This time there was no escape. He staggered into the room, pushed Anthony back on to the bed and gave him a love bite on one nipple. That was the cue for the terrified bloodstock agent to make a hasty exit. He hopped off the bed, grabbed a few belongings, fled down the corridor in his underpants and shot into the lift, heading for Phil Smith's room, where he spent the next few hours safely tucked up in the spare bed.

We'd all arranged to meet in the lobby soon after eight that morning for the taxi to take us to the airport. When Timmy stumbled out of the lift I could see that he'd been drinking heavily and hadn't managed much sleep. If I'd known then about Anthony's experience with him I'm sure the alarm bells would have been ringing. I think we all hoped Timmy would settle down once we reached the airport but he was still a bit of a pain there, running around, generally being a nuisance.

Hindsight is a wonderful thing yet knowing the state he was in we should probably never have let him on the plane, though that is easier said than done. We all have to take responsibility for that. Unfortunately he did board the flight and immediately started drinking again at the bar. All he was doing was topping up from a few hours earlier with one vodka and orange after another. Then he started getting abusive. It was madness.

Eventually they stopped serving Timmy drinks and somehow steered him back to his seat in the row behind mine where he continued to behave like a spoiled child by annoying everyone within earshot. Then, thankfully, he fell asleep. That should have been the end of it. But when he woke up a bit later he was straight out of his seat and up to the bar demanding another vodka and orange. Quite rightly the stewards refused to serve him.

I turned to Norman Williamson for assistance. If Timmy wouldn't listen to me I hoped he might take more notice of his fellow jockey. Norman agreed to come through to first class, grabbed hold of Timmy at the bar, steered him back to his seat and sat between him and the aisle to prevent him getting up again. That worked well until one of the stewards foolishly insisted that Norman should leave first class and return to his own seat.

Within minutes Timmy was up on his feet again, out of it, lurching towards the cockpit. I'm sure he thought the cockpit door was the entrance to the toilet. He was so far gone that when he couldn't open it he peed against the door. That was after he was alleged to have put his hand up the skirt of an air hostess. Personally, I've always doubted that. Yes, he was abusive, obnoxious and drunk, but I certainly didn't see any sign of an indecent assault.

You can't blame passengers for being frightened. There we were, thousands of feet up in the sky and someone, fuelled with strong drink, is banging and shouting, trying to force his way into the cockpit. In the immediate years after 9/11 in New York you could understand why the air crew were tough with Timmy. At first they were going to put him in a straitjacket and then, to my amazement, there was talk of making an emergency landing and dumping him off.

The trainer looks pleased as Sporazene and Ruby Walsh are led back in after completing my treble at Cheltenham on 18 March 2004.

Double top... trainer and jockey with their trophies after a fabulous meeting at Cheltenham.

All to play for as Thisthatandtother (Ruby Walsh) left goes on to beat Fondmort (Mick Fitzgerald) centre and Rathgar Beau in a thrilling finish to the 2005 Daily Telegraph Festival Trophy.

The one that got away. Silver Birch falls when leading the 2006 Grand National and brings down his stable companion Heroes Collonges. We then sold Silver Birch before he won the National a year later for trainer Gordon Elliott.

Champion at last on the final day of the 2005–06 season.

I was thrilled that Mum and Dad were there to help me celebrate at Sandown.

Paul Barber adds his congratulations at Sandown.

Cheers... David Nicholson, twice champion trainer, with his one-time head lad Clifford Baker and me at the party to celebrate my first trainer's title.

At the buckle end. Another anxious moment for Ruby Walsh on Kauto Star two from home in the Tingle Creek Chase at Sandown in December 2006.

Spring-heeled... Kauto Star on his way to his first victory in the King George VI Chase at Kempton in 2006.

Hair raising. Ruby Walsh sits tight as Kauto Star dives through the last fence as he wins the 2007 Gold Cup.

Centre of attraction... Kauto Star after his famous victory.

Denman (Colman Sweeney) makes a winning point-to-point debut at Liscarrol in March 2005. I bought him a few weeks later.

Denman (Ruby Walsh) is well clear in the Sun Alliance Chase in March 2007.

Harry Findlay salutes Denman after his thunderous triumph in the 2007 Hennessy Gold Cup.

In a world of their own... Denman and Ruby Walsh wing the last fence in the Lexus Chase at Leopardstown at Christmas 2007.

Ruby Walsh on his first visit to Ditcheat with his family as a youngster. From left Ted Walsh, Katie, Ruby, Ted junior, Jennifer, Helen and Paul Barber.

Denman (Sam Thomas) claims a stunning victory in the 2008 Gold Cup with stable mates Kauto Star and Neptunes Collonges second and third.

Denman leads the parade of champions through Ditcheat the following day.

Treble top. The first three in the Gold Cup safely back home.

Luckily for him that wasn't an option because we were over Siberia at the time.

I managed to help them calm him down by virtually sitting on him before he was forcibly led back down the aisle. Understandably, the person originally sitting next to Timmy didn't want him there for the rest of the flight. So we did a swap with me sitting in Timmy's seat while he was closest to the window beside me so that I could control him if necessary. First, though, I had to ask for some blankets to sit on because he had wet his seat. He continued to make a nuisance of himself for a while but then, thankfully, he fell asleep and stayed that way until we landed at Heathrow.

The next thing police cars appeared on either side of the plane as we taxied into position on the stand. Timmy woke up, looked out of the window, saw the police cars and asked why they were there. He had no idea. He soon sobered up when I explained, 'They are coming for you, Timmy.' Everyone was told to remain in their seats while the police boarded the plane. I remember that the two coppers were tall, stone-faced and armed. They stopped at our row, checked the seat numbers and reached out for me because I was in Timmy's seat.

'No, no, I'm not the one you want,' I said. They then turned their attention to Timmy, told him they were arresting him for assaulting a flight attendant and marched him off the plane. That was the last I saw of him. The flight was only thirteen hours but seemed to last forever.

Timmy's arrest and subsequent trial brought racing a barrowful of unwelcome headlines. I think the authorities had to take the matter seriously, yet part of me felt sorry for him because he clearly had a major drink problem and urgently needed help. He got it from Michael Caulfield, chief executive of the Jockeys Association, who advised him to check into the Priory, a branch of the alcohol rehab centre near Southampton, as quickly as possible. That helped him reach the career-saving decision to give up booze.

Timmy sensibly took a long sabbatical from riding while he sorted out his problems. In his absence I recruited Ruby Walsh and Barry Geraghty for the last ten days of the season. It turned out to be a glimpse of the future. Ruby rode a treble for me at Ayr on 20 April and Barry brought my score for the day to four on Valley Henry. A week later, at Sandown, Barry landed the Queen Mother Celebration Chase on Cenkos though Ruby had the last word by winning the final race of the season on Moving Earth.

By this stage my owners were already pressing me to sort out the riding arrangements for the future. Timmy Murphy had done well for us but was temporarily out of the picture and had blotted his copybook by his crazy behaviour on the trip to Japan. Hardly any of my owners wanted to support him after that because they felt he had embarrassed the stable which employed him. In some ways it was tough on Timmy, but he only had himself to blame after his behaviour on the flight to Heathrow.

Timmy was a top jockey, no question, and if he'd come to me to speak about his problems at the start of the season, instead of covering it all up, we might have been able to help him face his demons. A bit more communication from him would have made life a lot easier but that wasn't his way. Instead he bottled things up.

Ruby Walsh was the obvious choice to be stable jockey. This time he showed more interest in joining us, but was still reluctant to move full-time to England. We then turned our attention to Barry Geraghty, who was also unwilling to sever his ties in Ireland. At best he could ride part-time for us. That was an option but I was rather put off by his financial demands. He wanted the lot, a big retainer, taxi fares and others bits and pieces. When we put our cards on the table we were still miles apart. I was getting cold feet about the whole thing and wasn't sure we could ever reach a deal.

Ruby ended further debate by contacting us to say that he was ready to ride for us regularly in 2002–3 while continuing to race in Ireland for at least a couple of days a week. In a perfect world I'd have liked him on call seven days a week but that wasn't going to happen. What he was offering was a compromise. There were bound to be frustrations but we'd have to work through them.

Crucially, Ruby didn't want a retainer or any other financial incentive. Nor have we paid him a retainer in the years since. He is only interested in riding good horses. What we have had in place these past seven years is a gentleman's agreement which has proved to be a match made in heaven. He prefers not to have a retainer because that way he feels no one can demand that he be anywhere on a given day. If he wants to stay in Ireland for a particular horse he can and, equally, I can say, 'Sorry mate, I don't want you tomorrow. I'm using another of my jockeys.' Nor can my owners insist he rides their horses because they don't pay him for the privilege.

The arrangement is a bit like an open marriage where the two partners are firmly committed to each other for the long term but are free to play away from time to time! Ruby is usually here several days a week, most of all on Saturdays, when I need him, while on Thursdays and Sundays he tends to be in Ireland. It works pretty well. He is a brilliant jockey, as good as I've ever seen, and is a pleasure to deal with. If I ask him he'll come down to school a few horses when he is riding in England but we don't see that much of him. He has a heavy schedule and does so much travelling he doesn't need to wear himself out even more on six of mine before ten in the morning. I'd rather he's fresh for the afternoons.

I was determined to show my support for Timmy once his agent Chris Broad tipped me off that he was ready to return to the saddle after an absence of nine weeks. I welcomed the measures he'd taken to sort himself out and he didn't let me down when I booked him for Torn Silk at Worcester on 9 June. If Timmy was feeling pressure from all the adverse publicity on his second ride back it didn't show as he forced Torn Silk home in a tight finish with Joint Account.

I think we were all shocked when Timmy was sent to prison for six months after pleading guilty to charges of being drunk on board an aircraft and indecently assaulting an air stewardess. It was all done and dusted in three hours before he was driven away to Wormwood Scrubs. Given the problems on airlines at the time I suppose they were bound to make an example of him. A prison sentence would have finished many sportsmen but by sheer force of character Timmy has since got his career firmly back on track, culminating in his brilliant victory on Comply or Die in the 2008 Grand National. He deserves full marks for turning his life around.

I am still surprised that he pleaded guilty on the indecency charge without calling on people like me and Andy Stewart for witness statements. I'd happily have appeared in court to support him on that one and defend him to the hilt. But I wasn't given the chance. Drinking in excess is an illness and he had been ill for a long time before that fateful flight from Japan.

Although he was doing well as a jockey in those early days, everything I have heard since suggests he was badly in need of a father figure to make sure he stayed on the straight and narrow when he moved to England. In contrast, Ted Walsh was always there in the background to keep an eye on Ruby in his formative years as a jockey and point him in the right direction. Other lads who come here from Ireland need a bit of guidance, though unfortunately it isn't always there for them.

When Timmy came out of jail after three months he flew to Ireland to get himself fit riding out for his mentor, Michael Hourigan, before he was ready to race once more in England early in November. Starting afresh after a spell in prison must have been incredibly hard for him, especially knowing that he had blown his job with me. I admired his strength of character at such a difficult time and was delighted to provide the first winner of his comeback on Santenay at Wincanton on 9 November. He fully deserved a second chance.

18

He would have been locked up

It is said in racing that there is no secret so close as that between a trainer and his horse. That's a bit of a myth if you ask me because once you are running a business it doesn't pay to become too attached to the horses in your care. There are exceptions, of course, and even now, almost six years after his retirement a few weeks short of his fourteenth birthday, I am in no doubt that See More Business has been the most important horse in my career. I was so lucky to have him when I needed him most. He put my name in lights and was part of the furniture here for so long he seemed to have been going round almost as long as Big Ben.

I've trained a few better than Seemore, because he didn't quite have the class of Kauto Star, Denman, Azertyuiop or Master Minded. Nor was he the nicest citizen, particularly when he came back in from grass each July. Then he was anything but a pussycat, almost unrideable, turning himself inside out on the roads until he settled into the familiar routine of training.

If he was a human being he would probably have been locked up as a teenager as he had a nasty old temper on him. When he joined us he wasn't used to being tied up in his box while he was groomed each evening by Georgie Bown, who looked after him throughout his time here. He was so difficult about it I made him stand in his box for several hours tied up to a ring on the wall. He did his best to kill himself by angrily pulling against the chain so hard that he almost brought the stable down around his ears. We won in the end but if you took him on he'd fight you all the way. To clip him we had to slip a sedative into his feed or he'd chase us all out of the box. Many good horses have that mean, aggressive streak.

Seemore was basically a very tough, sound horse once he got over the early niggles of sore shins. He did once have a scare with a leg problem after his third hurdle win, when we left him alone for the rest of the season, but apart from that he was a wonderfully sound horse who retained his enthusiasm right to the end. That was the key to him.

He was his usual impossible self when he returned into training in July 2002. Though he'd soon be thirteen, there was no question of retirement. How could we pension him off so soon after he'd finished third to Best Mate in the Gold Cup? Things would have been different if he'd shown that he'd had enough. That autumn, however, he was so keen in his work we felt there were still races to be won with him.

Early in November we took him to Down Royal for the Grade 1 Championship Chase. It looked a match between him and Florida Pearl, but they were both beaten by a 20–1 shot, More Than A Stroll. The old boy more than paid for the trip by collecting £16,300 for finishing second. He showed an extra sparkle that season and was so full of himself he behaved like a horse half his age. The competitive edge that set him apart was there right to the end.

So none of us was surprised when Seemore landed the Rehearsal Chase at Chepstow in December, ridden by Andrew Thornton for the first time since the 1997 King George. The years rolled back as horse and rider rattled over the first six fences pretty much flat out before stretching clear of Bindaree. I thought it was a brilliant performance to give a stone and four pounds to that year's National winner and beat him out of sight. He was like a never-ending dream. A year earlier he had us all in bits as he lay prone by the second last fence for ages. Yet here he was winning again like a spring-heeled novice without a care in the world.

His next race in February brought the house down at Wincanton. It proved to be the final triumph of an unforgettable career that yielded a marvellous strike rate of 50 per cent with eighteen victories from thirty-six races and more than £700,000 in prize money. We were all in tears as he bounded clear in the CGA Chase at the venerable age of thirteen.

His performance that day was awesome. The way he trounced the favourite, Iris Bleu, six years his junior, I swear he could have gone round again. The regulars at Wincanton know a special horse when they see one and gave him an unbelievable reception. After that he was fully entitled to have one last crack at the Gold Cup in which he finished eighth to Best Mate. He ran with distinction in five Gold Cups and it would have been six but for foot and mouth in 2001.

We were thinking of letting Seemore bow out at Wincanton in the New Year until the decision was taken for us when he was struck down by a mystery illness just before Christmas 2003 which left him fighting for his life. He was such a hardy so and so he'd hardly missed any work in all the time he was at Ditcheat, yet within days he was in such a bad way we all feared the worst. He'd picked up some kind of infection or virus, had a soaring temperature and was so ill his droppings were more like water.

As a last resort we sent him to Liphook Equine Hospital in Hampshire. As he left the yard I was afraid I'd never see him again. While there he suffered an attack of colic. It was touch and go for a while until they put him on a drip and treated him with a course of drugs which, thankfully, set him on the road to recovery. I think it was only his toughness of spirit which got him through that ordeal during which he lost sixty kilos.

After such a fright retirement was a formality for See More Business. We were all touched by tributes to him in the papers. No horse could have achieved more for a young trainer than Seemore did for me. He took me to places I'd been dreaming about for years, was our first high-profile winner and stayed sound throughout his career. Yet for all the plaudits he received I've always felt he wasn't given his full dues. For me there will never be another one like him. He was unbeaten in three runs at Wincanton and received a great reception when he returned to the course in February to lead the runners to the start for the CGA Chase.

Clifford Baker thought so much of Seemore that he wouldn't let anyone else but Georgie near him. He led the string on him as a matter of course and had to be alert at feed time because the horse was so mean in full training he'd have taken a chunk out of him if he turned his back for a second. Seemore stayed in the yard for a while before moving to Paul's daughter-in-law, Emma, with the idea of starting a new life as a hunter. He was quite tricky at first, with an alarming habit of rearing up on his hind legs, but Emma spent a fair bit of time settling him down before enjoying a few quiet days on him with the Blackmore and Sparkford Vale Harriers.

He was really a bit too impatient to follow hounds, would never stand still and tended to launch himself like a missile at gates, hedges and rails. He was certainly not on his best behaviour on his return to Cheltenham on Countryside Day with several other past champions. The moment he reached the chute leading on to the course he began rearing up, dropped Joe Tizzard three times and tried to throw himself on the ground. He always did have a bit of a temper!

Hunting came to an end for Seemore after he did his best to kill Marcus Armytage at a meet nearby at North Barrow. Marcus rode no end of winners, including Mr Frisk in the 1990 Grand National, but he struggled to restrain Seemore once he'd jumped a few hedges and found the brakes didn't work when he tried to ease him back. To chill him out Marcus sensibly put him on point duty but that plan backfired when the field came cantering towards them.

Seemore reared up, landed on a rusty old gate, then came over backwards and got rid of Marcus, who escaped unscathed. The horse, however, collected a twelve-inch gash down his shoulder which needed stitching and took an age to heal. X-rays also revealed that he'd cracked a rib, so that was the end of hunting.

Emma looks after him as though he is the most important guest in a five-star hotel, which in a sense he is. During the summer he is turned out with another pensioner, Cenkos, and a few other horses. In the winter Seemore lives with the youngsters, is brought in when it is cold and wet and receives the best of food and attention. I can see him almost every day from my vantage point on the hill as I wait for the horses to breeze past on the all-weather gallop.

When we decided to retire him, Georgie Bown felt the loss so keenly she left the yard and disappeared. I'm pleased to say she returned after a year and is now one of my secretaries, which, of course, allows her to visit Seemore from time to time at Emma Barber's yard.

Cenkos was another hardy customer. It took me a while to realise that he needed an enormous amount of work to be at his best. Whatever you asked him to do he'd always come back for more. I worked the balls off him that autumn and was expecting a big show in the Tingle Creek Chase, which was billed as a two-horse race between Flagship Uberalles and Moscow Flyer. It proved to be one of the most satisfying results of my career with Cenkos and Ruby Walsh taking charge soon after Moscow Flyer and Barry Geraghty parted company at the fifth fence after colliding with Flagship Uberalles. Cenkos won easily by fourteen lengths. What pleased me most was the fact that I had the opportunity to set the record straight with Michael Kryzstofiak after Flagship came in a weary fourth.

Having Flagship taken away from me after I'd done so well with him hurt more than I care to say and exactly a year earlier at Sandown Michael had rubbed salt into the wound after my old horse had beaten Cenkos easily in the same race. Afterwards Michael smirked at me as he walked by and said, 'Happy Christmas, Mr Nicholls.' I was steaming and didn't know what to say.

Now, a year later, I had my chance to return the compliment. Spotting him waiting for Flagship, I wandered past, wished him a Happy Christmas and offered a smart remark which seemed to leave him speechless.

Ruby Walsh clocked up the air miles that winter as he flew over from Dublin and back two or three times a week. Having him on board was a huge plus and as the Cheltenham Festival approached I was on course for my best season after reaching my fastest century of winners on 6 February, over a month earlier than in 2002. Like a cricketer in search of a double century, I took a fresh guard and enjoyed a hat-trick at Newbury two days later. It takes years to build up a multi-talented squad of horses and, though I was lacking a serious Gold Cup contender, I had bags of promising youngsters coming through. One of them, Thisthatandtother, owned by Graham Roach, looked the part as he won three races, including the Tolworth Hurdle.

Young Devereaux was almost a veteran by then, at ten, but his legs were so fragile he ran only twelve times for me in seven years. When I did manage to get him to the races in one piece he was a big player and showed it by winning two valuable chases inside a month. He managed one more run that season before another long spell on the sidelines. If only he'd been born with a better set of wheels.

The ace up my sleeve for Cheltenham was Azertyuiop, who lived up to all my expectations over fences. He had size, pace and power for the job and was so athletic he was a natural when we schooled him at home in the autumn. Ruby was bowled over by the way he travelled on his debut at Market Rasen, where he won with ridiculous ease. He told me afterwards that never in his life had he ridden a horse that still hadn't settled by the time he arrived at the third last fence. He then looked every bit as good in two subsequent victories.

Ruby couldn't disguise his confidence when I asked him how he'd ride the horse in the Arkle. 'It doesn't matter,' he replied with a huge grin. I thought I had a decent second string in the shape of Le Roi Miguel, who fell early on leaving Ruby in the lead on Azertyuiop. It didn't make any difference. Horse and rider controlled the race from the front before galloping up the hill unchallenged to win by eleven lengths. It was a great way for us to start the meeting.

To have a winner so soon on the opening day of the Festival blows away all the pressure that builds up in the preceding weeks. For once I could relax and enjoy the meeting. Many people felt that a new star was born that day though the style of his victory wasn't much of a surprise to us. We'd known for some time that Azertyuiop had it all and two miles was his trip. With plenty of gears and speed to burn, he didn't need to be going any further.

Once again Andy Stewart drew a blank at Cheltenham, but it was a different story at Aintree, where he enjoyed a lucrative double. Le Duc, so talented but exasperating, set the ball rolling with a narrow success in the Four Year Old Hurdle. Ruby Walsh was at his very best that day, burying him in midfield before producing him with a strong run going to the last hurdle. Even so, Le Duc did his best to throw it away by edging persistently right across the runner-up, Spectroscope.

Two days later another of Andy's good horses, Le Roi Miguel, gained his first overdue success over fences by running away with the Maghull Novices' Chase with my other runner, Vol Solitaire, in second place. It was a result that set me believing my luck was about to change in the Grand National. Given my record in the race I should have known better. I felt I had the strongest possible hand with Ruby on the 7–1 favourite Shotgun Willy, so impressive at Haydock, and Paul Carberry and Ad Hoc seeking to make up for their misfortune twelve months earlier.

I'd done my best to protect Ad Hoc's handicap mark by keeping him to hurdles before switching him back to fences at Cheltenham once the weights were published but all my planning came to nothing when both horses were out of the race long before the end. Shotgun Willy was pulled up and Ad Hoc wasn't travelling as well as I'd have liked when he got rid of his rider after clouting the third fence on the second circuit. Horses sometimes don't jump so well the second time at Aintree. That was certainly the case with Ad Hoc, who didn't seem to want to know. It was left to Joe Tizzard and Montifault, a 33–1 shot, to fly the flag as they finished fifth.

There was a price to pay for Ad Hoc's excursion to Aintree. He returned with any number of cuts and bruises, including a nasty haematoma under his stomach. His season appeared to be over yet he surprised us all by the speed of his recovery. Sometimes it is better to keep them moving rather than leave them standing still in their boxes. Ad Hoc was so full of himself again within a week that I began to think of letting him tackle the Attheraces Gold Cup, better known as the Whitbread. It was a big ask, but he was giving me all the right signals in the final few days and did us proud by claiming his place in racing history by winning the race easily for the second time in three years.

Ad Hoc's tremendous success took the stable's earnings to £2.2 million at the end of my best season by some way, with 152 winners, but it wasn't enough to trouble Martin Pipe. Ruby Walsh had more than played his part. I'd have given anything for him to join me full-time but, hard as we tried to tempt him, he preferred to retain a degree of independence by continuing to ride in Ireland on a couple of days a week. Ruby showed just why I was so keen to sign him up by winning two big prizes for me at the Punchestown Festival on Sporazene and Le Roi Miguel.

19

An invitation from Clive Smith

Clive Smith appeared in my life one Sunday morning in August 2003. I was in the office on my own when I heard a voice call out, 'Anyone at home?' I popped my head out of the window and asked if I could help. Clive introduced himself, explained that he was passing on his way home from his brother's 60th birthday party, said he had horses with Martin Pipe, including Royal Auclair, and was looking for a change. The moment I heard that I shot down the stairs in record-breaking time.

As I showed Clive round the yard it became clear that he was keen to become more heavily involved as an owner. He'd done well building and running golf courses and named his first horse Hawthorn Hill Lad after a course he'd converted from the old racetrack of that name near Maidenhead. There was no turning back once the horse won on his debut with Jenny Pitman. He'd chosen his green, yellow and purple racing silks from the colours of Camberley Heath Golf Club.

Much later, Clive told me that he'd been hooked on racing since, standing on tiptoe as a small boy just inside the rails, he'd seen Doug Smith win the Ascot Gold Cup on Parthenon in 1950. He'd walked three miles to the course with his mother and brother from their home in Sunninghill and was bowled over by the colourful scenes. Hawthorn Hill Lad was followed by several other horses with Jenny, David Elsworth and, more recently, Martin Pipe. The best of them was Royal Auclair who won the Cathcart Chase in 2002.

Though Clive said he hadn't fallen out with Martin Pipe he'd become a bit disillusioned partly because his horses hadn't been running as often as he'd have liked. He was looking for another trainer with whom he could establish a closer relationship and hinted that, if things worked out, he was ready to pay serious money for more horses. After a lifetime of building up his business he'd reached a stage where he wanted to have some fun by making a major commitment to jump racing. As he left he asked me if I was interested in training Royal Auclair. A couple of days later he rang Martin to tell him the horse was moving to me along with Rainbow Frontier who hadn't raced for over two years.

Both had question marks hanging over them. Rainbow Frontier was a lost cause. I rang Clive after a month and said he was wasting his money keeping the horse with me as he was always lame after we tried to do a bit of work with him. Clive gave him away as a hack and confirmed that he could well be in the market for a decent horse.

Royal Auclair had a bit of a problem with his breathing. We first noticed him making a whistling sound as he popped over some fences in my outdoor school. As it wasn't too serious we decided to keep him going through the winter before having his wind done at the end of the season. Royal Auclair showed a deal of promise on his debut for me in finishing fourth in the Tripleprint Gold Cup at Cheltenham. He didn't win that season, chiefly because the handicapper didn't give him a chance, but he ran a series of fine races culminating in a short-head defeat in the Betfred Gold Cup.

Another new horse that season was Albuhera, a prolific winner with Mark Johnston on the flat before joining me. I think Mark is a terrific trainer who gets every ounce out of his horses and I particularly admire his stable motto 'Always Trying'. I wish I'd thought of it first. I like to think all of mine are always trying. I certainly never send out my jockeys with instructions to stop horses but there are occasions when they will benefit from an educational run to teach them to settle or jump. Albuhera, for instance, was horrific when we first schooled him, so clueless he backed off his hurdles if you let him and couldn't get six inches off the ground. Nor did he learn from several intensive schooling sessions.

To avoid a disaster on his debut at Chepstow in October 2003 I told Joe Tizzard his sole priority was to get the horse round in one piece. He was to drop Albuhera in, teach him to jump at racing pace and make sure he enjoyed himself. If the horse didn't win, no matter. Technically that is called schooling in public, but that is what we had to do if he was to progress over hurdles.

Joe followed his instructions so well that, despite a couple of hesitant leaps early on towards the rear, Albuhera was soon jumping like a natural as he moved up early in the straight before keeping on steadily to finish sixth of nine. Joe said he could have won, though Albuhera might not have jumped so well under pressure. Having that school round was the making of the horse. He then won three races on the bounce and six times that season.

What we did with Albuhera wasn't cheating because, if he'd jumped brilliantly from the start, he'd have won anyway despite Joe's orders. We never stop them. I've lost count of the number of times mine surprise me by winning despite my thinking they don't have an earthly chance. More than anything that is because they are all fit.

Early that winter I had a sharp reminder that jumping is the name of the game. In little more than a week my three best chasers all fell or got rid of their jockeys. Strong Flow started the trend by coming down four out when cruising at Aintree, Valley Henry then crashed heavily at Wetherby, before Azertyuiop, of all horses, dumped Mick Fitzgerald after blundering at the first in the Haldon Gold Cup.

I didn't think the sequence could get any worse until Poliantes collapsed and died moments after running the race of his life in finishing runner-up in the Paddy Power Gold Cup at Cheltenham for the second time. That was a body blow to everyone at the yard. Though you know these things occur from time to time it is always a nasty shock when it happens to one of yours.

We had such high hopes for Valley Henry, but he didn't always put his heart into racing and rather lost his way jumping. Paul Barber didn't have to think twice when a big offer came in for him from Howard Johnson on behalf of Graham Wylie. It was the right thing to sell because we'd gone as far as we could with Valley Henry. Towards the end that horse let all of us down. He didn't like the rain, the cold or hard work. For a cheap horse he did well and won some nice races but basically he wasn't tough enough for the job. One of Paul's great strengths is that he doesn't like standing still. He is always ready to sell and reinvest, something more owners should consider.

One that never ceased to surprise me was Rigmarole, owned by Wincanton's chairman, Mark Woodhouse, and his wife, Tessa. He began the season in May with defeat in an ordinary novice chase and twice ended up on the floor at Market Rasen when I switched him back to hurdles. After that his form was gilt-edged as he rattled up six victories, including the valuable Greatwood Hurdle at Cheltenham at 33–1 in November. He showed that was no fluke by taking the Bula Hurdle a month later at the same course at 25–1 before giving Mark and Tessa the thrill of a lifetime with a storming success in the Kingwell Hurdle at Wincanton.

Strong Flow was the most exciting young horse in the yard. I can remember the look of surprise on Ruby Walsh's face when I told him in May, just before he ran away with a valuable race at Kelso, that he'd win the Hennessy Gold Cup seven months later. In October, my belief in him was slightly dented by his fall at Liverpool. That left me in the position of having to give him a confidence-booster eleven days before Newbury. The timing wasn't ideal, but I needn't have worried as Strong Flow jumped like an old hand at Newton Abbot on his way to a bloodless victory.

I began to lose my nerve as the day of the Hennessy approached. It is one of the toughest, most competitive staying handicaps of the year and I was concerned at pitching Strong Flow against seasoned chasers on his fifth start over fences. I knew beyond doubt that this was a special horse, a champion of the future, and I didn't want to be over-facing him too soon. We'd had one blip at Aintree and the last thing I needed was for him to end up on the floor again. If he had turned upside down at Newbury people would have been lining up to shoot me.

So many things were buzzing around in my head I didn't know which way to turn. I'm not normally negative but that was one time when I was tempted to err on the side of caution. When I told Ruby I wished I'd entered the horse in the novice chase he replied, 'I'm glad you didn't.' I changed my mind several times before Ruby persuaded me we should have a go. Convinced that Strong Flow was the best he'd ridden, he was all for running. Yet even on the way to Newbury I was almost trying to find a way out of it. In the end we were brave and luckily it paid off.

I had a big fright when Strong Flow almost ended up on the floor after an almighty blunder at the ninth fence. Ruby told me later that the horse's tail came over his head and he almost disappeared out of the back door. That was the only alarm in a race they turned into a procession in the closing stages with Strong Flow coming home four-teen lengths clear of Joss Naylor. It was an awesome performance and a special victory for me in a race I'd won as a jockey on Broadheath and Playschool.

Strong Flow belonged to Barry Marshall, who spent much of the year on business in Russia. I thought the horse was definitely as good as anything I'd trained at that stage. The Gold Cup was an option but I was much keener on him tackling the Sun Alliance Chase at the Festival for which he was already a warm favourite. Sadly, Cheltenham was out of the question after he tried to demolish the last fence on the first circuit on his way to winning the Feltham Novices' Chase at Kempton.

The legacy of that horrific blunder was a fractured knee which ruled him out for the remainder of the season and eventually brought a premature end to his career. The knee was still troubling him after six months' box rest. Some mornings that summer he was so lame he was on three legs. We sent him to Newmarket early in August where X-rays taken by Ian Wright pinpointed a small, sharp splinter of bone floating in his knee. As he flexed his knee it was a bit like having someone run a razor blade across the point of the original injury. No wonder he was lame.

Strong Flow took a while to recover from surgery. Our one aim was to bring him to his peak in time for the 2005 Gold Cup. He showed a fair bit of promise on the gallops, too, but on the track he just wasn't the same as before. After a dreadful run of fatalities and injuries, Barry's family couldn't cope with another setback for Strong Flow the following season. I could hardly blame them when he took the decision to pull out of racing.

I've tended to buy most of my horses from France over the last ten years, but as you don't want to have all your eggs in one basket I continued to do business with the legendary horseman Tom Costello, who ran a superbly organised operation near Shannon airport until his death in June 2009.

Strong Flow was one of the first horses I bought from Tom, who usually kept his cards close to his chest. On that visit, however, with Paul Barber, I sensed he was extra keen to do business with me, perhaps because I was doing so well. Some time earlier Paul had marked his card by asking him to let us know if he had an emerging star for sale. We got the call after Strong Flow won a point-to-point, flew over and bought him along with a couple of others.

We gave just over £100,000 for Strong Flow. There were several others interested in buying him but Tom was so desperate to bring me on board that he made sure we took him home. He would have seen it as a long-term investment for team Costello. I was hugely impressed with Tom's set-up, which he ran with his sons. They had done plenty of work with all the horses we saw including loose schooling. You could tell they already had a fair bit of time and money invested in them. They were specially trained and far from the big, backward, unbroken types that English trainers once bought from Ireland. It was clearly an advantage that you wouldn't need to wait two years before running them.

I always enjoyed my annual shopping trip to Tom Costello. He made me laugh by saying every horse he pulled out of its box was the best pedigree in the book. He'd look me in the eye and try to keep a straight face as he suggested, 'This could be the next Best Mate. His mother was very good, the family is chock full of winners and you'll regret it for the rest of your life if you leave this one behind.' He'd then wind up the ante by letting slip that Henrietta Knight and Terry Biddlecombe were calling in the next day.

Tom was a brilliant salesman though in the past few years his sons have had more to do with the selling. At first I used to let Paul Barber do the wheeling and dealing because he was an old hand at it. Now, after watching and learning, I'm happy to make the decisions. Tom and his sons would start off at one point, we'd begin at a much lower figure and if we didn't agree we didn't buy. We'd usually go out with the idea of finding one and end up with five!

Azertyuiop was a typical French-bred, tall, imposing and precocious. After his early departure at Exeter he definitely needed the race when he met the two-mile champion, Moscow Flyer, for the first time in the Tingle Creek Chase at Sandown in December 2003. Moscow Flyer had the better of the argument that day. Azertyuiop was surprisingly fresh for one of mine and took ages to settle before blowing up after the Pond fence. As that was effectively his first race of the season he was nowhere near his best though he still finished a fair way in front of Le Roi Miguel and Cenkos. Ruby and I both felt we had a good chance of turning the tables at Cheltenham.

The autobiography of footballer Len Shackleton famously included a blank page under the heading 'What the average club director knows about football'. It would be misleading and unfair of me to put racehorse owners in the same bracket when you consider that their enthusiasm and hard cash bankroll the sport. I always try to be 100 per cent honest with my owners and keep them informed at every turn, to the point that I seem to be on the phone all day long. That way they have no cause to complain.

I have had my moments with a few who wanted to make all the decisions without understanding the full picture. John Francome, who briefly trained himself, warned me that you can be as rude as you like about an owner's wife but can't insult his horses! How true. Maybe it's because they don't want to hear the truth.

When I started training, one or two of my owners tried to bully me but I soon put a stop to that. As I tend to call a spade a spade I've told a few of my clients to take their horses elsewhere if they didn't like what I was doing. The best line of defence is usually attack. Normally they ring up the next day, apologise and back down. If they don't then the horses are on their way. It is fair to say my owners are usually fine. When a problem occurs it usually starts with their friends who think they know it all and chip away against me behind my back.

None of my owners exasperated me as much as Oliver Carter, who died in 2009. He was a monstrously difficult character who combined outrageous expectation with a cantankerous manner which left no room for negotiation. If they were all like him I'd have given up training years ago and tried something less stressful. As a farmer, trainer, dealer, owner and racecourse proprietor, Oliver was something of a legend in the West Country for more than half a century, particularly in his own mind! He was also a collision of contradictions, which helps explain why I found him unplayable for the short period I trained for him.

I first got to know him when I fell off two of his horses as an amateur. I could hardly blame him when he said, 'Boy, you will never ride another one for me.' To be fair to him he had a great deal of success as a permit trainer, most notably winning the 1976 Whitbread Gold Cup with Otter Way. By 2003, when he was well over eighty, it was obvious to me he was struggling to get his horses fit. One of his, called Venn Ottery, kept taking my eye at the races. He was a gorgeous horse, a tall, rangy sort who pulled like mad, raced with the choke fully out and then got so tired he never finished his races. He ran in a few point-to-points, too, without a prayer of getting the trip, wore a cross noseband and was usually pulled up exhausted by halfway.

I loved the horse from a distance and kept teasing Oliver about him. I'd say, 'He's getting fatter every time you run him. Why don't you send him to me to sort him out?' I kept this up for a couple of years before he took the bait over Christmas 2003 though with Oliver nothing was straightforward. He agreed to drop Venn Ottery off at Ditcheat then added that he never paid training fees. In that case, I countered, he could keep the horse even though I was itching to get my hands on him.

After a brief stand-off we reached an agreement whereby, while no training fees would change hands, he would pay £1,000 into my Weatherbys' account to be passed on to my daughter Megan every time the horse won. Oliver thought he had the best of that particular deal at that stage since Venn Ottery had run twenty-six times for him without winning. That season alone he'd been beaten nine times, most recently in December at Uttoxeter where, starting at 100–1, he finished tailed off last. If I could turn him around he was going to be unbelievably well handicapped.

The hill at Ditcheat proved to be a tremendous shock to Venn Ottery. First time he barely reached halfway before stopping to a walk like an overweight runner at the end of the marathon. He was even more unfit than I had guessed so we drew up a demanding schedule to get the weight off him. It started with an hour on the mechanical horse walker, followed by another hour out with first lot, and a further session on the walker. He then did another hour or two on the walker in the afternoon. Soon he was able to canter once up the hill, then twice. In another couple of weeks we had him cantering three times in the morning and once more in the afternoon, followed by two hours on the walker.

The transformation in Venn Ottery in six weeks was astonishing. He'd arrived looking like a bloated tank. Now he was hard and fit, cruising upsides the good horses, and sprinting along the flat gallop with the best of them. It was time to give him a few entries. First stop was a maiden chase on 18 February at Leicester for which most of the papers had Nicky Henderson's Tollbrae down as a good thing. We were pleased for him to make the market for us.

Everyone in the yard backed Venn Ottery. He was probably the biggest certainty that ever left Ditcheat. I told Joe Tizzard to be positive by making use of his pace and fitness. As Venn Ottery made a bit of a noise we put on a tongue tie to help his breathing. He played his part by winning easily at 15–8 and was unrecognisable from the horse that had struggled to finish his races in the past.

Venn Ottery was a revelation as he notched up a hat-trick in little more than a fortnight. That was £3,000 safely in the bank for Megan. I then made the mistake of running him in very soft ground at Market Rasen, where he did well to finish second. Two days later he showed his true form on more suitable going at Hereford by defying a seven-pound penalty with ridiculous ease.

Oliver being Oliver, he had already given him an entry in the Queen Mother Champion Chase for which he'd backed him at 1000–1. I had bigger fish to fry in that race and had no doubt Venn Ottery should have been aimed at the Arkle Chase bar the fact that he hadn't been entered. Though the horse was a novice Oliver insisted on going for gold and drove me mad by interfering with my jockey arrangements.

With Ruby on Azertyuiop and Mick Fitzgerald on Cenkos, it made sense for Joe to ride Venn Ottery but his owner wouldn't play ball. He stubbornly refused to use Joe, who'd already won twice on the horse, and insisted on booking Timmy Murphy. I wasn't having that but you couldn't reason with Oliver because he was beyond argument. A long row ended with me telling him he could do what he liked because I didn't give two hoots. Oliver then declared Timmy for Venn Ottery but, crucially, forgot to declare the tongue tie, which was an expensive mistake.

Even without it he travelled like a dream through the race to the point where he was still lying second two fences from home. Timmy must have been pinching himself, but I knew the horse would stop without the tongue tie and that's what happened. Suddenly he was like a car that had run out of petrol as he struggled on bravely in slow motion to collect over £6,000 for finishing fifth.

I was furious at a wasted opportunity for Venn Ottery though he would never have troubled Azertyuiop. Half an hour later, I had a full-blown row with Oliver in the owners' and trainers' bar. He was at his obnoxious worst that day, totally unreasonable. No one in their right mind would have put up with what he was saying. The horse had earned him a bundle of money since he'd joined me but all I was getting was grief. He kept having a go at me even though he was the one who forgot to declare the tongue strap.

Eventually I lost the plot and told him, 'Oliver, the horse is up there in the stable yard. Go and pick it up and take it home because I don't want to see it or you again.' That should have been the end of it until his granddaughter brokered an uneasy truce between us. Even so, I knew I was coming to the end of the line with Oliver Carter. He would have given an aspirin a headache.

Venn Ottery ran three more times for me without success before Oliver took him back in mid-April. I was sad to lose the horse, who had huge ability, but I wasn't sorry to see the back of his owner. What followed in the next three years was a disgrace. In that time Venn Ottery performed poorly for five different trainers, including Martin Pipe, and even ran, so help me, in the Cheltenham Gold Cup at Oliver's insistence, but never looked remotely like winning again. At one stage Oliver rang asking me to take the horse back but he was such a pain I wasn't even tempted.

Venn Ottery should have been retired but Oliver kept running him, often against the best, which was totally wrong. I was disgusted to see him make a comeback aged twelve for Sue Gardner in a Grade 2 chase against Well Chief at Newbury in February 2007 and outraged when he injured himself so badly in the race he had to be put down. Venn Ottery should never have been allowed to run that day. For me it was a straightforward case of abuse and a shocking end to a horse that had given us so much pleasure. I often wonder how far he could have gone if he'd started his racing life with me.

The aggravation with Oliver Carter was the only downside for me during a fabulous run at the 2004 Cheltenham Festival, which yielded four winners. After a series of minor reverses on the first day when some of mine failed to fire, Azertyuiop justified my faith in him with a stunning victory in the Queen Mother Champion Chase. The race was billed as a match between him and Moscow Flyer, who unseated Barry Geraghty four from home just as Ruby Walsh was winding up the tempo on Azertyuiop, who winged the last few fences before charging up the hill like a fresh horse. He was at his absolute peak that day and I had no doubt he was the best two-mile chaser I'd trained. I was thrilled for his owner, John Hales, who'd been devastated by the loss of his great chaser One Man a few years earlier. Now he had another champion in his colours.

At the start of the week every trainer will tell you with absolute honesty that he would readily settle for one winner at the Festival. On Thursday I enjoyed three in less than two hours. The best came first that day, mainly because Earthmover surely set a record that will never be matched when he won the Foxhunters for the second time at the grand old age of thirteen, six years after his first success in the race when he was trained by Richard Barber.

Shortly after that initial victory his owner, Roger Penny, received a letter from Sir Robert Ogden offering to buy the horse. Roger could have named his own price but he wasn't interested in selling and never had cause to regret that decision because Earthmover turned out to be a horse in a lifetime. He was one of those supremely honest characters who make jump racing such a brilliant sport though initially we used to call him Fencemover because he gave them no respect and terrified his jockeys.

He was also tough beyond belief to survive a dreadful injury he sustained when he fell at Newton Abbot on his first run for me in November 1998. He seemed all right at first then began bleeding internally and by the time we got him home he had a massive haematoma on his left side running all the way down to his stomach. We were all convinced he was going to die that night. He was sweating and in a lot of pain as our vet, Brian Eagles, tried to save him.

Brian couldn't lance the point of the swelling for ten days until he was sure the bleeding had stopped. Then, once he had made a two-inch incision, a torrent of black, clotted blood poured out of the wound. Clifford said he had never seen so much come out of a horse. He turned the corner after that though the muscle wastage was so extreme you could put your hand in a gap between his front legs.

Having survived that ordeal, Earthmover progressed to be a high-class handicapper, winning plenty of races and even running in the Grand National on a couple of occasions. Because he always tried his heart out and didn't know how to give himself an easy time Earthmover was soon in the unforgiving grip of the handicapper. Genuine horses like him who shoot up the ratings for running well every time don't come down at the same speed. As age, hard races and injuries take their toll you are often left with animals whose ability no longer matches the handicappers' exalted view of them. When pleas for leniency fall on deaf ears you are snookered.

As Earthmover had started life in the hunting field it made sense to qualify him for hunt races again in 2002–3. I've had a lot of stick for doing the same thing with quite a few of my old soldiers. Surely horses like him who put so much into their racing deserve another chance in the evening of their careers? They have done a lot for the sport, so why can't they have a little bit back by running in hunter chases when they are not up to winning anything else? Earthmover was sound, loved life, relished our environment, kept coming back for more and was always hunted hard by the girls in the yard. He deserved his second chance in hunter chasers. The switch was rewarded when he finished fourth for me in the 2003 Foxhunters.

Roger Penny could have retired Earthmover after that but the old horse enjoyed his racing so much we decided to keep him in training. He repaid that decision with a thunderous success in the 2004 Foxhunters, ridden by Rilly Goschen, a hard-working point-to-point stalwart who kept him wide at my suggestion before taking command in the final three-quarters of a mile. That triumph was probably the highlight of Rilly's life. Roger immediately announced that he was giving all the prize money to a hospice in Bristol for terminally ill children. Earthmover is now going great guns team chasing.

The day got better when St Pirran landed a gamble in the Grand Annual. The race had been the target since he came back to me from Graham Roach the previous August after almost two years out with a leg problem. Early comers managed to get on at 20–1 before the odds tumbled to 4–1 on the day. Ruby settled St Pirran towards the rear, apparently without a care in the world, and allowed him to creep into the race running down the hill before producing him like a winged assassin to cut down the leader, Ground Ball, at the last fence. It was beautiful to watch.

As darkness began to fall Sporazene completed my treble in the County Hurdle. There was a bit of controversy about that one because I couldn't run the top weight, Rigmarole, after he picked up a knock in finishing eighth in the Champion Hurdle two days earlier. That left Sporazene topping the weights on a handy ten stone thirteen pounds with most of the runners out of the handicap. There was a lot of fuss about it at the time with trainers and bookmakers complaining that

I'd given myself an unfair advantage. The stewards called an inquiry but I hadn't broken any rules and once I produced a vet's certificate to show that Rigmarole was lame the matter was closed.

The controversy was caused by the fact that I had to declare Rigmarole for Thursday before he had run on Tuesday. If he had fallen at the first in the Champion Hurdle I could have run him again forty-eight hours later. I didn't feel any guilt because I played by the rules of the time to the benefit of Sporazene's owners. I took advantage of a loophole but if Rigmarole had been fit on the Thursday I'd have run him again just to shut everyone up.

My success at Cheltenham briefly lifted me to the top of the trainers' table but Martin Pipe was right on my tail and past experience had taught me not to take anything for granted. I had a few big shots left to fire but was short of a serious Grand National candidate that spring and was always likely to be overwhelmed by sheer numbers in the closing weeks of the season. Pipe, for instance, ran seven in the National. Lord Atterbury was the only one to get round, but in finishing third he contributed £66,000 to his trainer's tally.

Our annual duel for the title was pretty much over after that, though Cenkos did his bit by winning the Queen Mother Celebration Chase at Sandown on the closing day of the season. Pipe, however, had the final say by fielding seven in the Betfred Gold Cup, including the 33–1 chance Puntal, who pipped Royal Auclair by a nostril. My horses earned £2,191,810 that season but it wasn't quite enough to topple the champion from his perch. I couldn't see how I was ever going to beat him.

20

Why the hot tub had to go

The Norwegian hot tub I installed in the garden soon after Bridget left was a great source of entertainment in the years that followed. My girlfriends at the time liked nothing more than jumping into it on a warm summer's evening and helping me work my way through a bottle of ice cold champagne as the sun went down. Megan then gave the game away when my sister Julie came to stay. Seeing Julie preparing to climb in wearing her bikini, Megan assured her, 'You can't do that, Aunty. You have to take all your clothes off in the tub. That's what Dad's girlfriends do!' Out of the mouths of babes.

I had a lot of fun in that hot tub, which provided a great way to relax after a stressful day. It also offered me the best chat-up line I've ever used. 'Would you like to see my hot tub?' never failed. There was nothing better than lying back in the water with a warm-eyed companion sharing a bottle of bubbly on a starlit night.

Eventually, though, I decided the tub had to go after things got a bit out of hand at three in the morning when Mick Fitzgerald and I ended up frolicking with a couple of girls who had better remain anonymous. If pictures of that episode ever reached the *Sun* we would all have been in trouble. I sold the tub within days to the first bidder, who happened to be Earthmover's owner, Roger Penny, though he might not have paid so much if he knew its full history.

In the years following the breakdown of my second marriage I seemed to gain the reputation of something of a ladies' man. The truth was rather different. Yes, I had plenty of girlfriends and love female company, but with two failed marriages behind me there was no way I was prepared to let any of them get too close to me. Anyway, I didn't have the time to devote to a long-term relationship, one that might lead to marriage. As I've said, I'm not the easiest to live with because the training and the horses always come first. That's not much of a basis for contentment at home, more a recipe for aggravation.

If you are going to do this job properly you have to be single-minded to the point where domestic life is not the priority. I've never been able to devote much time to family life and I'm unlikely to change now. Everything revolves around the horses. Girls flitted in and out of my life but most of them wanted more commitment than I was prepared to give and I can't blame them for that.

Graham Roach once told me an amusing theory that all women start off hoping to marry a prince. My experience has taught me that if they can't manage that then the next best in line is a racehorse trainer though I'm not sure it is the perfect cocktail for marital harmony. Yes, there were days when I was lonely after Bridget left but usually I was so busy I didn't have much time for myself, let alone anyone else.

My sister Julie says that I have made a lot of sacrifices to make it to the top. I don't quite see it that way but will admit that a few years ago I was briefly tempted to give everything up here, walk away from Ditcheat and start all over again in New Zealand. It happened after the break-up of a particularly intense relationship with a lovely girl. I was in a bit of a muddle at the time, worrying about the reaction to the split and what everyone was thinking about me. Luckily, the feeling soon passed and I've learned to cope better with this type of situation.

My domestic arrangements changed in the months after I met Georgie Browne, whose marriage to the ex-jockey Luke Harvey was over almost before it started. As she was a smart-looking girl I took the chance to chat her up after one of mine, Cerium, beat her horse Phar Bleu at Cheltenham in November 2004. At the time she was training at her home near Lambourn. We then had our first date at the Race-horse Owners Dinner in London in December. A few days later I wasn't best pleased to see an item linking us in the *Daily Mail* diary, which immediately put an end to all other relationships.

Georgie and I saw each other regularly after that. Even so, I couldn't believe my ears when she told me in April, on the eve of the Grand National, that she was pregnant. That wasn't planned and consequently things had to change quickly. Georgie moved into Highbridge that July, gave up her training licence and has been here ever since. Our daughter Olivia was born on 13 December. The birth happened while I was listening on my mobile phone to the commentary on one of mine, Stavordale Lad, finishing second at Folkestone. Olivia is a lovely little girl, full of mischief and gets on really well with Megan. I wish I had more time to spend with them. I'm sure that must sound sad to many people. Although racing and business still come first, Georgie, Megan and Olivia mean everything to me.

One of the tasks that demands my attention is searching for new horses. Shopping for decent young prospects is not an exact science. Just ask Clive Smith. When he asked me to find him a horse that could go to the top I recommended Garde Champetre, who showed he had all the qualities to make a top-class chaser when he beat Monet's Garden and Inglis Drever on his final start over hurdles for me at Aintree in April 2004. He was owned by the Million in Mind partnership who sell all their horses at the end of each season and I was desperate to keep him.

Clive was up for the challenge when I told him I thought Garde Champetre was on a par with See More Business at that early stage of his career, but on the day he was hosting the final of the Lagonda Challenge, a golf event he sponsors each year for promising amateurs. So he was on the end of the phone as I bid in vain for Garde Champetre at Doncaster. Prices went through the roof that week with two stores each making 185,000 guineas.

That was nothing compared to Garde Champetre who ended up being sold for a world record price for an NH horse after a fiercely fought bidding war that escalated miles beyond his reserve. I thought for a moment I had him at 490,000 guineas, then someone else stepped in before he was knocked down for 530,000 to J. P. McManus, who was part-owner of Manchester United at the time. I thought I had lost a superstar but time would show that we had an incredibly lucky escape because Garde Champetre was subsequently injured that summer and never reached the heights I expected though he has enjoyed a terrific revival in cross-country races.

After missing out at Doncaster, we switched our attention across the English Channel. Ten years ago, with the help of Anthony Bromley, I started buying more horses from France, partly because prices in Ireland had become too steep. I was also encouraged by the way French horses tended to be more precocious than the traditional National Hunt stock in Ireland that can take an age to reach their peak. Anthony has some excellent scouts and had been tracking a horse called Kauto Star for some time though there was one major snag. His trainer, Serge Foucher, had no intention of selling and, crucially, he owned a share in the horse.

Things changed rapidly after Kauto Star won a Grade 3 race for four-year-olds at Auteuil on the Sunday after Garde Champetre slipped through the net. Twenty-four hours later Anthony was tipped off that the principal owner, Claude Cohen, would be interested in a deal if the price was right. He immediately arranged for videos of Kauto Star's Auteuil race to be sent to me and Clive. I was impressed and luckily Clive, too, really liked what he saw. With others showing an interest we had to move quickly. On Wednesday, Anthony bid on Clive's behalf and a day later a price was agreed provided the horse passed the vet. That is when we hit a snag that nearly scuppered the deal.

Foucher seemed happy enough to let Anthony and our vet, Buffy Shirley-Beavan, watch the horse in his work at the training centre of Senonnes in the west of France, but the trainer had disappeared when the moment came for Buffy to scope Kauto Star. Nor was the horse in cooperative mood when she tried to feed the tube up his nostrils. Without a scope we couldn't check his larynx or see if he'd bled. If a horse is resistant to this procedure you can dope him to get the job done. But to do it Buffy needed the trainer's permission and he was nowhere to be seen and wasn't answering his phone.

Normally I wouldn't dream of buying a horse without having it scoped but with Clive's encouragement I made an exception with Kauto Star and neither of us has had any cause to regret it. After some frantic phone calls, Kauto Star became his property at a cost of €400,000 and by the time he had snapped up another French prospect, Le Seychellois, he had two exciting chasers for much the same price that he had bid for Garde Champetre.

I have some sympathy for Serge Foucher, who appeared on French TV three years later speaking like a grieving parent who had lost his favourite child. He revealed that there were tears all round when Kauto Star left his yard because he knew he would never train another one like him. Foucher had bought the horse at six months old and was forced to geld him because he was so nasty in his box. Apparently he was nervous, distrustful of humans and impossibly difficult when it came to breaking him in.

It was obvious that he could run. He was only two when he earned the nickname 'l'Extraterrestre' after taking off with his rider during a routine canter and passing the entire string of horses ahead of him. Like so many French horses, Kauto Star was jumping fences like a natural twice a week in the autumn as a two-year-old and ran in the first three-year-old hurdle of the season. He had, suggested Foucher, a temperament of steel.

Kauto Star was a bag of nerves when he arrived at Ditcheat in June 2004. My first impression as he came off the lorry was that he was surprisingly tall for a four-year-old but also narrow and very lean. I was thrilled to see that he moved like a gifted athlete and had a real presence about him. After a busy time he'd earned a long summer's break, which he enjoyed with several others in a paddock beside my house at Highbridge. Since Kauto Star had already achieved so much in France and was bought to go chasing, I left him in the field for another month when the others came back into training. There was no need to hurry. Once he came in he was so sharp in his work he could lie up with the best.

His jumping in my outdoor school set my pulse racing and he certainly looked the part when he stormed to victory on his English debut in a decent novice chase at Newbury on 29 December with Foreman, fourth in the Champion Hurdle, beaten nine lengths. I ran him in a tongue strap as a precaution, mainly because he'd always worn one in France. Now it is too late to take it off. I was a bit suspicious of his breathing at first as he definitely made a little noise breezing up the hill. It soon cleared and I've not had a moment's worry about his breathing since.

Kauto Star didn't waste much time in the air at Newbury. If anything he was a bit too brave. No one was more impressed than Ruby Walsh, who came back grinning from ear to ear which told me everything I needed to know before he spoke. We both felt we had a serious Arkle candidate on our hands. I then took him to Exeter at the end of January for a race that cut up so badly only two took him on. He cruised through the race, enjoying a nice school in public until he spoiled the script by getting in a bit too tight to the second last fence, clipped the top and turned over.

Ruby remounted in the blink of an eye and, without irons, set off in pursuit of Mistral de la Cour, who'd seized a long lead. It looked an impossible task, but normal rules do not apply to this horse who winged the last fence and made up so much ground on the run-in that he would have got back up again in one more stride.

Kauto Star's dramatic fall was hardly an ideal preparation for Cheltenham though I still felt he was the one they all had to beat in the Arkle. He was sound when he returned to Ditcheat that night but our hopes were in ruins the next morning when we found that he was lame behind. It was difficult to pinpoint the problem until X-rays established that he had a hairline fracture of a bone in his near hind hock. He wouldn't be running anywhere for months.

The injury to Kauto Star led to a heated public debate about the wisdom of remounting a horse after he has fallen. Once the RSPCA repeated its call for the practice to be banned, Ruby came in for a fair bit of stick, which I thought was totally unfair because if he had won he would have been a hero. We are talking about a split-second decision. Remounting that day at Exeter was second nature to Ruby who is a brilliant horseman and unbelievably competitive. If Kauto Star had been obviously injured or out of contention when he came down Ruby wouldn't have reacted as he did because the welfare of horses is uppermost in all our minds.

If a rule is brought in to ban remounting then I'm sure everyone will readily accept it and should any of my owners ask my jockeys not to remount if they fall that is fine with me, too. At the time Ruby was fully entitled to do what he did because he felt he had a chance of winning the race. I would have done exactly the same if I'd been in his position and was pleased to see Tony McCoy rush to Ruby's defence. He spoke with the authority of a man who had remounted and finished alone in a race on Family Business at Southwell in which all seven runners famously fell or were unseated.

Kauto Star's untimely injury proved to be the making of him, though I didn't think so at the time. Looking back now I'm sure it was a big plus that we didn't end up running him in the Arkle, which was likely to be too sharp for him. As he'd already won over two and a half miles in France I was always a little concerned at running him over two miles on good ground.

Knowing what I do now I realise that the Sun Alliance over three miles, not the Arkle, was the right target if he'd been fit. I guarantee if he'd run in the Sun Alliance he would have been hard to beat. Instead, he spent three months restricted to box rest while the injury healed without the need for surgery before he spent an hour each day on the horse walker. Only then was he able to start his summer holiday.

Shortly before Kauto Star ran for me for the first time, Noble Action took me to a notable milestone at Folkestone by providing me with the 1,000th winner of my career. That was a figure way beyond my wildest dreams when I had started training. It had taken me thirteen years of hard slog and, with a strong team in the yard and more owners eager to join the party, I hoped there was even better to come.

Azertyuiop returned to action with a stylish success under top weight in the Haldon Gold Cup, which helped erase the memory of his early departure in the race the previous year. That set him up nicely for a return match with Moscow Flyer in the Tingle Creek Chase at Sandown but this time we were the ones to leave the track wondering what might have been. John Hales, in particular, was so unhappy he chose to go public in his criticism of Ruby after Moscow Flyer saw off Azertyuiop by one and a half lengths at the end of a tremendous duel.

John told reporters that Ruby should have put Moscow Flyer under pressure when he was breathing down his neck going to the Pond fence, the third last. He was incensed because Ruby didn't ride the horse in the way we had discussed in the paddock. There is no malice in John, who is one of the kindest men you will ever meet, but when it comes to his horses he wears his heart on his sleeve and can get fired up if things go wrong. Perhaps he would have been better keeping his own counsel yet, as the man who paid the bills for Azertyuiop, he was entitled to his opinion. Privately I thought he was probably right but I kept my views to myself then because I didn't want to be seen knocking a jockey whose instinct for doing the right thing in a race has provided me with so many important victories.

Even the greatest jockeys make the odd mistake and that was one of Ruby's. I still believe Azertyuiop might have won that day if he'd been more positive. If my jockeys jump to the front I always tell them not to give away the advantage by reining back. I wanted Ruby to track Moscow Flyer before setting Azertyuiop alight turning for home. He was in the perfect position to do so, too, as he jumped the last fence down the back, travelling like a demon. But instead of kicking on and seizing the initiative, he took a pull and chose to sit and wait two lengths behind Moscow Flyer who gained vital ground at the Pond fence while Azertyuiop landed in a bit of a heap and never quite managed to claw back the deficit. If Ruby had moved upsides Moscow Flyer before taking him on he would have been two lengths closer at the Pond fence and would at least have gone very close to winning.

I spoke to Ruby about it a couple of days later. While I'm not sure he entirely agreed with me we both knew that he'd have to use more positive tactics next time if we were to beat Moscow Flyer, one of the best two-mile chasers for years. First, though, I took quite a gamble by upping Azertyuiop to three miles in the King George VI Chase on Boxing Day, which led to a tug of war over Ruby.

Initially, he was going to ride Le Roi Miguel for Andy Stewart but Ruby was keen to switch mounts once I decided to run Azertyuiop. It took a fair bit of diplomacy on my part to sort that one out before I booked Paul Carberry for Le Roi Miguel. Maybe I should have been a politician! In the end neither troubled Kicking King, an outstanding chaser who won the Gold Cup three months later. Though we couldn't be sure Azertyuiop would stay three miles we decided to ride him positively in the hope that he would last home. He was still travelling comfortably close behind Kicking King approaching the last bend but was unable to make any impression in the straight and did well to keep on for third place, beaten less than four lengths, with Le Roi Miguel a long way back in fourth.

That Christmas everyone was shocked by the terrible impact of the tsunami disaster in the Far East in which thousands lost their lives. It happened at the time my staff won £8,000 donated by bookmaker Stan James to the leading stable at the two-day Kempton meeting. People in racing are not the best paid in the world so I was immensely proud when my staff decided to give every penny of their prize to the Tsunami Appeal.

I then topped it up with £2,000 from my winning percentage after Silver Birch, owned by Paul Barber and Des Nichols, gave me my first success in the Coral Welsh National. When I informed Steve Fisher, boss of Stan James, that he should pass on the money direct to the appeal he reacted generously by pledging that his firm would match our contribution of £10,000.

Though the ground was as deep as it gets at Chepstow I was beginning to think that Silver Birch could be the horse to end my drought at Aintree. He'd taken to the big National fences like a duck to water in winning the Becher Chase in November and stamina was clearly not an issue. Given his subsequent record at Aintree perhaps he was the one but he never made it to the course in April because, a month before the race, we found a little bit of heat in one of his legs. Another chance had passed me by.

I was all for the decision to increase the Cheltenham Festival to four days that year but it looked like being a long week after the comprehensive defeat of Azertyuiop on the Wednesday. By then I was regretting the decision to run him in the King George. I suspect that race finished him; that stretching his stamina to the limit got to the bottom of him so that he was never quite as good afterwards. He had another hard race when he was all out to hold off Well Chief at Newbury and was a huge disappointment at Cheltenham, where he didn't travel with any fluency and was never in contention though he struggled on to finish third, fifteen lengths behind Moscow Flyer.

It was hard to take in because he'd been gliding through his work at home, going up the hill three times a day. I didn't know what to think. Thisthatandtother lifted my spirits by gaining the big race success he deserved in the Daily Telegraph Trophy on the Thursday before Sleeping Knight, who was blind in one eye, closed the week for me on a winning note in the Foxhunters.

Six years earlier I'd promised myself I'd never again let myself get involved in a repeat of the undignified scrap for the trainers' championship with Martin Pipe late in April 1999. I still have the scars to show from that one. After a fruitful Cheltenham, with the horses in rampant form, I realised I was back in with a good chance of beating him. At a stroke all my best intentions went out of the window.

Results at Aintree were vital to maintain the momentum of the stable. Sleeping Knight played his part by winning a valuable handicap, others collected useful place money and Royal Auclair topped the lot by earning £154,000 for finishing second in the Grand National to Hedgehunter. After so many crushing disappointments in the race I was thrilled to have a horse involved at the end of the race though Royal Auclair and Christian Williams never for a moment looked like reeling in Hedgehunter and Ruby Walsh, who romped home by fourteen lengths. With Pipe drawing a blank at the meeting maybe the tide was finally turning in my favour.

Three days after the Grand National I made the mistake of ringing Pipe's office a few minutes before declaration time to ask if Well Chief would be running at Cheltenham the next day. As the automatic top weight, Well Chief's presence would have made a big difference to the amount my pair Le Roi Miguel and Mouseski had to carry, but I was told that no decision had yet been made, so had to declare mine, not knowing what was happening. That was taking gamesmanship to a new level. When the declarations came through Well Chief's name was missing.

I headed for Scotland that weekend hoping to provide Ruby Walsh with a record-breaking fourth success in a Grand National in one season, following on from Silver Birch, Hedgehunter and Numbersix-valverde in Ireland. Despite taking a hefty bump at the second last fence, which cost him vital momentum, he looked like achieving it, too, as he produced Cornish Rebel with a typically well-timed challenge approaching the final jump. The horse, however, was not nearly as straightforward as his jockey. Thinking he'd done enough once he hit the front on the flat, he pricked his ears and was caught and passed by Joes Edge in the last couple of strides.

Channel 4 showed pictures of me riding every bit as strong a finish as Ruby as I bounded through the enclosures like a greyhound, shouting Cornish Rebel home, until I realised that we might have been denied by Joes Edge. Afterwards I was kicking myself for not putting blinkers on Cornish Rebel. I'm sure they would have made the difference by helping him concentrate. The photo finish print showed that he had lost by little more than a centimetre. The difference in prize money was £43,000 so, with a week to go, Pipe's lead was down to £38,371.

The dramatic finale to the season was played out against an increasingly acrimonious background as Pipe sent horses all over the country in his eagerness to hold on to his lead. With three days to go I'd cut that to £16,587 and managed to claw back another £2,160 by winning an appeal over a runner that had previously been demoted at Exeter.

On the Friday, Pipe conjured up thirty-four runners at four meetings around the country. I was hardly going to run up the white flag at that late stage and hand the title to him on a plate. To match him I ended up being as aggressive as him. Once again it was getting out of hand. I ran fifteen that Friday, including Andreas who was hacking up at Perth until he came down at the last fence leaving Pipe's Sardagna to take the first prize of £8,398. Perhaps the gods were trying to tell me something.

All week I thought my banker for the weekend was The Persuader, who looked sure to start favourite in the Bonus King Hurdle which opened the card at Sandown on Saturday. So you can imagine my feelings when he failed to get into the race thanks mainly to Pipe declaring ten of the twenty runners. It was hard to avoid the conclusion that it was done to keep mine out. Amazingly, six more of his were eliminated along with The Persuader. My assistant, Dan Skelton, rang his yard a few minutes before declaration time to find out about his running plans. Once again we were told they still hadn't decided. Nothing new then.

On the day of the race three of Pipe's ten were withdrawn, one Inch Pride, with a vet's certificate, and two more, Medison and Escompteur, after a request from the trainer that they be examined by the Jockey Club's vet at Sandown. Crucially, all three had raced in the previous forty-eight hours. So The Persuader could have run after all but with no reserve system in place he remained in his box at Ditcheat. That was bad enough but the sight of Pipe's hurdler Sindapour trailing in last in that race, looking absolutely exhausted, was the final straw for many lovers of jump racing.

Only Pipe knows what he was doing sending the horse to Sandown to race less than twenty hours after he lay prone on the ground at the final hurdle at Newton Abbot following the most horrifying fall. Dan Skelton, who was there that evening, thought Sindapour was dead.

The RSPCA immediately became involved. Their spokesman, David Muir, was particularly incensed at the appearance of Pipe's Commercial Flyer in Sindapour's race. That was his third race in three days. Muir told reporters, 'I don't think it is conducive to equine welfare. In fact I think it is outrageous that a horse runs three days in a row.'

Just reading Commercial Flyer's exhausting schedule made my eyes water. He'd won at Ayr the previous Friday. Then he was again sent from Somerset to Scotland where he managed to win on successive days at Perth, on Thursday and Friday, before the long haul through the night back to Somerset. Commercial Flyer can hardly have slept before he was loaded back on to the horsebox for Sandown early on Saturday and was probably suffering from jetlag as he finished a weary fifth.

I knew my fate by then because, realistically, I had to win both the Celebration Chase and the Betfred Gold Cup to have any chance of overtaking Pipe. Most of all, I was pinning my hopes on a revival by Azertyuiop who continued to work like a top-class horse at home. The race developed into a duel between him and Well Chief, a horse I've always admired. After leading at the eighth fence, Azertyuiop was headed at the last by Well Chief and couldn't find any more on the flat. At some point in the race he struck into himself so badly on his near foreleg that he never ran again. I knew it was serious as the wound had gone through the skin and the tendon sheath into the tendon. Although I was sick to my stomach about what had happened, I made a point of shaking Pipe's hand and saying well done before heading for the vet's box, where I spent the rest of the afternoon with Azertyuiop.

That was one of the worst days of my life because I thought the world of Azertyuiop. I hate it when any horse is injured and he was one of the best I've ever trained. We'd enjoyed a lot of good days together but I was pretty sure he wouldn't race again. The course vet, Simon Knapp, did a brilliant job. Once he'd cleaned and stitched the wound and put him on a high-level course of antibiotics he moved the horse to his clinic a few miles away to keep an eye on him over the next few days. It was easy to think I shouldn't have run Azertyuiop that day of all days; then again, he could have been injured at any time. It happens to so many sportsmen and athletes.

Driving home that evening from Sandown I was as low as I've ever been, beyond consolation. I felt sorry for myself and sadder for Azertyuiop. His career-ending injury was the final straw on an afternoon when I found myself runner-up in the trainers' championship for the seventh consecutive year. I'd enjoyed a fabulous season with 153 winners, more than ever before, and £2.75 million in prize money.

So many people wanted me to be champion. I was gutted and felt I'd let down everyone who was willing me on at the final hurdle. It wasn't just about me; there was everyone at the yard to consider.

There is no end of pressure to succeed for the team. What on earth did I have to do to beat Pipe? Once again he had 450 more runners than me. Give me one hundred of them and I'd have finished on top.

Pipe's resolve to hang on to his crown at any price was roundly condemned in the days that followed. Charlie Brooks, once a trainer himself, didn't pull any punches in the *Daily Telegraph* as he tore into Pipe for running Sindapour at Sandown so soon after that horrid fall at Newton Abbot. 'Didn't Pipe have six others to try to win the blasted race?' asked Brooks before adding, 'It was, in the words of Josh Gifford, criminal.' Brooks concluded that Pipe had given every animal rights group a free shot and in doing so had betrayed his fellow trainers and the sport.

Pat Murphy, another trainer, was equally scathing in his column in the *Bristol Evening Post* as he suggested that horses were abused in Pipe's desperation to keep his crown. The public weren't slow to show their feelings either. I had lots of messages of support, including one from Ian Jenkins, who lived close to Pipe's yard.

It began: 'I felt I had to write to say how sorry I was to see that, according to the media, you "lost" the race for the trainers' title to that devious little shit Martin Pipe. Any fair-minded analysis of the figures will show that you won – and handsomely. It will not have escaped your notice that in terms of winners or runners to prize money your record was unquestionably better than his, without your having to resort to his questionable tactics.'

21

Champion at last

My black mood didn't last much longer than twenty-four hours after the heartache of Sandown, though my dad, who probably knows better, says it took me a fair bit longer to perk up. Badly in need of a short break, I jumped at the chance to join Paul Barber on a trip to Ireland the following weekend where one of his young pointers, Willyanwoody, was expected to win at the Muskerry Foxhounds meeting in County Cork. The weather was foul, with heavy rain driving across the course at Dawstown, and our afternoon wasn't improved by the sight of Willyanwoody falling heavily at the fifth fence.

On days like this, Irish hospitality helps keep out the cold and we didn't need much persuasion to accept Adrian Maguire's offer to show us a horse that had been on the market for six weeks since winning a point-to-point on his debut at Liscaroll. Paul had been tipped off about Denman by his friend Tom O'Mahoney the day after that race, but wasn't tempted because the owners were initially asking silly money given that he'd already undergone an operation to correct a breathing defect after he was withdrawn from Tattersalls Derby Sale the previous summer. Other interested parties had already seen Denman, including Best Mate's trainer, Henrietta Knight, who was probably put off by the knowledge of that wind operation.

The moment Denman was led out of his box I was bowled over by his presence and raw power. He was my ideal type of horse, a great big strong, scopey sort, correctly put together and a lovely walker who, with any luck would make up into a chaser in a couple of years' time. Denman had only taken a few steps when I told Adrian I'd definitely have him. The words were hardly out of my mouth before Paul countered, 'No you won't. I'm having him.'

He was a little concerned about Denman's wind op but I felt that was a bonus. 'The way I see it that has saved you from spending £1,000 on having it done at a later date in England,' I suggested. Adrian then showed us the tape of Denman's pointing win in which he pulled hard, jumped fluently and was running away from start to finish. After seeing it I couldn't believe he hadn't already been sold. He was out of an outstanding brood mare, Polly Puttens, who produced nine winners from nine offspring that raced. Paul did the deal on the spot, quickly settling on a price of €120,000. Soon Denman was on his way to Ditcheat to join Paul's other horses out in the field. He then rang Harry Findlay who readily agreed to take a half-share.

Denman was such a big horse. It took me an age to get him fit that autumn and we didn't really know what to expect when he ran for the first time over hurdles at Wincanton on 23 October. That was a bit of a fact-finding mission to help us decide whether to keep him over hurdles or switch him to fences. He was just another horse when we started him off, looked a bit of a lazy slob walking round the roads and didn't show me anything on the gallops, though he did his best to run away with his riders from time to time. He certainly didn't stand out back then.

With Ruby Walsh busy in Ireland, one of my youngsters, Christian Williams, rode Denman who pulled hard throughout and showed his inexperience by running green and ducking and diving on the run-in before staying on strongly to beat Lyes Green by one and a quarter lengths. It was hardly a performance to set the pulse racing though Christian was highly impressed.

Less than three weeks later Denman really looked the part back at Wincanton as he bolted in by sixteen lengths from the odds-on favourite Karanja. I'm not sure Christian intended to make all the running but he didn't have much choice once Denman charged into the lead. Turning for home on the final bend he drifted left-handed but it didn't interrupt his momentum and once Christian gave him a smack he took off and finished so strongly it was a job to pull him up. Christian was full of it afterwards, as excited as I've ever seen him. He had no doubt the horse was a machine and assured me Denman was the best horse I'd ever trained. I told him he was mad but time would prove he wasn't far wrong.

Next up was the Grade 1 Challow Hurdle at Cheltenham on New

Year's Day. With six dual winners in the race it looked seriously competitive but Denman blew them all away as he bounded clear by twenty-one lengths. This time it was the turn of Ruby Walsh to be overwhelmed by the potential of the horse who was already looking like our banker for the Festival.

Another shaping with immense promise was Kauto Star who, despite needing the run badly, showed that he'd made a full recovery from his hock injury by finishing a creditable second to Monkerhostin in the Haldon Gold Cup on 1 November. I'd have been happy for him to finish in the first four; a clear round was the priority since he was still virtually a novice up against battle-hardened handicappers. I was thrilled to have him back and certain I could get him straighter for the Tingle Creek Chase at Sandown where we booked Mick Fitzgerald as Ruby Walsh was on the injured list with a dislocated shoulder.

Kauto Star offered a tantalising glimpse of the future as he won the battle of the young guns at Sandown. Aged five, he was still learning his trade in his fourth race over fences but you wouldn't have known it as he winged round the course on his way to a decisive victory over Ashley Brook. I warned Mick not to get into a battle with the front-running Ashley Brook on such testing ground, but Kauto Star was going so well he let him breeze into the lead at the third last fence before he idled and edged left on the run-in. It is always nice to have one with so much potential but even better when you see him go and prove himself like that in a Grade 1 race. Kauto Star was all class and beginning to relax. We were still learning about him and Mick thought he would be even better going left-handed.

My horses were in great form in the weeks leading up to Christmas to the point where I suddenly found my name at the top of the trainers' table. Nothing, though, prepared me for the shock of my trio filling the first three places in the Coral Welsh National. With the blinkers back on, L'Aventure was left clear when One Knight came down at the last fence and would probably have won anyway. There was a distance back to Heros Collonges, with Cornish Rebel a neck-away third. I ended a brilliant day's work by winning the last two races on the card.

The hot streak continued into January when I came close to doing a Frankie Dettori by almost going through the card at Wincanton on 21 January. In the end I had to settle for six out of the seven winners and was surprised to discover I was the first trainer in Britain to do so. I couldn't have written the script any better at my local course, which is only ten minutes' drive from our yard.

I've had seven winners in a day at different meetings but this was a record I'll never forget. Ruby Walsh nearly missed all the fun. He wasn't sure about flying over because his dad Ted wanted him for Southern Vic at Naas. I'm glad I won that particular tug of war and so was Ruby after riding five of our winners at Wincanton.

I didn't set out with the intention of going through the card. Given what can and often does happen in jump racing, I don't think you could possibly plan a thing like that. To illustrate the point my nap of the day, Le Volfoni, was beaten at Lingfield! It wasn't all bad news, though, as anyone who put my six winners together in an accumulator was rewarded with a return of 1,766–1.

Raffaello set the ball rolling before Ballez let the side down in the second race. I hoped a set of blinkers might bring about some improvement but he quickly lost interest and was soon on the transfer list. After that it was plain sailing. East Lawyer hacked up in the third before Ruby earned his corn in two tight finishes on The Luder and Almost Broke. Not many jockeys would have won on Almost Broke, who needed some vintage assistance from the saddle to help him catch Dunbrody Millar in the last fifty yards. Liam Heard, one of my conditionals, then enjoyed his moment in the sun on Nippy Des Mottes before Ruby brought a fabulous afternoon to a stunning climax by hacking up on Bold Fire.

Sometimes success can be difficult to deal with. Initially I was quite embarrassed by all the fuss at Wincanton. I felt a bit like the greedy boy at school who pinches all the best sweets before any of his classmates can get their hands in the jar. Yet there were so many positives from the day, which was sponsored by Connaught, who also support my yard. Almost Broke brought up my fastest century of winners and by the end of an extraordinary afternoon I'd stretched my lead over Martin Pipe to £433,000. That alone was a great excuse for a terrific party at my home which lasted well into the early hours. After the heartache of the previous few years I wasn't taking the championship for granted. This time, though, I'd only have myself to blame if I didn't manage to seize the crown from Pipe. Cheltenham and Aintree would settle it and I had plenty of ammunition for both.

A cold snap in February left me facing a dilemma with Kauto Star who badly needed race practice before the Champion Chase. I'd planned to complete his preparation for the Game Spirit Chase at Newbury. Once that was frozen off the race was transferred to Lingfield but I wasn't prepared to risk him there on bottomless ground. Exeter came to the rescue by letting me give him a full-blown racecourse school a fortnight before the big race.

Clive Smith travelled with me to watch Ruby put Kauto Star through his paces upsides Joe Tizzard on Cenkos. The speedo on the groundsman's truck was nudging 40mph as we tracked Kauto Star soaring over his fences in such a confident manner, and Ruby's eyes sparkled with delight as he hosed him down afterwards.

That thunderous workout proved to be a false dawn. Of all my runners at Cheltenham Kauto Star was the one who had everything geared towards winning at the Festival. In countless interviews in the weeks leading up to the meeting I made no secret of my belief in him. That's probably why he started 2–1 favourite.

We soon knew our fate. Kauto Star set off racing keener than Ruby would have wanted and fell so heavily at the third fence he was lucky to escape with his life. It happened without warning as he stood off too far, stepped at the fence, burst through it and sprawled on landing, bringing down Dempsey. Basically, he was a bit too bold and brave, a trait that has been there throughout his career.

It was a horrible fall made worse by the kicking he got as horses galloped over him. The most serious damage was inflicted by Moscow Flyer who caught him painfully on his off-hind fetlock joint, which came up like a balloon that night. We were worried that he'd broken something but the X-rays were clear, which was great news because plaster casts come hardest to those with wings on their heels. Even so, Kauto Star was pretty battered with a few lumps and bumps on his legs. That terrible fall left me thinking that things were happening a bit too quickly for him over two miles. We would have to look at different options in the future.

Clifford Baker spent a lot of time hosing his fetlock joint to settle it down; then it was a case of keeping the horse on the move. We did harbour hopes of bringing him back for one more race at the end of the season but he didn't recover in time, so we gave him a school over fences before turning him out for the summer.

Kauto Star's dramatic exit came on a typically roller-coaster day at the Festival. It began with the unexpected defeat of Denman in the opening Sun Alliance Novices' Hurdle and then got markedly better as Star de Mohaison landed the Sun Alliance Chase. Denman's defeat by the leading Irish fancy, Nicanor, was a shock to me. I suspect it was partly down to the fact that Ruby didn't know the horse very well because he'd only ridden him once.

As they didn't go a great gallop and Denman was pretty keen I'd like to have seen Ruby make more use of him racing down the far side. I blame myself for not being more positive in my instructions and suggested afterwards that we might have won if he'd been more aggressive on Denman. Ruby wasn't convinced but twelve months later admitted that I was right. We were still learning about the horse.

There was a second possible excuse for Denman who was unusually dull in his coat. Two weeks later he looked much better. He is a liver chestnut, which is quite an unusual colour, and chestnuts are generally much slower to come in their coats because they don't appreciate cold weather; I'm sure that was true of Denman once his coat was clipped late in January. Now I don't clip him after November; it's made a big difference. Sometimes at Christmas he looks dreadful, like a woolly, shaggy thing but come the Festival his coat is spot-on and that is what matters. For the record, I think you will find that not one chestnut won at Cheltenham that week.

Ruby could have ridden Star de Mohaison, but preferred Our Ben, who blundered his way out of the race early on. Barry Geraghty partnered Star de Mohaison who'd been threatening to win a decent prize for a while and franked the form at Aintree. I hoped he could go to the top.

That was the first year I travelled to Cheltenham and back in a helicopter. Suddenly a journey of up to three hours each way was transformed into a half-hour jaunt. It made the days much less stressful, allowing me to watch the horses work in the morning and do various other jobs before jumping into the helicopter in the paddock beside Highbridge. Each evening I was home by six o'clock. I'd have done it years before if I'd been able to afford it.

Ruby and I began that Festival on a winning note with Noland in the Supreme Novices' Hurdle and ended it in style as the quirky ex-flat horse Desert Quest landed a bit of a gamble in the County Hurdle.

Noland came from out of the clouds to snatch the verdict from Straw Bear in the last stride. He looked well out of it two hurdles from home and was still seven lengths down at the last before an irresistible run took him to the front.

My lead in the trainers' championship had increased to almost £750,000 by the opening day of Aintree where Martin Pipe hit back with Celestial Gold in the Betfair Bowl. With the Grand National to come and the champion fielding runners everywhere it still wasn't over, so I was surprised to hear that he had conceded the title to me on his website. Apparently he wanted to be the first to congratulate me!

It was very good of him but there was no way I was starting the celebrations until it was mathematically impossible for him to overtake me. Secretly I hoped that one of my six runners in the Grand National would provide the victory to seal the trainers' crown but, given my record, that was highly unlikely. Sure enough, they were all out of it after little more than a circuit. Crucially, though, Pipe didn't enjoy any better luck. I headed south in high spirits ready for a long night at Dan Skelton's 21st birthday party.

The moment I walked in they started playing Queen's 'We Are The Champions'. That really got to me. Maybe it was true at last, I thought, wiping a tear from my eye. The number of people who came up to me at the races the following week to offer their congratulations finally convinced me that I'd done it. The relief was immense. For the first time in seven years I wouldn't be looking over my shoulder in the closing weeks. I can't begin to put into words how good it felt not having to endure the stress of the closing weeks in past years. That was a huge bonus after what had happened twelve months earlier, when Martin and I ended up punching ourselves to a standstill like two bare-knuckle prizefighters. That had been horrible.

This time Cheltenham proved the turning point though at the start of the week it could have gone either way. Obviously it helped that the horses stayed healthy all year. Although I was champion at last I felt I'd learned more about training in this season than in any of the last few years.

What Martin had achieved as champion fifteen times was incredible. We were never likely to be drinking companions because we came from different generations. Nor did I particularly appreciate the way he'd sometimes walk by me at the races without so much as a nod or a smile. But you had to admire the way he produced hundreds of winners year after year. His record is there in the history books for all to see. He was the one who set the standard.

I always hoped to be champion trainer one day but that is not the reason I am doing the job. To train lovely horses for good owners is a great way of life, yet first and foremost it is a business. From modest beginnings I've created quite an industry in Ditcheat and am responsible for a lot of livelihoods. I'm extremely proud of what I've built up since I started with eight horses and a few bob in my pocket back in 1991.

I adore what I do. Racing has always come first in my life to the extent that it takes up all my time. If you want to succeed you have to put everything into it and there was no danger of my taking my foot off the throttle now that the championship was finally mine. I don't regret for a minute that I've made a fair few sacrifices along the way. I guess that is the price champions pay in all sports. I am every bit as keen now as when I started. More so, if anything, with all these nice horses in my care. As each season ends I can't wait for the new one to spark into life in October.

I woke up on 29 April full of excitement at the prospect of collecting my first champion's trophy at Sandown that afternoon. I'd waited so long for the moment and couldn't believe what I was hearing when Martin Pipe announced his retirement on Channel 4's *The Morning Line*. That caught everyone out. Talk about raining on my parade. I was gobsmacked at Pipe's timing. Then again, perhaps I shouldn't have been surprised.

I made sure it didn't spoil my day. Whatever my feelings, it must have been tough for Pipe to be knocked off his perch after all those years. They say that statistics never lie and mine was the name on top of the trainers' table that night with earnings of £2,402,374. Life doesn't get any better.

It wasn't all plain sailing. One that slipped through the net was Silver Birch who was among a batch we sent to the sales in May. He was a huge disappointment that season, lost his way completely, finished distressed on two occasions and fell in the Grand National. His owners, Des Nichols, Paul Barber, and I were all agreed he had to go after talking to our vet, who felt he had a few issues, including the suspicion of a heart murmur. If I knew then what I do now about stomach ulcers I'd probably have given Silver Birch another chance because he was giving some signs that he was suffering from that problem. It can happen when horses are stressed and is not an easy thing to spot.

Silver Birch was sold for 20,000 guineas to a young Irish trainer, Gordon Elliott, who planned to aim him at cross-country races. Gordon did such a great job with Silver Birch he ended up winning the 2007 John Smith's Grand National at 33–1. Full marks to him for a tremendous training feat. Des Nichols eased the pain by having a large punt on Silver Birch. Paul Barber, being such a sportsman, was just pleased to see his old horse deliver in the race we always thought was made for him.

Wags in the Manor Inn at Ditcheat weren't slow to rub it in. They put up a large sign above the bar saying 'Grand National winners bought and sold. Apply lunchtimes to Paul Barber's Bloodstock Services'. Thanks, guys.

Towards the end of my championship season I briefly turned my attention to flat racing. As I'd long fancied having an interest in a couple of two-year-olds I splashed out on a quarter share in one with Ron Hodges and also took a third share in another bought at the breeze-ups by Alan King. Neither turned out to be much good, though Alan managed to win a small race with Beverly Hill Billy. I sold my shares in both when some of my owners suggested I could be guilty of a conflict of interest once Beverly Hill Billy looked like going over hurdles. That was a shame but I didn't need the hassle. It remains an ambition of mine to train a two-year-old winner and I don't rule it out in the future.

I enjoyed an entertaining diversion in Paris in May with a pal, Dave Staddon, as guests of Harry Findlay at the European Cup Final at the Stade de France. It was a fantastic occasion, particularly for Harry, who'd been backing Barcelona for months and picked up a fortune when they beat Arsenal 2–1. However, travelling to the ground on the Metro in boiling hot temperatures wasn't my idea of fun. The return journey was even worse as we didn't have tickets and had to jump over the barriers to reach the train. In addition, we had loads of abuse from Arsenal fans as we made the mistake of wearing Barcelona scarves and rosettes given to us by Harry.

I'd long promised myself that if I ever became champion trainer I'd throw a huge party to thank everyone who'd been part of my life and helped me achieve it. It was a brilliant night which contained a few surprises, including an emotional speech by Paul Barber before he presented me with a superb leather-bound album containing a photographic record of many of the best moments of my career. It is very much like the red book they used to hand to the victim on *This Is Your Life*. I thought it was a lovely gesture.

John Francome then stole the show with a virtuoso performance as a stand-up comic by telling a series of risqué stories that had people in stitches. Only he could get away with it. If a defamation lawyer had been in the audience he'd have been made for life! John also conducted an entertaining auction in aid of the jockey J. P. McNamara who suffered serious spinal injuries shortly after riding for me in the Grand National. I donated a year's training fees and several of my owners offered generous items which helped raise £50,000 for JP. I am thrilled to say he has since made an excellent recovery.

22

A £1 million bonus

Kauto Star had me scratching my head that summer because I knew instinctively that I still hadn't found the key to him. His time at Ditcheat had yielded two memorable successes and two falls which could have ended his career. He was a bit like a teenage football prodigy who spends too much time on the treatment table. Now he needed to step up to the mark with a sustained run in the Premier League. Aware that things might have happened too quickly for him at Cheltenham, I sent him to Aintree late in October for the Old Roan Chase anticipating that the step-up to two and a half miles on a sharp track would suit him well.

Although I was hoping for a big show I didn't expect him to win in a runaway style that opened up all sorts of exciting options for the future. Kauto Star cruised through the race jumping fluently, led three out and galloped a long way clear of another of mine, Armaturk, a reliable yardstick. I tried not to get carried away because he was on a decent mark against some exposed handicappers. Ruby, however, was bubbling. He rang me that night saying the horse was ideal for the King George VI Chase. I trumped that by suggesting he could win the Gold Cup.

The only way to find out if Kauto Star had sufficient stamina was to try him over three miles, so I ran him next in the Betfair Chase. The opposition looked formidable with several hardy campaigners including Kingscliff, L'Ami and Beef or Salmon all lured to Haydock by a £1 million bonus offered by Betfair for any horse that won their race, the King George or Lexus Chase and then the Gold Cup. They had the form in the book while Kauto Star still had questions to answer.

It wasn't a contest as Kauto Star won in a canter by seventeen lengths from Beef or Salmon. It was an awesome performance, which, at a stroke, changed the landscape of steeplechasing. I didn't need to ask Ruby what he thought. Just one look at his face as he came back smiling broadly was enough to tell me he already felt that the Gold Cup was ours for the taking. Kauto Star jumped, travelled and showed us for sure that he stayed every yard of three miles. What could possibly beat him at Cheltenham if he stayed in one piece? And if we took in the King George along the way he had a major chance of becoming the first horse to land the massive bonus.

Before Clive Smith flew off for a short holiday we agreed that Kauto Star would go straight to Kempton. Why risk the Betfair million by racing him again beforehand? So I was surprised to receive a text from Clive the following weekend asking me to consider running Kauto Star in the Tingle Creek Chase six days later. Initially, I was 100 per cent against the idea as we'd spent a fair amount of time teaching the horse to settle. Why jeopardise all that hard work by revving him up against the best two milers around? I texted Clive saying the Tingle Creek came too soon after Haydock, adding that if the horse was older it might have been worth considering.

Clive, though, was not for turning. He's one of those enthusiastic owners who believe horses are there to race. Kauto Star was in the form of his life and guaranteed to start favourite if he turned up at Sandown. We had to give it a go. Clive's persuasive testimony gradually won me round to the point where I agreed to make a decision later in the week.

For a second opinion I rang Ruby Walsh who, at first, also questioned the wisdom of bringing Kauto Star back in trip. 'It's not a great idea because it will only get him racing too keen in the King George. Don't do it,' he advised. Deep down I thought he was right.

By the time Ruby rang back two minutes later he'd changed his mind. 'I was wrong,' he said. 'We've got to go for it because we could all be dead next year,' he added with irresistible Irish logic. I was in touch with Clive all week, aware that Kauto Star was giving me the right signals. Since he was bouncing and squealing at home I declared him for Sandown encouraged by the prospect of testing conditions that would make the Tingle Creek more of a test of stamina.

Full marks to Clive. Kauto Star's stylish success at Sandown was down to him. When I looked at the race that morning I realised I'd have been hopping mad if I hadn't made the entry. It would have been crazy for him to be idle in his box at home. Once again he was hugely impressive as he pulled seven lengths clear of Voy Por Ustedes, who went on to win the Champion Chase at Cheltenham. My fears of dropping back in trip proved groundless though he did clatter through the second last fence in a carefree manner that became increasingly familiar that winter.

Ruby played down the mistake, saying, 'He's learned from past errors and never looked like lying down', before adding, 'Long before my time they talked in glowing terms of Arkle working alongside his stable companion Flyingbolt. That's the level of this fellow.' It was some tribute from a man who doesn't hand out compliments lightly.

Kauto Star fulfilled all our expectations in the King George VI Chase. He was out on his own that day despite two horrific blunders that would have put most horses on the floor. When I looked at the video later I realised how close we'd come to disaster. The first mistake at the fourth last fence was so bad I don't know how Ruby survived it, yet a few moments later Kauto Star bounded into the lead absolutely full of running. The race was already over bar a fall which nearly happened at the final fence where he seemed to lose concentration and tried to step through it. Once again Ruby sat tight.

I think those two errors happened partly because Ruby and I decided he needed to be saving a bit and not letting Kauto Star stride on at Kempton, which is basically a speed track. Nor did it help that I'd probably confused the poor horse by switching him from three miles to two and quickly back to three again. Not many chasers could cope with that and win each time.

Pictures of Kauto Star's last-fence howler dominated the racing pages the next day. When he meets one on a decent stride his jumping is breathtaking, but if he's not sure he has his own way of getting from one side to the other and sometimes it is not very pretty. I think he was set in his ways by then. Even so he was proving to be one of those rare horses that change people's lives.

Suddenly Clive Smith was looking at a £1 million pay day at Cheltenham in March. First, though, Kauto Star displayed the reckless bravado of a kamikaze pilot as he tried to demolish the last fence at Newbury in the Aon Chase, which was supposed to be a relaxed dress rehearsal. This time he misjudged his takeoff so badly he landed with both knees in the fence. Perhaps he enjoys living dangerously.

Thankfully, though, he has such marvellous balance that he managed to stay upright and see off the late challenge of L'Ami.

These X-certificate mistakes were threatening to shorten my life. I'd almost come to expect them. I didn't know why he was doing it and couldn't understand what was going through his head. After almost twenty races he should have known better and no amount of schooling was going to help because he was always foot-perfect at home. Though his jumping was a concern he always seemed to survive and it really bugged me that people were getting hysterical about it. I tried to persuade myself it wasn't as big a problem as everyone was suggesting.

As I trawled through tapes of his races looking for clues, it was encouraging to recall that he was foot-perfect at Aintree and Haydock. In his other three wins he'd jumped brilliantly bar one or two lapses towards the end, when he tended to hang left looking for the rail. It was as if he was panicking, uncertain what to do. That's when the mistakes occurred. He jumped left at the last fence on his debut in this country at Newbury two years earlier and again in the Aon Chase. After walking round Cheltenham a week before the Festival, I was confident that the nature of the left-handed track would be fine for him. There was a rail on the inside the whole way round and I'd be asking Ruby to stay tight on it.

I felt the key to the Gold Cup was getting Kauto Star switched off and was glad the race was on the final day because Ruby, like all sportsmen, can get a bit wound up and is often better on the last day than the first. Hopefully he would have had a winner or two by then.

Although Kauto Star was the ace in my Festival pack, I had several other major players, most notably his new next-door neighbour, Denman, who was a raging-hot favourite for the Sun Alliance Chase after rattling up a four-timer. We moved him into the adjoining box in Millionaire's Corner at the start of the season partly because its extra space suits our bigger horses. Subconsciously perhaps I was also acknowledging his potential in switching him to the stable previously occupied by Strong Flow.

For such a large horse Denman was incredibly athletic in my outdoor school when we popped him over fences. As he's a hard horse to get fit first time we started him off over two miles at Exeter with the prime objective being a nice clear round. There were one or two doubters afterwards because he didn't win doing handstands but I was thrilled with the way he jumped and knew there was much better to come.

Next we gave him an early sight of the fences at Cheltenham where he beat Don't Push It well enough despite veering left-handed on the run-in. Having to knuckle down and battle probably taught him more than all his previous races put together. Until then, I suspect, it was all a game to Denman. He was hugely talented and really looked the part when we stepped him up to three miles at Newbury a month before the Festival, ridden, for the first time, by Sam Thomas. For a high-mettled racehorse he was wonderfully uncomplicated with a huge, raking stride and limitless stamina. All we had to do was wind him up, give him bags of work and let him go. He made all the running at Newbury and pulverised the opposition. Given a clear round I couldn't see him being beaten at Cheltenham. His part-owner, Harry Findlay, clearly felt the same because he'd been backing the horse for months and stood to win several hundred thousand pounds.

The countdown to Cheltenham 2007 was more hectic than ever before with huge media interest in Kauto Star who was being hailed as the natural successor to Best Mate. On a press morning at Ditcheat late in February there were upwards of forty snappers, scribblers and camera crews milling around the yard as I paraded twenty-five of my Cheltenham runners. I also took part in half a dozen Festival preview nights, which have mushroomed in the past few years. In Ireland things often don't get under way until 10.00 p.m. with up to 1,500 punters and enthusiasts hanging on to your every word as the clock nudges past midnight. Then the party really starts!

Though I'd never approached Cheltenham with such a strong team I was still empty-handed on Tuesday evening. Granit Jack, a gorgeous looking grey, ran a cracker to be second in the opening Supreme Novices' Hurdle before Twist Magic turned over at the second last in the Arkle Chase when full of running.

Wednesday was a great deal better thanks to the thunderous triumph of Denman in the Sun Alliance Chase. He looked a monster in the paddock, much better in his coat than the previous year, jumped beautifully, was always up with the pace, moved into over-drive at the third last and was soon running in a race of his own. It was a performance which left everyone who saw it reaching for the superlatives. Now, for sure, we had two Gold Cup horses for the following season. The biggest headache would be keeping them apart.

As Denman puts so much into everything he does, I felt he'd done enough. It needs an enormous amount of graft to bring him to peak fitness. Like elite athletes preparing for the Olympics, he'd put in a lot of hard miles to get to Cheltenham. He was unbeaten in five chases and the best was yet to come. Denman wasn't the only family member at work that day. His full brother, Silverburn, was far from disgraced in finishing fourth in the Ballymore Properties Hurdle. Taranis kept up the momentum on Thursday with a gutsy success in the Ryanair Chase. He'd been consistent all season, mostly over hurdles, and did well to hang on from Old Vic after being left in front at the fourth last.

After three hectic days I was beginning to feel the strain at a meeting which always provides a searching examination of endurance . . . and that was before it was extended to four days! Normally I thrive on pressure but so many people wanted to talk about Kauto Star on the Thursday that by the end of the afternoon I couldn't wait to jump into the helicopter for the short hop back to Ditcheat. Usually I can get by with no more than four hours sleep, but I barely slept the night before Kauto Star's date with destiny. So much was at stake.

Tossing and turning restlessly in bed I was encouraged by Clifford Baker's belief that the horse had blossomed since Newbury and was arriving at Cheltenham in the very peak of condition. Surely only bad luck could rob him of the race that matters most in the National Hunt calendar? Then I'd drop off to sleep and wake up reliving the nightmare of his last-fence blunders at Kempton and Newbury. Niggling away at me was the thought that people could keep knocking a horse who'd already achieved so much in the last few months. Why pick holes in him because he made the odd mistake? All the hysteria was definitely getting to me and with nineteen runners there was also the danger of Kauto Star encountering trouble in running.

Ruby and I had a long talk about tactics. The plan was for him to give Kauto Star a chance early on and settle him in mid-field down the inner before making his move whenever he wanted once he faced up to the last two fences. Some people questioned whether he'd stay the Gold Cup trip but I had no worries, particularly on good ground. At Haydock, for instance, he could have gone round again. What we didn't want was a slog on bottomless ground. On ratings and form Kauto Star was the best horse in the race. In my book, if he stood up the others couldn't beat him. That might change in time but for the moment he was every bit as dominant as Tiger Woods at the start of a Major.

Watching my horses in action has always been an ordeal and it seems to be getting worse with the years. It's partly a feeling of helplessness knowing you can't do any more once they leave the paddock. From that point they are out of your control. By then I'm a bag of nerves. Normally during a race at the big meetings I try to hide away somewhere on my own, safe from the prying eyes of television cameras. I have one or two favourite spots at Cheltenham, usually near a TV monitor. I'll listen to the commentary without watching the action then occasionally peep at the screen as the race comes to the boil.

That's how it was for me once Kauto Star reached the start. I wanted to watch him more than I can say, but the moment the tapes rose I had to turn away and trust in the skill of Ruby Walsh to deliver the dream. For the best part of three miles I was lost in my own little world, tense beyond belief, listening to the voice of the course commentator assuring everyone that Kauto Star was moving easily and then, thrillingly, closing on the leading pack running down the hill for the final time.

I missed the blistering display of acceleration rounding the bend into the straight which propelled Kauto Star from mid-field into the lead in less time than it takes to tell. That's when my resolve cracked. I hadn't seen much of the race up to then but I am only human. How could I continue to turn away a moment longer when the roars of the crowd were telling me that Kauto Star was about to claim his place in history? I picked up the action just in time to see him wing the second last fence with a clear lead. It gave me a huge lift to see that he was still moving with a powerful rhythm while those behind him were all under the pump.

One more clean jump and the prize was ours. Surely to God he'd get it right this time. With victory beckoning as he approached the fateful last fence, everyone had their eyes shut, including me. Maybe Kauto Star shut his eyes, too. I should have known what was coming because it had been happening all season. He started to edge left looking for the rail, lost concentration and got in a bit tight before launching himself recklessly at the fence. In the end he jumped through it rather than over it, parting the birch with his front legs as if it was made of paper.

It was a heart-stopping moment which will live long in the memory, but he is as nimble as a cat, found a leg somehow and landed safe on the other side. Some jockeys might have been dislodged but Ruby was ready for it and never looked like falling off. Behind them Tony McCoy was getting up a head of steam on Exotic Dancer, who began to close on the final, unforgiving hill. Kauto Star, however, wasn't stopping and stayed on to claim a famous victory by two and a half lengths. I never had any doubts that he was the real deal but after the nerve-racking tension of the past six weeks my first reaction was one of overwhelming relief.

Late that night, watching the race properly for the first time, I realised how clever Ruby had been to avoid any trouble by opting to make his move on the outside. It was a good Gold Cup, they hadn't gone a great pace and seven or eight were still in with a shout after the third last. If Ruby had stuck to his original plan to challenge down the inner he might have ended up with as much daylight as a coalminer at midnight. He knew, instinctively, that route was too risky.

What he didn't anticipate was that Kauto Star would take off with him once he switched to the outside and asked him to quicken. As his turbo kicked in the searing burst of speed that took him clear of the pack in an instant sealed the result. The way he put lengths between himself and the rest was amazing and showed how much he had left in the tank. It was a bit like watching a world-class sprinter mow down the opposition in the King's Stand Stakes at Royal Ascot, except that he did it at the end of three miles.

The hour after Kauto Star's immense victory passed in a blur of presentations, interviews, celebrations and tears of emotion. I think I was kissed by more women in those sixty minutes than in the rest of my life. I didn't realise I was so popular. Everyone was overwhelmed by the enormity of Kauto Star's achievement. To have won all those Grade 1 races in the same season in the grand manner was truly exceptional.

At the press conference conducted in a little marquee behind the weighing room Clive was asked how much he'd won on Kauto Star.

He admitted that he'd been backing Kauto Star for months and had topped it up on the day with another hefty wager. First-prize money in the Gold Cup came to £242,335. In addition, Clive pocketed £750,000 from the Betfair million with £100,000 each to Ruby and me and £50,000 to my stable staff. Then there was the best part of another £200,000 to come to Kauto Star's owner for winning the Order of Merit. These were unprecedented figures for a jumps horse.

You are never given much time to savour the moment in this sport. The press immediately began quizzing me on the date when Kauto Star and Denman would clash for the first time. I knew the answer already because I'd been thinking about it for months but for once I wasn't prepared to play their game. That could wait for another day. It wouldn't be at Kempton at Christmas, I hinted, because the track wouldn't suit Denman. Though I didn't say so it was already clear to me that the showdown the whole of racing seemed to be demanding wouldn't take place for twelve months. I didn't doubt that when it happened Kauto Star would come out on top. So much for inside information!

Andreas then completed an astonishing afternoon for me by landing the Grand Annual Chase. Ouninpohja, arguably the quickest horse I've ever trained, should probably have made it five for the week in the County Hurdle. He was talented and wayward in equal measure, a right monkey who worked like an aeroplane when he was in the mood. I love the challenge of these tricky ex-flat horses, got him super fit, tried to iron out some of his kinks and asked Ruby to wait as long as he dared before putting his head in front on the line. Unfortunately, Ouninpohja struck the front too soon, hung to the right and was caught in the final hundred yards by Pedrobob. When I suggested to Ruby that he might have delayed his challenge longer he shrugged, smiled and gave me a look which said louder than words that nothing much mattered once we had the Gold Cup in the bag!

That night we had the mother of all parties at the Manor Inn in the village. Things got a bit out of hand with people coming from miles around to enjoy free drinks, which flowed well into the early hours. I was horrified when the bill arrived on my desk; it was massive, well into five figures. Though Clive hadn't been near the pub that night he insisted on paying for it all, which was incredibly generous.

I was so wound up I didn't sleep any better that night and was downstairs again soon after five, watching the video of Kauto Star time and again. The celebrations resumed later in the morning when Clive joined in the fun as we paraded our Festival winners through the village. A couple of weeks later I took around sixty stable staff out to dinner at the Queen's Arms. It was the least I could do after all their hard work and support.

Before Cheltenham I'd booked a week's holiday in Barbados with Georgie starting two days after the Festival. I'd done it partly as a form of defence in case Kauto Star was beaten in the Gold Cup. That way, I thought, I could mope around on the beach without anyone seeing the depth of my misery. A week in the Caribbean would also prevent me getting a lot of hassle if things didn't go our way in the Gold Cup. I was already regretting that decision. The moment Kauto Star won I knew I didn't want to go. Given half a chance I'd have cancelled the tickets and stayed at Ditcheat with the celebrations in full swing.

At the airport on Sunday I bought every paper I could find and spent half the flight leafing through all the reports from Cheltenham. I'm not a great one for switching off on holiday but was so tired I slept in late for the first three days, which was a rare luxury. I stayed in touch with my office by fax and could be found most mornings watching a few races in the betting shop in Bridgetown. That is one of life's enriching experiences with all sorts of colourful characters crowding round the screens shouting home their fancies. It is brilliant entertainment. Much to my embarrassment they treated me as something of a celebrity.

Though I probably needed that break, I couldn't wait to return home for the closing weeks of the season with my second championship already guaranteed. With the help of some physio Twist Magic bounced back in triumph at Aintree where normal service was resumed as my four runners in the Grand National failed to finish. Perhaps they should move the race to Cheltenham!

Neptune Collonges then brought the curtain down on a fabulous season by winning the Grade 1 Guinness Gold Cup at Punchestown. In doing so he paid a massive compliment to Kauto Star who beat him easily at Cheltenham. Neptune was a bit of a late developer. When he arrived from France as a four-year-old he was so small and narrow that

I thought they must have sent the wrong horse as a wind-up. The physical transformation since then has been little short of miraculous.

On the eve of Royal Ascot, Clive Smith threw a brilliant party to honour Kauto Star at his own golf club, which was decked out in his racing colours of yellow, green and purple. It began with a champagne reception before dinner with videos, speeches and a cabaret to follow. What I remember most was the sight of Clive taking part in an acrobatic Cossack dance that would have finished most people half his age.

Then it was time for the holiday of a lifetime. With the money I won from the Order of Merit I flew my family club class to Barbados where I'd hired a big house on the beach. It was an overdue thank you to Mum and Dad and to my sister, Julie, her husband, Geoff, and their children, Amy and Harry, along with Georgie, Megan and Olivia. We had a terrific time though I paid a painful price for showing off my waterskiing skills to Megan. When I came off at high speed I hit the water so hard I aggravated an old back injury and spent the next few days having treatment. There is no fool like an old fool!

23

The longest night of my life

Gamblers don't come any more fearless than Harry Findlay. He has won and lost fortunes on a late goal, a swashbuckling century, a missed putt or a wayward forehand in a Wimbledon final. Harry's big-punting way of life is a source of constant fascination to the tabloids who faithfully record tales of his big wins on sporting icons like Roger Federer and Tiger Woods. When Harry is lumping on large, as he puts it, he thinks nothing of having £100,000 or more on a player or a horse at odds of 1–4 or even shorter.

Just listening to him talking about his bets terrifies me but he seems to need the adrenalin rush that comes from dancing so close to the fire. I guess it is the same for trapeze artists and lion tamers. It's just as well he gets it right a fair bit of the time, yet he is only human and when he makes a mistake or a misjudgement the bill can run into seven figures. I should know because I was with him in Cardiff in October 2007 on the night he lost £2.6 million when the favourites, New Zealand, were bundled out of the Rugby World Cup by France.

Harry had spent much of the previous two years backing New Zealand to win the World Cup at all available odds, from 4–5 to 2–5. He thought they were a class apart, wouldn't hear of defeat and persuaded several of his friends, including his gardener, to dig deeply into their savings and support the All Blacks. Most of them, I suspect, had far more on than they could afford. Paul Barber, his son, Chris, and I were guests of Harry in his box at the Millennium Stadium on the night of the fateful quarter-final. The mood was distinctly upbeat as twenty of us sipped pink champagne over dinner before the game. Harry and his pals wouldn't hear of defeat and were happy enough when New Zealand led 13–3 at half-time

Then the sky began to fall in. France scored two tries, New Zealand lost their rhythm, missed a couple of kicks and suddenly the unthink-able was happening before our eyes as the unconsidered outsiders seized a 20–18 lead with two minutes to go. The sense of panic, of numb disbelief among the All Blacks down on the pitch was mirrored by the atmosphere in Harry's box. Some of his guests were crying. Swept along by Harry's unshakeable faith in New Zealand, they were facing painfully large losses. For Paul, Chris and myself it was like being at a wedding party that unexpectedly turned into a funeral.

The last sixty seconds were incredibly tense as New Zealand pushed relentlessly forward looking for the score that wouldn't come. At the final whistle I had the uncomfortable feeling that I was intruding on private grief in a morgue. Everyone was stunned. What could I say? What could anyone say? The three of us edged towards the door, crept out and closed it quietly behind us before fleeing into the night. We were all shaken by the experience but not half as much as Harry and his pals who had 'done their brains'.

Much later Harry suggested to me that playing under the closed roof at Cardiff had cost New Zealand dear. He blamed in turn the pitch, injuries to four All Blacks in six minutes, and the referee for making two crucial mistakes. He may well have been right for all I know but that was scant consolation.

I remember him saying, 'People at the ground spoke of a smell of death and decay in the All Blacks dressing room. I promise it was the same in my box.' I wouldn't argue with that. It has been said that he lost £3 million but he assured me the true figure was £2.6 million. How many punters can take a hit like that?

I had a pretty bad day myself when Kauto Star was beaten on his return at Aintree three weeks later. It wasn't the greatest shock as he had to concede a stone to Monet's Garden and, unusually for him, hadn't schooled well earlier in the week. Whatever the reason he was lethargic throughout, ran lazily and looked as though he'd be well beaten before rallying to finish a length and a half behind Monet's Garden. It was unlike him to be so quiet. Maybe he had a bad journey or an off day, but I changed his work routine after that. Until then he'd been galloping with the quickest horses at home. I suspect that he was doing too much. To help get him back to his best and rekindle his enthusiasm I put him upsides some slower ones in the mornings.

A season that promised so much was turned on its head on a bleak day at Cheltenham when two of my best young horses were killed in the space of an hour. First Willyanwoody landed directly on Ruby Walsh with a sickening force as he turned a somersault. It was the type of fall that can finish the careers of horse and rider. For Willyanwoody it was the end. He broke his back and was swiftly put down. Nor did it look good for Ruby who was in terrible pain when he came back in the ambulance. Given the nature of the fall he was lucky to escape with nothing more than a dislocated shoulder.

His injury left me without a rider for Granit Jack, a horse I fancied like mad in the Paddy Power Chase. Almost every jockey at Cheltenham was already involved in the race but my good conditional Liam Heard was already dashing to the course from Uttoxeter for a later ride. As he'd schooled Granit Jack at home he was the obvious choice. After a brief chat with the horse's owner, John Hales, it was agreed that if Liam arrived in time he could ride Granite Jack. If not we'd withdraw him.

No one, not even Ruby, could have ridden a better race than Liam Heard on Granit Jack, the 3–1 favourite, who looked sure to win as he eased into the lead two fences out. He jumped it perfectly, took a stride, then knuckled over and broke his neck. It was a shocking death for a horse I was sure would go to the top. I thought so much of him I'd already backed him for the Champion Chase. My mind was in turmoil as I ran down to the fence where I did my best to console Liam who was in tears. Nobody could possibly blame him. I told him he'd done everything right but I'm not sure he was listening. The horse was tanking along then out of the blue we had a tragedy. It was so sad for everyone.

John Hales and his wife, Pat, were in pieces. I did my best to lift their spirits and spoke to John again that night before licking my own wounds. I was convinced Granit Jack didn't deserve to fall. It was as if his own momentum took him down yet he'd already won four chases in France before joining me and his schooling had been exemplary. Running through the tape time and again that evening I tried to pinpoint a reason for his sudden exit. Later I visited the scene with Simon Claisse, the clerk of the course, who subsequently made a few minor changes by putting a bit more belly in the fence and levelling the ground a fraction in front of it.

That was the worst day I've ever experienced as a trainer. Losing the two horses and seeing Ruby stretchered off left me in such a state I didn't get any sleep that night. As someone who is always positive I know it doesn't pay to dwell on what has gone wrong in the past. That will only drive you mad. However bad the pain, you have to move on. At least in racing there is always another day, another race and another horse to focus on.

After a tortuous night, I returned to Cheltenham buoyed by the knowledge that Sir Alex Ferguson would be coming down to Ditcheat after racing. As a close friend of Ged Mason he'd just bought a half-share in What A Friend and another, horse Quell The Storm, and wanted to have a look round the yard. It was fascinating to chat to Sir Alex on the journey back to Ditcheat, listening to his views on Posh and Becks and other big names he'd handled over the years. That was the most interesting two hours I've ever spent in a car. We discovered that our jobs have much in common. He has a squad of players and I have a squad of horses. Some, he explained, could turn out for every game of the season, twice a week if necessary. Others had to be rested for up to three weeks. It's the same with horses who have to be treated on an individual basis, too.

At the end of each season we both have to weed out a few of the older, more experienced members of the team and replace them with younger recruits who, hopefully, will make the grade in time. If we sell at the right time they can make a lot of money. Hang on to them for too long and you are probably looking at a free transfer. The same applies to star strikers and veteran chasers. To stay at the top we both have to wheel and deal in the market. I'm sure the key to being a manager or trainer is building up a reliable team of people who will work with you.

Over dinner that evening Sir Alex explained that he had enjoyed racing as a way of relaxation ever since his first visit to Cheltenham some years ago. He and Ged stayed in a hotel nearby and were up early the next morning to watch the horses on the gallops. They were both tickled pink when What A Friend won for them at Chepstow after Christmas.

With Ruby Walsh on the easy list I had some important decisions to make about his replacement. My second jockey, Sam Thomas, was in pole position. I'd signed him up the previous season when it became clear that Christian Williams would be out of action for many months with career-threatening injuries from a fall the day before he was due to start riding out for me after the summer break. It was tough on Christian, but I needed a regular back-up for Ruby and Sam fitted the bill. Before then he'd been riding the odd one for us while retaining his links with Venetia Williams but, by this stage, crucially, I had first call on him.

First up for Sam was Kauto Star in the Betfair Chase at Haydock. Initially, Clive Smith wanted to book Mick Fitzgerald but I persuaded him it was important to keep faith with Sam who was part of the team and riding well. Ruby helped out by passing on some useful advice on Kauto Star.

I told Sam he had my full confidence and that he should be in no doubt that he was on the best horse in the race. The plan was to drop in behind and give the horse a chance but if he was going well down the back straight Sam shouldn't be afraid to seize the initiative. That's just how things worked out. Kauto Star led soon after halfway, stepped up the tempo in the home straight, made his usual mistake at the last and kept on strongly to see off Exotic Dancer. The wheels were back on the wagon. It was a crucial success for Kauto Star and an even bigger one for his young jockey. Clive and I did briefly discuss giving Kauto Star another shot at the Tingle Creek, but thought better of it, which left the way clear for Twist Magic to win it.

Harry Findlay was probably still badly in need of a pick-me-up after his bruising experience in Cardiff. He got one when Denman, ridden by Sam Thomas, stormed to victory in the Hennessy Cognac Gold Cup at Newbury in a manner that advertised his claims as the biggest danger of all to Kauto Star in March. Harry picked out the Hennessy for Denman months before the race and seemed relieved when he realised I was just as keen as him.

The Hennessy has always been an ideal race for second-season chasers. Denman is a big, gross horse, at 580 kilos probably the heaviest of all mine when he comes in from grass. That is why I was worried that he'd need his first race after a long summer's break. Given that he had top weight at Newbury and still looked a shade on the burly side to me, I wasn't that confident.

You can look back now and say he had two stone in hand but it wasn't so obvious going into the race. Maybe I didn't yet appreciate how good he was. I certainly knew a few minutes later as he routed a decent field of handicappers after tanking into the lead a mile from home. It was a truly awesome performance which left me wondering what he might do when he was fully wound up. The key was the way he readily settled for Sam in the first mile. It was an excellent result following Kauto Star's return to form a week earlier and I was thrilled to become the first trainer to win the Hennessy twice, both as a jockey and trainer. Afterwards everyone wanted to know when the big two would finally meet. I made it clear it wouldn't happen until Chelten-ham and added that the gap between them was going to close. Ladbrokes obviously felt it had closed as they priced up the pair at 2–1 for the Gold Cup.

With Kauto Star heading back to Kempton on 26 December and Denman in Ireland two days later, it was going to be a tense Christ-mas. The prospect of our two heavyweights strutting their stuff inspired Ruby Walsh to rush back sooner than was sensible or advis-able. I'd have done exactly the same if I was in his shoes; and had done so many times when I was a jockey.

If it hadn't been for Kauto Star and Denman, Ruby wouldn't have been back before Christmas because he wasn't fit. Once he passed the doctor he did have one ride in Ireland to prove to me that he was up to it. I wasn't convinced but neither was I prepared to stand in his way. Ruby is a world-class rider, he's totally professional and he was saying he was ready. Once he told me that I had to accept it, though privately I had no doubt he was some way short of 100 per cent.

I made a mistake in letting Ruby ride the hard-pulling Silverburn an hour before the King George. Sam Thomas should have been on that one. Silverburn did his best to undo all the fine work of Ruby's medical team by tugging his arms out for two and a half miles before finishing third. Watching him whistle round looking uncomfortable I realised I should have put my foot down on that one. The horse's owner, Paul Green, was irate afterwards. In fact, Ruby didn't ride the horse again that season.

There was no need for cautious tactics in the King George. Now we knew for sure that Kauto Star stayed three miles so well I suggested that if he was going well down the back stretch Ruby should kick on and win the race there and then, which is exactly what he did. The

A lap of honour. Master Minded becomes the first five-year-old to win the 2008 Queen Mother Champion Chase.

Celestial Halo makes all the running in the 2008 Triumph Hurdle.

Neptune Collonges (Ruby Walsh) gains a well-deserved success in the Guinness Gold Cup at Punchestown in April 2008.

Roll on the winter... Ruby Walsh in playful mood after winning the Galway Plate on Oslot in July 2008.

Denman takes time out to smell the flowers in the main yard at Ditcheat.

Next-door neighbours. Kauto Star and Denman.

A study in elegance. Kauto Star and Ruby Walsh gain a third successive victory in the King George VI Chase at Kempton on 26 December 2008.

Sir Alex Ferguson in jaunty mood after the victory of his horse What A Friend at Chepstow in December 2007.

Master Minded gave me a big scare after his runaway success in the Victor Chandler Chase at Ascot in February 2009.

Master Minded gains a second success in the 2009 Queen Mother Champion Chase.

A few minutes later Clive Smith holds aloft the trophy with Ruby Walsh.

A picture postcard scene... Kauto Star (Clifford Baker) and Denman (Georgie Browne) lead the string up the hill on a snowy morning at Ditcheat early in 2009.

Kauto Star reclaims his crown with an unforgettable victory in the 2009 Gold Cup. I was amazed that Denman ran so well in second place after his heart problem.

Four of the best on holiday in the paddock beside my home, Highbridge. From left, Master Minded, Kauto Star, Big Bucks and Denman.

Jubilant scenes at Cheltenham after Big Bucks lands the Ladbroke's World Hurdle in March 2009.

A proud moment for the Stewart family after the brilliant success of Big Bucks.

Starting young... Olivia looks the part on her pony Oakey.

Georgie, Megan and Olivia with Denman the day after he won the Gold Cup.

With Georgie at Royal
Ascot in 2009.

A winning team... Megan on G Whizz
(left) edges ahead to win at Stafford
Cross in Devon in April 2009.

Two for the future... Megan
with her cousin Harry Derham
who already rides out for me
at weekends and in his school
holidays.

A pair of old softies enjoying a
quiet moment.   That's me and
Denman.

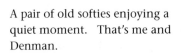

horse was even more impressive this time and fully deserved the rave reviews he received in the papers.

Two days later it was the turn of Denman. We chose the Lexus Chase at Leopardstown because it was a valuable Grade 1 race on easy ground on a left-handed track. The going was testing even by Irish standards, but that wasn't a concern because it can never be too soft for Denman. Three other British horses travelled over with only Mossbank and Beef or Salmon representing the home side. None of them troubled Denman who led at the third fence, was always in command and willingly pulled clear again on the run-in. He does more at home some mornings. It was yet another mighty display yet some observers tried to pick holes in the form. They must have been looking at another race.

Though I didn't realise it at the time a third superstar was already in residence at Ditcheat. Clive Smith had bought Master Minded back in May and immediately recouped a decent chunk of his purchase money when he finished second in his colours at Auteuil a few days later, ridden by Ruby Walsh. We'd been tracking the horse for ages, first tried to buy him in October 2006 when he won over hurdles and finally managed to do a deal after he'd fallen for the second time in four attempts over fences.

It wasn't the ideal profile for a new recruit, but we knew his trainer, Guillaume Macaire, thought the world of the horse and suspected he'd tried to put off would-be purchasers by winning a chase with him in April when he was barely four years old. Crucially, that ruled him out of novice chases in England. Clive, however, wouldn't be denied. He liked the tapes of Master Minded's races, was at the front of the queue thanks to Anthony Bromley's persistence and had the money in his pocket following the exploits of Kauto Star.

A price of €300,000 was agreed, provided he could run in Macaire's name at Auteuil on 27 May. We enjoyed a fun weekend in Paris brightened by the sight of Master Minded cruising through the race and jumping flamboyantly before tiring and finishing second over two and a half miles. Macaire wanted to keep him for another week or two before sending him to England but I wasn't having that because I knew he wouldn't be able to resist running the horse again. There would be no French leave for Master Minded as my own lorry was already at Auteuil. He looked lean and light when he arrived at

Ditcheat, in need of a long holiday. As Clive already had an ace up his sleeve I suggested that we could afford to be patient with Master Minded in his first season, run him in one or two graduation chases then start looking at some big prizes the following year.

We were certainly in no rush with Master Minded. He was out in the field for fully three months and came in so late he wasn't ready to run until December. Clive kept hinting that I should enter him in the Champion Chase at Cheltenham, which I thought was way over the top. I countered by saying that he lacked experience, was a bit too brave in schooling sessions and we shouldn't be too ambitious to start with.

Master Minded's first race at Exeter shortly before Christmas seemed to confirm my view. He got no further than the third, a ditch, where he stood off too far, landed on the fence and shot Sam into orbit. At that stage he had more courage than sense. If he continued like that it was bound to end in tears. So it was a case of back to basics for Master Minded with the most intensive education in jumping. I had him in my outdoor school every day popping over barrels, poles and ditches, you name it, until the penny dropped.

When he ran again in a handicap at Sandown early in the New Year my instructions to Ruby couldn't have been clearer. Worried about the test of jumping posed by the Railway fences I assured him the only priority was a clear round. 'He is one for the future but still has plenty to learn about jumping. Be sure you look after him,' I said.

Master Minded travelled and jumped so well that Ruby never had an anxious moment as he brought him clear to win with any amount of hand. Watching on TV from Chepstow I thought it was a superb performance given his patchy record over fences. When I spoke to Ruby later I asked if he felt Master Minded was good enough to enter in the Champion Chase.

'No, I don't think so. He wants two and a half miles and would be better going right-handed,' he replied. Those words persuaded me that the Ryanair Chase was the right option for Master Minded at Cheltenham, though, conscious of Clive's views, I also entered him in the Champion Chase.

It took Master Minded a while to settle into our routine. We'd had to build him up and concentrate on his jumping. Then he began to blossom. In the month after Sandown I've never known a horse improve as much as him. He turned inside out, put on condition and was unrecognisable from the lean, light-framed individual who joined us in May. His exploits on the gallops were of such a high order I felt justified in letting him work on the bottom gallop upsides Kauto Star who is a machine at home. I couldn't believe my eyes when Master Minded edged ahead in the last furlong, absolutely running away. Nor could Clifford Baker, who usually rides Kauto Star at home. Clifford was speechless for an hour afterwards because his horse had come off second best. He thought there must be something wrong with Kauto Star.

Four days later I pitched Master Minded against the two-mile champion, Voy Por Ustedes, in the Game Spirit Chase. We had nothing to lose and, with luck, the race would show us where to go next with him. On the way to Newbury I told Anthony Bromley that Master Minded would win. He thought I was mad. I got much the same reaction from Ruby in the paddock. He looked at me as if I was stupid until I said, 'I'm telling you chap this horse has improved enormously. If there is no gallop, don't be frightened to press on and make all.'

Master Minded lived up to all my expectations with an astonishing victory from the front that had the bookies running for cover. He gave an exhibition round of jumping, enjoyed a short breather on the final bend then bounded clear again before Voy Por Ustedes stayed on to narrow the gap to five lengths. Ruby was beside himself in the winners' enclosure. 'You were right. This will win the Champion Chase,' he told me. Two months earlier Master Minded had been any price you like for the race. Now he was the new favourite with most firms. I was so excited about the thought of him at Cheltenham, aware that he wasn't yet fully fit, and would improve again for the run.

Master Minded was my third winner of the afternoon at Newbury with the banker, Denman, still to come. He was ridden by Sam Thomas at the request of Paul Barber and Harry Findlay so Ruby found himself in the bizarre position of competing against him on Regal Heights for Donald McCain.

In an ideal world Ruby would have preferred to wait until the last minute before choosing between Kauto Star and Denman in the Gold Cup. You could hardly blame him for wishing to keep all his options open. Paul and Harry, however, forced an early decision by insisting that Denman's big-race jockey should ride him at Newbury. Ruby had a few days to make up his mind, though I was confident he'd side with Kauto Star. How could he get off the reigning champion? It wasn't simply a question of being loyal to Clive Smith and Kauto Star. If he'd wanted to ride Denman, he'd have done so. But in picking Kauto Star he thought he was on the better horse; and so did I at the time.

Once that was settled Sam took over on Denman who delivered a performance of savage intensity on his final public appearance before the showdown with Kauto Star. Unbeaten in eight chases he looked a giant in every sense of the word as he hacked up by twenty lengths from Regal Heights despite being heavily eased on the run-in.

A week later it was the turn of Kauto Star to top the bill with a flawless display in the Commercial First Ascot Chase over two and a half miles. With so much at stake I'd been a nervous wreck all week and was only able to relax once Kauto Star eased clear of his old rival Monet's Garden in the final furlong. Then my heart missed a beat as I spotted him take a couple of false steps on his way back to the winners' enclosure. The next moment he was fine. Perhaps he was more tired than I imagined. I assumed no one else had noticed and was relieved to see Kauto Star walking 100 per cent sound as he was led away afterwards.

Just to be sure, I checked again with my travelling head lass, Donna Blake, before I left the course. She assured me that Kauto Star was fine when he was led out of his box at the racecourse stables for a pick of grass. So I set off for home in a jaunty mood, delighted that my two Gold Cup contenders had come through their prep races without harm. We had two outstanding horses and two confident jockeys, both of whom thought they were going to win the big race.

Then my mobile rang with the kind of news that all racehorse trainers dread. Donna was calling to tell me that Kauto Star was badly lame behind when they went to put him in the lorry. The racecourse vet, suspecting that he'd twisted his off-hind fetlock joint, had strapped up the damage and put it in plaster. If the vet was right it was curtains for him in the Gold Cup.

Donna added that X-rays taken on the spot failed to show any kind of injury in the area of the fetlock joint. I seized on that piece of information like a drowning man reaching for a lifebelt. I also knew in my heart of hearts that if the injury was that serious he wouldn't have been sound an hour earlier while having a pick of grass. Maybe we still had a chance. The Ascot vets were talking about sending Kauto Star to Newmarket for further examination. That was the last thing I wanted so I told Donna to bring him home to Ditcheat.

While all this was happening someone at the racecourse stables must have been straight on to Betfair, laying him for the Gold Cup. As his price began to drift alarmingly the newspapers got hold of the story. Some bookies suspended betting on the Gold Cup. Already sick with worry, I had to field a series of calls from journalists asking if all was well with Kauto Star.

I wasn't in a position to say anything until I'd spoken to Clive and he wasn't answering his phone. When I did get through I gave him the bad news and explained that I wouldn't really know what the problem was until we examined him at Ditcheat. I must have had a hundred calls that evening which all added to the pressure. My phone was in meltdown. Eventually I told the Press Association that I'd be making a statement after the horse had been checked over by my own vet, Buffy Shirley-Beavan, in the morning.

Every minute seemed like an hour until Donna drove into the yard shortly after nine. Kauto Star didn't seem badly lame as we put him in his box, then stripped off the strapping from his leg so that we could have a good look at it. There wasn't a sign of swelling or pain in or around the joint. That was definitely a bonus.

A concerned observer in all this was Paul Barber who was distraught at the prospect of Kauto Star missing the Gold Cup. 'You've got to get him to Cheltenham because it will not be a proper Gold Cup without him,' he said. It was more an order than a request because he wasn't interested in Denman gaining a hollow victory in the race while his mate was still in his box at home. I remember Paul adding, 'If either one of these horses doesn't make it to Cheltenham it will be so strange, like kissing your own sister.'

Paul watched as Clifford Baker removed the shoe on Kauto Star's off-hind foot so that I could test it to see if there was any pressure. When I squeezed at one particular point Kauto Star almost jumped through the roof. His foot was really warm to the touch and we began to suspect that it could simply be a case of pus in his foot. It had probably been brewing for twenty-four hours before Ascot and the race brought it out, leaving him in serious discomfort.

I rang Clive once more, explained what we'd found and said Clifford and I were 99 per cent certain the problem was pus in the foot. If that was the case he'd be fine within a couple of days. With horses you can never be sure and I didn't sleep that night as I tossed and turned hoping for the best and fearing the worst. It was the longest night of my life.

The next morning Paul Barber and I were both in the yard soon after six, peering anxiously into Kauto Star's box. When Buffy arrived she quickly confirmed our diagnosis; once she dug a small hole in his foot pus came pouring out. The sense of relief in the camp was overwhelming as Buffy poulticed the wound and pronounced that the patient could be led out for a short walk later in the morning. Kauto Star was sound by then and almost sound at the trot. The crisis was over.

By the afternoon he'd recovered sufficiently to go on the horse walker for half an hour. The next day you would never have known he'd had a problem. Best of all, he didn't miss any work as he was due a couple of days on the easy list after Ascot. He was led out for a walk again on Monday, with the shoe back on, and was back cantering by Wednesday. By then he was definitely in better shape than his trainer.

24

A promoter's dream

Mention of the 2008 Cheltenham Festival stirs up a host of unforgettable images in my mind though I returned home empty-handed after the opening day. Next morning I woke to hear that Wednesday's card had fallen victim to high winds with parts of the tented village taking off in the direction of Tewkesbury. Among the events blown off course was the Champion Chase. Cheltenham moved with commendable speed to reschedule it as part of a ten-race card on Thursday.

The delay had me 'walking my box' overnight but it didn't harm Master Minded who became the first five-year-old to win the Champion Chase with a towering performance that had anoraks comparing him favourably with legendary two milers from the past. I'd never seen anything like it. Nor had many others, including the official handicapper, who subsequently raised him to a mark of 186, which made him the highest-rated chaser in the land ahead of Denman (182) and Kauto Star (179). That was a bit like going from camp six to the summit of Everest in one bound.

Master Minded travelled like a dream, jumped flawlessly, cruised into the lead at the fifth last and flew home an astonishing nineteen lengths clear of Voy Por Ustedes. I thought he'd win but not like that. He was awesome in full flight and Ruby confirmed that he was pulling his arms out at every stage.

I was too wound up to eat anything on Gold Cup day so my mum took my seat at lunch. All I could manage was a handful of jellybeans every time I walked in or out of the marquee where I usually take a couple of large tables with some of my owners. Nor do I drink much apart from a glass or two of champagne once it's all over. With nine races shoe-horned into the card it was going to be a seriously long day.

Head-to-head confrontations in racing don't come any bigger than the one between Kauto Star and Denman in the 2008 Gold Cup. Media interest in their duel was heightened by the fact that they lived in adjoining boxes in Millionaire's Corner opposite my office. It was a promoter's dream, the classic sporting collision between the supreme, stylish artist and the big-punching fighter. It was right up there with Ali v Frazier, Coe v Ovett, Nadal v Federer or Grundy v Bustino. None of them were next-door neighbours, as far as I know.

The Gold Cup was shaping up to be the most exciting race of my life, one that everyone in racing wanted to see. While it was great for the sport I was finding the build-up increasingly nerve-wracking. Above all I hoped that I didn't let anyone down, that both horses would be in peak form on the day. Their form during the season put them head and shoulders above everything else. The most important thing was that they both came back to their boxes safe and sound.

Kauto Star was the reigning champion, as good a chaser as we've seen for years. Precociously gifted and sleekly athletic, he tends to glide through his races and his last two victories, I felt, were his best ever. I'd never seen him better and would have been amazed if Ruby Walsh deserted him. Whatever beat him would have to be a superstar. Of course it was possible Denman was in that category but no one could be sure on what he'd done so far.

Denman, the challenger, was a raw-boned giant of a horse, un-defeated over fences. Taller and heavier than Kauto Star he possesses a ground-devouring stride, unlimited stamina and a ruthless racing style that intimidates his rivals. I know in my own mind that very few people could train Denman. He can be so difficult; if I was easy on him he'd never win a race. No chance. If you saw him at home trundling up the hill you'd think he was a slow old hunter. In fact, he is quite slow but also a relentless galloper who needs a huge amount of work to get fit. You have to be positive and get on with it to the point where I sometimes work him the day before he runs. You can only win with horses who race like him if they are 100 per cent fit. Given his aggressive style of running it was obvious that he'd be handy from the start though I warned Paul and Harry that you can get a good stayer beaten in the Gold Cup by making too much use of him.

I've never dared work the two together on my flat gallop, mostly because Denman takes such a hold that I often wonder if he is going to stop when he reaches the end. Sometimes I have to step out in front of him to make sure he pulls up. My interest in the Gold Cup included Neptune Collonges, who had more than earned his place in the line-up. After winning on the horse twice Liam Heard deserved to keep the ride until he lost out when John Hales booked Mick Fitzgerald without consulting me. I wasn't happy about it, but John wouldn't back down. We nearly fell out over that one.

Aware that I had six entries, including Turko and Star de Mohaison, some commentators assumed that I was trying to emulate Michael Dickinson's amazing feat of saddling the first five in the 1983 Gold Cup. I'm sure his record is safe. Running five or six doesn't interest me. The others were there in case something happened to the front two though Star de Mohaison was going to run until the ground turned against him. All I wanted was for one of them to win.

I'd have been surprised if anything beat mine, yet strange things can happen in the Gold Cup as I know to my cost after See More Business was carried out in 1999. I was sure Kauto Star would take a deal of beating. Though I didn't say so publicly I couldn't see him failing.

What did concern me a little was the knowledge that Arkle broke the heart of Mill House in the 1964 Gold Cup. Normally, I'm sure they get over losing. Obviously something had to give, but I didn't want the one that came off second best returning to Ditcheat broken-hearted. For months the race had been billed as the big showdown. They both had to go for the Gold Cup for the sake of racing. That was the dream. I wanted them to meet as much as everyone else because I am a fan, too.

Celestial Halo gave us all a lift in the first race on the Friday in the JCB Triumph Hurdle by providing Andy Stewart and his family with their first success at the Festival after so many near misses. Andy has been coming to Cheltenham for forty years since his first day trip on a coach from London as a teenager. We gelded Celestial Halo as soon as he joined me after finishing seventh in the 2007 St Leger. He'd won impressively on his hurdles debut before disappointing at Doncaster partly because Ruby Walsh gave him a negative ride from mid-field. The winner got first run on us that day.

Determined that it shouldn't happen again I kept revving Ruby up, impressing on him that there would be no hanging about at Cheltenham. As we knew the horse stayed well and had a high cruising speed, I urged him to be positive and serve it up to the favourite, Franchoek, when the tapes rose. The plan worked to perfection as Celestial Halo led all the way and saw off the persistent challenge of Franchoek. It was a great result for everyone at the yard because Andy is the most generous of owners. The moment he has a winner he always sends a large present to be shared among the staff.

Just over an hour later I was giving last-minute instructions to my three jockeys in the paddock before the Gold Cup. I tried not to overcomplicate things as they already knew pretty much what they were going to do. There was no question of team tactics. Each jockey was expected to play his cards to his horse's strengths. Of the three, Ruby hardly needed any advice. He had so much confidence in Kauto Star, had ridden him to perfection twelve months earlier and would employ similar tactics again before trying to outspeed Denman as the race came to the boil. Having ridden the other two he was well aware of the dangers of letting Denman get too far ahead.

I told Mick to be prepared to make the running if no one wanted to go on. Neptune Collonges needs to be flat out the whole way. That's what suits him best. Mick should bounce him out in front, set a decent gallop and, if something else took over, then gratefully accept a tow. I wanted Sam to give Denman a chance early on, track the leaders for a circuit, then nose ahead and try to stretch the field going away from the stands. Whatever happened I didn't want him taking a pull on Denman, breaking his rhythm. 'If he wants to be galloping let him gallop, then let him roll on the second circuit. Above all, be positive' were my last words to him.

As the runners filed out on to the course, I drifted away to watch the race on my own. The previous year a camera crew wouldn't leave me alone during the Gold Cup until I gave them a red card. I found their intrusive behaviour highly embarrassing and made it clear that there wouldn't be any interviews this time if they continued to film my every move. Then it was a case of tucking myself away beside a TV screen outside the little Tote tent near the weighing room.

With three contenders and so much at stake I saw a fair bit more than the previous year as Denman set out to ambush his neighbour. The writing was on the wall at halfway when Kauto Star made crucial mistakes at the two fences approaching the stands just as Denman was winding up the tempo. Paul Barber suggested later that Denman took Kauto Star out of his comfort zone, but it wasn't as simple as that. Those errors cost him dear at a crucial point of the race. If he'd winged them he'd have been much closer to the leader. Instead, he was already in trouble when Sam started turning the screw heading out on the second circuit.

For me the race was already over because Denman was moving so powerfully in the lead that, barring a last-minute drama, the prize was his. Neptune Collonges was running the race of his life in second place with Kauto Star just behind trying so hard to close the gap. This was tougher than anything he'd experienced before. It was a much sterner task than the previous year and he was going down with all guns blazing despite not jumping with his usual fleet-footed fluency.

Down the hill and round the final bend Denman was pounding along several lengths clear with victory beckoning, yet Kauto Star never gave up the chase. He moved into second place after the third last and was just starting to close on the leader a fraction when he made yet another mistake at the final fence which cost him vital momentum. Denman was away and gone by then, thrusting home for a fabulous success. Some way behind him his two stable companions had a rare old scrap before Kauto Star took second place by a whisker from Neptune Collonges.

It had been a hell of a horserace and there was pandemonium afterwards as racegoers rushed to acclaim steeplechasing's new hero. I hadn't expected it to turn out this way and didn't really know which one to cheer as an unforgettable race came to an astonishing climax. I loved the ruthless style of Denman as he galloped and jumped them all into submission, but was equally proud of the way the other pair fought to the end. They all covered themselves in glory in filling the first three places.

Ruby and I were both shocked by the result. I was in the strange position of being in two camps. As things turned out he was in the wrong camp. Channel 4's Derek Thompson later added to Ruby's misery by asking if he regretted choosing Kauto Star! It was the most stupid question I've ever heard. Ruby told him exactly what he thought of him before terminating the interview.

The scenes in the paddock were amazing as we waited for the horses to return. John Hales was beside himself as he assured everyone within earshot, 'We nearly beat Kauto, we nearly beat Kauto.' A few yards away Clive Smith was clearly downhearted at seeing his pride and joy lose his crown. I walked over, shook his hand and said there would be other days for Kauto Star.

Nearby Harry Findlay was besieged by a scrum of pressmen. As a dedicated self-publicist he is an interview waiting to happen, an open mouth in search of a microphone. Just one question will set him off for five minutes. Beside him Paul Barber, not for the first time, could hardly get a word in. No wonder they are known as the Odd Couple! Harry then fired up John Hales by thanking him for all his help. Unfortunately, in the heat of the moment, John took that to mean we'd deliberately run Neptune Collonges to set the race up for Denman. It was nonsense, of course, but at first John didn't see it that way. Once again I had to pour oil on troubled waters.

When See More Business won back in 1999 Paul missed leading him in because he became caught up in the scrum approaching the winners' enclosure. This time, once Paul dropped back, I stopped the cavalcade for a few seconds so that he could take his rightful place at Denman's head. The reception the three horses received from one of the most knowledgeable crowds in sport was out of this world. I think everyone at Cheltenham realised they had witnessed one of the great moments of racing history.

Standing on the podium a few minutes later I had to pinch myself. Thirty years earlier I was just starting out in point-to-points. Looking back now, my riding career was so long ago it has no significance in my life. Winning the Gold Cup for the third time, however, was beyond my wildest dreams. It was brilliant to have Megan with me on that day above all others. I tried to impress on her that it wasn't always like this though I'm not sure she believed me.

I was proud, too, of the team who had helped me bring all three horses to Cheltenham in peak condition. There are so many cogs in the wheel, none more important than my head lad, Clifford Baker, who was there to enjoy the moment. Harry Fry, my new pupil assistant, could hardly believe his luck. In the space of twenty-four hours at his first Festival he was the man responsible for taking Master Minded and then Denman to the box where the winners are dope-tested. The magic of those two days will live with him forever.

That evening thirty of us celebrated in style over dinner at the Manor Inn, before Harry Findlay's party turned up just as the meal was over. I'm not sure they were too interested in eating by then but the kitchen managed to rustle up some fish and chips. For me the relief that it was all over was immense. I think I felt more pressure in the lead-up to that Cheltenham than ever before.

I watched the Gold Cup replay at least ten times that night before we went out, when we got back and again in the quiet hours before dawn. I'd follow a different horse each time, then rewind the tape and start again. Although I've trained myself to get by on two, three or four hours sleep a night I do get tired in the busiest times. Sometimes I seem to survive on pure adrenalin. I was totally drained by Friday night, almost on my knees, yet there's nothing better after a major victory than switching on the video and watching it all unfold again and again.

In the morning in my office I was reduced to tears watching Channel 4's reprise of the Gold Cup on *The Morning Line*. The enormity of it all hit me then. Talk about mixed emotions. There were tears of joy at the way Denman exceeded my expectations by dominating one of the best Gold Cup fields for many years. Obviously he was better than any of us had realised. At the same time I was upset for Kauto Star, gutted and a little bit shocked that a brilliant horse had just had his colours lowered by his mate. Even now watching the replay of that race gets me going.

My feeling at the time was that the baton had changed hands, that Denman was always likely to outstay Kauto Star at Cheltenham over the Gold Cup distance. Put the race on at Kempton over three miles and you'd surely get a different result. Clive Smith didn't agree. A few weeks later he assured me that his horse would turn the tables in 2009. That's positive thinking for you.

At lunchtime on Saturday we paraded the three Gold Cup horses through the village together with Master Minded and Celestial Halo before another party in the pub. In the weeks that followed I had dozens of letters, cards and faxes from friends and well-wishers. I was touched to hear from Jenny Barons who had done so much to launch me on my career as a trainer.

There was no question of Denman running again that season because he was absolutely knackered. I could see that as he walked back into the winners' enclosure. He puts his heart and soul into everything he does, was out on his feet afterwards, steaming hot and took two hours to cool down at Cheltenham. My travelling head girl, Donna Blake, had never seen anything like it. She kept washing him off with cold water, trying to cool him down. That night he seemed to recover quickly, though it took him the best part of three weeks to get over his hard race.

Denman spent most of the time in his box with his backside to the door, showing no interest in what was going on in the yard. He rarely lies down but as Dan checked round late at night over the next couple of weeks he was almost always asleep on the floor. He had given everything in the Gold Cup, and more, until he had nothing left. It got right to the bottom of him.

Clive Smith was keen to allow Kauto Star the chance to go out on a winning note at Aintree which would help him seal the Order of Merit for the second year running. I was fully in agreement once the horse showed me he was bouncing again and wouldn't be meeting anything of the calibre of Denman.

Strictly on form, Kauto Star looked to be a penalty kick in the Totesport Bowl but it didn't work out that way as Our Vic came with a sustained run to catch him on the line. Ruby and I both got it badly wrong that day. Conscious that I'd asked him to be more positive than usual he took on Our Vic earlier than necessary and suddenly found himself in a prolonged battle once Kauto Star blundered badly at the second last fence when in command. After that it wasn't pretty viewing as Kauto Star struggled to last home.

I suggested Ruby should watch the video once and throw it away. Later I texted him saying that was one of the worst rides he'd given one of mine and one of my worst training performances. He texted straight back, agreeing with me. That was typically honest of him. Between us we'd cocked it up. Nothing more needed to be said. I think we get on so well because we are open with each other. He's the one out there on the track making instant decisions and it's not often I have reason to complain. When I do have something critical to say we talk it over and move on.

We suffered a further reverse that day when Celestial Halo was soundly beaten by Binocular. Things improved on Friday as Big Bucks, Gwanako and Pierrot Lunaire achieved a treble. Although

Gwanako is only a pony he soared over the National fences in the Topham Chase as if he was on springs.

Watching him was just what I needed after the shock of seeing Master Minded, a 2–5 shot, firmly put in his place by Voy Por Ustedes in the Melling Chase over two and a half miles. With the benefit of hindsight it was clearly a mistake to take him to Aintree, which we chose in preference to Punchestown where the ground was likely to be too quick for him. We were probably all guilty of believing he was a steering job at Aintree and I still think he'd have gone close if he hadn't tried to demolish the same fence that Kauto Star hit the previous day. Landing on it knocked all the stuffing out of Master Minded, leaving him winded like a boxer who'd taken a low blow. After that it was game, set and match to his old rival who fully deserved his triumph.

Some people thought Master Minded was starting to tire as he approached the second last fence upsides the winner. I'm far from convinced about that because his wasn't the mistake of a tired horse. In time I'm sure Master Minded will stay every yard of two and a half miles, particularly on a speed track like Aintree. Clive Smith has even talked to me about the horse getting three miles in the King George at Kempton.

The defeats of Kauto Star and Master Minded at Liverpool proved to be a rare reverse in a record-breaking season by my horses. Neptune Collonges and Twist Magic kept up the momentum by winning at the Punchestown Festival before Poquelin and Andreas rounded off an exceptional campaign with a big race double on the final day at Sandown. That brought the stable's earnings for the season to £3,646,511, which was more than Aidan O'Brien collected as champion flat trainer in Britain the previous summer. It was a massive total for a jumping yard.

Three days later I celebrated in style at Old Trafford with Dan Skelton, Clifford Baker and Harry Fry as Manchester United made it through to the final of the European Cup by beating Barcelona 1–0 in the second leg of the semi-final. For me the best part of the trip was being shown round United's training ground at Carrington by Sir Alex Ferguson the next morning. Wherever I looked there were photographs on the walls of successful teams past and present. When I asked why there were so many photos he explained his belief that it is vital to get into the minds of his players from the start that sport is all about winning. I feel exactly the same.

In the restaurant some of the players I'd seen in action the previous night were tucking into breakfast. It looked a great deal healthier than the bacon, mushroom and sausage baps some of us devour at Ditcheat after first lot. Nutrition and science are clearly part of United's training regime. I was fascinated to discover that some players need to be rehydrated the morning after a game.

I love talking to Sir Alex who is wise beyond words in the way of the world and retains tremendous enthusiasm for his role as a manager. Even now, in his late sixties, he is usually the first one to turn up at Carrington in the mornings. I hope I am exactly the same at that age. You pick up so many useful hints from a man like him. I know I'd jump at the chance to spend a few days with him on the training ground, watching how he handles his players. He calls me two or three times a week, loves to back a winner and has a great sense of humour.

25

My way

Training horses is not an exact science. We are all trying to win as many races as possible but probably use any number of different methods to achieve it. My way is not necessarily the right way for others but it is the one I know and trust after 1,700 winners in eighteen years as a trainer.

Jump racing has changed enormously since I started out as an amateur jockey. Back then everyone in the industry – horses, jockeys, trainers and stable staff – had a chance to recharge their batteries during a two-month summer break in June and July. Now we have wall-to-wall racing, twelve months of the year, though I've never been a great fan of summer jumping. I might keep a handful of top-of-the-ground horses going through May but every summer the two yards at Ditcheat are empty for a minimum of twenty-eight days. That is a golden rule. We use that time to steam-clean every box and carry out maintenance and building work that can't be done when the yards are occupied.

Every year I say we can't squeeze in any more horses at Manor Farm but you should never say never, and in 2008, after talking to Paul Barber, I put up a block of eight wooden stables in an area that used to be our car park. This brought the total to eighty-two with another thirty-three at Highbridge. Then there are the horses at our satellite yard run by Richard Barber and others with Emma Barber, Chloe Roddick and Dave Stadden. As one or two fall by the wayside through injury we bring in others to fill the boxes so that over the season I will run around 160 horses.

In 2008 I also spent a fortune upgrading the facilities, including improving the drainage and the shape of the start of the uphill all-weather gallop and replacing its 'eco track' surface. Once or twice in the past I've been horrified to see part of the gallop swept away by floods. Now the drainage is so efficient I hope we've prevented it happening again.

One of the best things Paul Barber taught me was to use my bank's money to my advantage. Four years ago, when I completely renewed the bottom gallop, I took out a short-term loan of £250,000 to pay for it and started charging my owners a gallop fee. I saw it as an investment in the business. Long before then I'd reached the stage where I couldn't expect Paul to pay for improvements. In 2008 I'd just paid off that loan then was straight into negotiations for another bank loan for fresh work on the top gallop and outdoor school. This time it was costing me the best part of £175,000, which is frightening, but it had to be done. Every time I've earned a few bob from a good season I've always reinvested in the facilities.

That hill gallop is the best in the world but it is high-maintenance. A few years ago, on a night of storms and torrential rain, half of the surface slid down the steep slope in a full-blown avalanche which almost took me with it. Concerned at the volume of rain that had fallen I turned out with Paul Barber at around two in the morning to inspect the damage during a break in the weather. He remained at the top of the hill while I drove towards the bottom, parked my truck and stepped on to the grass in eerie silence.

The next moment Paul rang with an urgent warning: 'Quick, quick, it's coming. Get out of the way,' he began before a wall of woodchip and water fully ten foot high came tumbling down the slope with terrifying force and swept past a few feet from where I stood. Had I been on the gallop at the time they would probably still be searching for me now. Most of the surface ended up in the road at the bottom of the hill in a torrent of water. Once daylight came, Paul and his son, Chris, organised a team to scrape up the woodchip and put it back in place on the hill.

At the end of each season some horses return home to their owners or to studs who have staff to keep an eye on them while they are turned out. Others stay with me in fields beside my home at Highbridge. In the summer after the 2008 Gold Cup Denman and Kauto Star were turned out with two others, Master Minded and Big Bucks, next to my house. It didn't seem such a good idea in June when most of the paddock was flooded several feet deep after torrential rain. Next morning I discovered the quartet grazing together on the only bit of ground not under water. A couple of hundred yards away the river was pouring over the bridge and running down the road like a waterfall into a house in Alhampton I had briefly considered buying.

The annual cycle starts again when the horses return to Ditcheat by mid-July. By then they will have had the best of the summer grass. I always think eight weeks out is enough. Leave them in the field any longer and they will be so fat it can take an age to get the excess weight off them. It's far from ideal allowing them to become too gross. These days, professional athletes and footballers don't let themselves go on holiday. They have to keep reasonably fit. Turning horses out for so long is something of a time-honoured, old-fashioned English thing. In France, by contrast, the horses hardly move out of training at all. I can see the sense in that.

One day our two yards are as deserted as a seaside resort in midwinter. The next they are humming with activity again. Within a week we will have well over a hundred horses in training in the two yards. It's a bit like a new term at school. There are fresh faces, both equine and human, but the core members of the team return year after year. You can't do too much at first with horses that have been on holiday so initially exercise is restricted to walking on the roads and sessions on the mechanical walker.

Trotting on the roads is not an option. Do that with them for three weeks and they can actually put on weight. Dick Baimbridge always used to say that horses were not designed for roads and roads were not designed for horses. After seven to ten days walking they are ready to start gentle canters on the uphill all-weather gallop. From that point they will canter every day. Next we begin to build them up with two and then three canters when we need them. Usually it takes around twelve weeks before they are fit enough to win.

It is a gradual process and there is no rush because hardly any of the horses will be racing for at least three months. What's the point when the ground is usually too quick until the rain arrives in October? When I first started training I was much more impatient and tended to press on as soon as possible. Back then, with a handful of moderate horses, I had to take every opportunity that came my way if I was going to succeed. Some never made it to the track. Others ran only once or twice before they were gone. Now I can afford to wait and do not need to press any buttons until the end of September.

Horses are creatures of habit. Keep them to the same routine and they are happy. My philosophy is to work them hard to get them fit then work them hard to keep them fit. There will then come a time when you have to back off them for a bit before virtually starting again.

We ride out three lots a morning, never more. That means we are quite labour-intensive. With upwards of fifty on the payroll in the two yards at Ditcheat our wage bill is quite high, but the results justify the outlay. In sport as in business you have to invest in good staff. If we started cutting corners and having four or five lots it would not work.

It is important that the work is all done before the yard closes down each day at 12.30. The staff then come back at 3.00 p.m. Each lad or lass looks after four horses and helps tidy up the yard before Clifford starts the evening feed. Usually everyone has left for home by 5.30 p.m.

Jump racing is a game for young people, apart from the key positions, so, like lots of stables, we have quite a high turnover. They tend to stay for two, three or four years, then leave to get married and have children or maybe want a change, because the hours can be a bit unsocial. The lads earn good wages and excellent bonuses with their share of the pool money from all our winners. Hopefully they all have a good time while they are with us. The team we have at the moment is the best ever.

Jumping is the name of the game but schooling horses in the autumn used to be a bit of a nightmare, particularly in dry spells. That has all changed since I built the outdoor school at Highbridge. I use it virtually every day, one morning putting the youngsters through their paces over the smaller obstacles, the next sending experienced handicappers or maybe Kauto Star or Denman repeatedly over a couple of fences to keep their eye in.

Horses tend to enjoy their time in the school and I love watching them. They need to be sharp, alert and athletic in equal measure because they are into a tight turn three or four strides after landing. They will jump the fences several times going left-handed, and will then pop over the same jumps going the other way. To help their concentration we put big blue barrels in the open ditch. That really makes them respect the fences. My view is that older horses in particular need to school three or four days before they run to stretch everything, which is all part of the training.

The jockeys in the yard take turns to do the schooling. In addition Sam Thomas and Christian Williams will come down to help out whenever I ask. Ruby Walsh is a master of schooling and loves doing it. He is a joy to watch as he makes sure the horses go his pace, not theirs. His hands always seem to be on their withers so that he is never interfering with their mouths.

For seventeen years I didn't have a hurdle on the place, just baby fences. That changed last winter when I was sent two sets of 'Easyfix' plastic hurdles which are now used on some courses in Ireland. I am now a convert to the point that I wonder how I managed without them. They are quite solid, fairly upright, and do not encourage horses to take liberties. I schooled all my Cheltenham hurdlers over them at Highbridge before the 2009 Festival and couldn't have been happier with them.

I used to enjoy riding out but some mornings a busy trainer needs to be in three places at once and I haven't sat on a horse for ten years apart from hacking back on one that got loose on the gallops. To be riding round the roads for an hour would be a total waste of time. Nor, sadly, do I go hunting any more, which was something I really used to enjoy. I don't miss it because I don't have time to miss it. I had a long innings with bags of hunting as a kid and years of race riding but that's all over now though I enjoyed a brief comeback in 2006 when I took Megan for a ride as a treat on her 9th birthday. She was on her pony, Charlie, and I rode Atom Re as we cantered along the sand gallop, then walked along the road before hacking side by side up the hill gallop. No prizes for guessing which one of us was blowing hard at the top.

I leave many of the day-to-day decisions in the yard to Clifford Baker who knows exactly how I want things to be done. We both believe that stable hygiene is vital to keep out bugs and viruses. There can be no sloppiness or short cuts to ensuring the horses keep a clean bill of health. In the yard if anything needs sorting out Clifford is the man to do it.

He is the first one into the yard in the mornings long before dawn and often the last to leave at night. We feed Vixen nuts together with haylage supplied by Paul Barber from his farm in Dorset. The horses love it. In addition we give them all a scoop of electrolytes and some vitamin E twice a week and the night after they have run. The combination of nuts and haylage provides quite a high-protein diet so you have to be positive and work the horses hard. Our results suggest the system works fine.

We don't have particular work mornings. Instead, each day we tend to arrange things to fit in with each horse's racing programme. Nor do ours do a lot of galloping because some are doing fast work every day. It is a question of mix and match. Some will have a blow out twenty-four hours before they run. Others will work three days before they race.

I remember Jenny Barons advising me to run them hard up to Christmas, give them a break and then step up the work again. That's what we tend to do and it fits well with our vaccination programme. We vaccinate twice a year, when they come back in the summer and again at the beginning of January, which is usually a quiet month. Racehorses are athletes, not pets. They are all individuals but you can't wrap them up in cotton wool because, if they can't stand the training, they will not stand the racing.

Traditionally, trainers walk round with their head lads at evening stables, checking the horses. We prefer to do it separately. Clifford starts looking round at four and if I'm not racing I set off half an hour behind him; then we compare notes. He's been doing the job so long, first for David Nicholson, and now me, that he can often identify an injury, ailment or little niggling problem and treat it before any damage is done. That's probably one of the reasons why the vets are not always in the yard and also helps keep the costs down for the owners. Brian Eagles, a first-class vet for us, was a big help for a dozen years, though he only used to come in one afternoon a week, except in emergencies. Buffy Shirley-Beavan, who took over from him, is excellent, too, yet is only here perhaps one morning a week.

A lot of training is common sense. I used to weigh the horses an awful lot. Not any more because I found the figures could be misleading. We might weigh them when they come back into training and maybe once a month. Sometimes weighing the horses complicates things. It's a help but only in moderation. Imagine trying to weigh a hundred horses on the scales during a hectic morning.

Nor do we carry out the many blood tests or trachea washes which some trainers swear by. Never have done. Of all our horses that ran at the Cheltenham Festival in 2009 not one had a blood test or tracheal wash. I don't consider blood tests unless I think a horse has a problem or if I want to find out why one has run moderately. Nor do I think that horses can possibly enjoy the experience of a tracheal wash when a tube is fed up the nose into the lungs before some liquid is squirted in there, then drawn back to see if there is any sign of infection.

My view, and Clifford's, is that if you get the work into the horses and they are looking good and eating well there is no need for any tests. If, on the other hand, they are working moderately or not eating then we back off them. Our record speaks for itself. If you know they are right why take blood tests? Otherwise you can end up with your vet training your horses. It's fair to say that Clifford and I rely to a large extent on the evidence of our eyes over modern science. However, if one runs well below form we will have a look afterwards to try to discover the reason.

An increasing number of horses these days seem to suffer from ailments that affect their breathing and thus their performance. When it happens I send them off for a wind operation to Geoff Lane, an outstanding vet who specialises in this type of surgery. In the summer of 2008 he operated on more than twenty of ours. There was a time when some of my owners didn't like the idea but the success rate has been so high that there is no argument now. The sooner you have it done the better, after you have identified the problem, because once a horse's breathing is damaged irreversibly you have no chance of a recovery.

The first sign of trouble usually comes when we hear a horse making a whistling noise as it canters up the hill, or maybe in the outdoor school. Others will only make a noise when they tire in a race. If we have one with suspect breathing we immediately call in Geoff to carry out a scoping. Often he will advise operating straightaway, although sometimes he will suggest giving the horse another run or two with a tongue tie to see what happens.

Geoff usually comes to Ditcheat at the end of the season to check over any horses showing signs of a wind infirmity. He pops a scope up their nose into the back of the throat and with the help of a tiny digital camera examines the larynx either on a screen or through an eyepiece. It is fascinating to watch him at work.

People in racing would be surprised to discover just how many National Hunt horses suffer from minor respiratory impediments. Geoff makes the point that the smallest blockage can make a big difference to a horse's performance. He uses the analogy of washing-up water in a kitchen sink. If a little bit of potato peel becomes stuck in the hole when you pull out the plug it will seriously slow up the speed with which the water drains away. The same, he says, applies to horses. The smallest obstruction will markedly reduce the amount of air reaching the lungs. Apparently there are many forms of airway obstruction that occur in horses. Often horses will have several minor problems at the same time.

Geoff has refined an operation to put things right. Much to my embarrassment, he now calls it the 'Nicholls'. This involves combination surgery, under full general anaesthetic, which basically requires tightening up the soft palate and smoothing out the lining of the voice box by removing any existing blockages.

It is easy to understand Geoff's view that partial asphyxiation is an unpleasant sensation for horses at full gallop. Who can blame them for quickly going off the idea of racing if they repeatedly experience respiratory problems? Some do not even make a noise because they ease off and drop themselves out the moment they feel that something unpleasant is about to happen. If you or I struggled for breath every time we ran we'd be frightened to death. It is no wonder that horses who can't breathe properly suffer secondary problems such as bleeding.

Apparently Geoff's standard wind operation is quite similar to the procedure carried out to prevent humans snoring! The causes are much the same, too. Our horses travel to the equine hospital he uses on the border of Devon and Somerset twenty-four hours before surgery and return here a day or two later for a month's box rest. Then they can come back into training. Each operation takes less than an hour but includes an anaesthetic. It is not considered major surgery, more a case of making minor adjustments to horses suffering from fairly small obstructions. It has made a massive difference to our results.

Sometimes, as in the case of Twist Magic, I will ask Geoff to operate on a horse that has shown no symptoms of a wind problem, not even after a scope. This normally involves the ones that work really well at home but don't perform on the track. Before the op Twist Magic wasn't finishing his races. Afterwards, bingo! He was a new horse, might well have won the Arkle but for falling two out and then won a Grade 1 chase at Aintree next time and more Grade 1s the following season. Others to have done spectacularly well include Oslot and Oumeyade. Taranis is another transformed by Geoff's magic touch.

It is a big bonus to have the backing of our sponsors Connaught. They put a deal of money into the yard one way and another. In return their name and logo are carried on our horseboxes, on the stylish jackets which they supply to all our staff, our paddock sheets and on the silks of all our runners. Hopefully they get a lot out of it in return. Connaught were certainly keen to sign up again for another four years immediately after the 2009 Cheltenham Festival, with an option for a further two years. I'm pleased to say I've trained quite a few winners for Mark Tincknell, the chairman of Connaught, who is a great personal friend.

In the office, Georgie Bown, who looked after See More Business, has been with me for a dozen years and Sarah West is now my PA. I couldn't have a better, more efficient pair of girls to protect me from drowning in a sea of bureaucracy. They get on well and take some of the pressure away from me. I can find my way round a computer but I leave most of the paperwork to them. Georgie and Sarah are part of a surprisingly young team. Clifford and I are the oldest by far, apart from my dad. Most of the staff are in their twenties. Dan is still only twenty-four and Harry Fry, another assistant, is twenty-two. We are all going forward together.

As we expanded in the early days I quickly realised I couldn't do all the jobs myself. With such a big operation you have to delegate. Usually I prefer to promote from within. If you put your trust in people they tend to respond to the challenge. When Jeremy Young left I chose one of my jockeys, Bobby McNally, as his successor as assistant trainer, and when Bobby returned to Ireland to resume riding I gave the job to Dan Skelton even though he was only nineteen at the time and had been here barely a month. I couldn't be more pleased with him. Equally, when my travelling head lad, Neil Baskwill, moved on I didn't hesitate to promote Donna Blake.

There are so many benefits to training in Ditcheat that I couldn't imagine moving elsewhere. The only downside is the constant danger of an accident with the horses on the roads each morning. There have been a few close shaves but the only serious injury occurred when Ornais, spooked by another horse, decided to jump on the back of a passing trailer. That put him out of action for a few months. We've had the odd horse upside down in the ditch but local drivers are very good when they see our string approaching. So, too, are the drivers of the big articulated lorries bringing milk to Paul's cheese factory in the village. The lorries do give me nightmares but the horses are used to them now and we all have to exist together.

One morning late in 2006 a couple of our unraced three-year-olds managed to jump out of a field and gallop over two miles down the nearby A371 in thick fog. In the frantic chase that followed Rose Loxton, one of our most experienced girls, managed to reverse her car straight into the side of my Range Rover. At least the errant pair were unscathed. Paul Barber was highly amused by the incident once he knew the duo were safe. 'Don't worry about your vehicle,' he said. 'Those youngsters are much more valuable!'

When accidents happen and horses are injured or killed I always try to contact their owners as soon as possible. Passing on bad news is just about the hardest part of my job and one I dread, but it has to be done. The least an owner deserves is to hear it direct from the trainer. So I pick up the phone straightaway, explain what has happened and worry like mad afterwards because losing a horse hits me hard, too.

I used to have a rule that if I didn't catch up with every owner in the week I'd spend Sunday morning in the office speaking to all of them on the phone. Now, with Sunday racing, that is not often possible. It is important for owners that they can contact me at any time. They are able to do just that as my mobile is on 24/7. Texting also helps. It means I don't have any time to myself but that is how it has always been.

Planning the detail of my owners' party each year, and organising the glossy brochure that goes with it, takes up a fair bit of time in the summer. It is my chance to say thank you for all the support I have had over the previous twelve months. Usually we parade the horses before a long lunch for upwards of three hundred guests with a bit of entertainment or cabaret. Things have certainly moved on since around sixty people turned up to my first owners' party in September 1992. We paraded about fifteen horses in steady rain before taking cover in the little conservatory which was my office in the days when I lived in the yard. Some of those present that day have supported me through thick and thin down the years. They include Paul Barber, Colin Lewis and Des Nichols.

I decided to change the format for the big day in September 2008, with disastrous results. The idea was to parade all the horses at Ditcheat before everyone moved on to a marquee in the paddock at Highbridge for a mega party to celebrate our 1–2–3 in the Gold Cup. Storms of biblical proportions then left the marquee waterlogged and the adjoining car park resembling a lake. So we had to cancel the celebrations at the last minute.

One way or another stress is my constant companion for twelve months of the year. It appears in many forms though most of the time I manage to disguise how much day-to-day things affect me. I keep it within if I can. You learn to cope with disappointments and problems, that whatever happens you have to deal with it and move on. If I couldn't handle the stress I couldn't continue in the job. I thrive on it in a lot of ways and couldn't do anything else. People say I should take my foot off the throttle by playing golf a couple of times a week but that is not for me. I don't think you can do this job properly and play golf at the same time.

I'm not a good sleeper, though. Some nights I spend an hour going through the entries in bed before falling asleep. Then I'll be wide awake at three or five, with a thousand thoughts buzzing round my head before nodding off again. To help me through the night I often watch replays of my horses running the previous day on the large TV at the end of my bed. If I don't view them at night then I never get to see them. Obviously it helps that I can survive on little sleep. I am usually awake long before the alarm goes off at 6.20 and off to the yard by seven. The first task with Clifford and Dan is to go through the work list, which is a bit like tackling a giant jigsaw puzzle. Matching the most suitable rider to each particular horse is one of the most important jobs of the day.

Every morning there are entries to be done five days in advance of the race and confirmations to be made for those running the next day. I still do all the entries myself and spend hours and hours going through the options; in the car, in bed and, yes, sometimes, on the loo. By keeping first lot at 8.00 a.m. summer and winter, and second lot two hours later, I have the best part of an hour to sort out final plans for the next day's runners. That is the key time when I have to be on the ball despite the distraction of constant phone calls and texts.

In many ways work is my relaxation. I love being at home, going into the yard early every morning, working away in the office and watching the horses going through their paces on the gallops and in the outdoor school. There is never a dull moment. Then, if I am not racing, I meet Paul Barber in the pub at around 12.30, have a glass or two of Coca-Cola, before grabbing a sandwich and a twenty-minute nap on the sofa. Then it's back to the yard early in the afternoon.

These days Dan Skelton, Robert Baker or Georgie will usually drive when I go racing. That gives me the chance to deal with more paperwork and snatch a few minutes shuteye before the phone wakes me up again. It is a never-ending cycle with new challenges every day and I couldn't imagine doing anything else.

26

Who the hell are you?

Old-timers will tell you that training racehorses involves months of misery and moments of magic. I promise it is much better than that. But everyone at Ditcheat was feeling down the day in September last year that Denman set off for Newmarket for treatment for a major heart problem. At the back of our minds, as his horsebox pulled out of the yard, was the awful prospect that we might never see him again.

When he came back from grass it didn't take us long to realise that he might have a little defect. The signs were there from the start. He was hot all day, didn't look happy, wasn't eating and had traces of blood in his nose. Denman has always been a bit idle and crafty in the early weeks of exercise, lumbering along the roads like a bit of a slob, without a care in the world. Once again he showed little or no inclination to exert himself as we stepped up his regular canters. Nor was he performing up the hill.

Almost as soon as he started cantering we had niggling doubts about his wellbeing. At first we put down his lack of motivation to a change of rider. Jess Allen, his regular partner for two and a half years, had left to have a baby shortly after the Gold Cup. Jess is ideal for Denman. A strong, no-nonsense rider, she knows she has to bully him to make him do more than he wants. It is not a question of giving him a hard time, more a case of motivating him to put his best foot forward.

With Jess away until at least Christmas I asked Sarah West, my PA, to take over on Denman. She was so looking forward to sitting on this wonderful racing machine. Soon, though, she was unable to hide the disappointment on her face as she came back in most mornings. Sarah couldn't believe he was the same horse. She is a decent rider but, hard as she tried, she couldn't make Denman pick up the bit. He showed no interest walking round the roads and ambled along like an old horse on his daily canters. In short, he didn't want to go. Clifford told Sarah not to worry, that the horse was always like that but she was so gobsmacked she hinted that he felt more like a hunter.

I knew for sure that we were in big trouble after Sam Thomas popped Denman over a few fences in the outdoor school at Highbridge. As the idea was to wake the horse up I was encouraged by the sight of him dropping Sam the moment he stepped into the arena but it was all downhill after that. Denman jumped without any zest and was out on his feet after two circuits of the tight school. He couldn't have gone any further.

I called in Buffy Shirley-Beavan who took various tests the next morning before his usual exercise and checked him over again after he had breezed along the bottom gallop. We were all stunned by the verdict. Apparently, Denman was suffering from atrial fibrillation of the heart, a form of irregular heartbeat. Basically, his heart was beating out of rhythm. There was no question of him racing in that condition and, without treatment, explained Buffy, retirement beckoned. She recommended that we send him to the veterinary practice Rossdales in Newmarket who would attempt to return his heartbeat to normal. There were risks attached, she added, but if we didn't deal with it straightaway his career was over.

I was out of my mind with worry on 22 September as Denman left for Newmarket. I knew there was a chance that he might not be coming back as horses can die from the treatment. Yet without it he was finished as a racehorse. We had to try and there was comfort that he was in the best hands with Celia Marr at Rossdales.

Kauto Star seemed to be caught up in the downbeat mood in the yard while Denman was away. He missed his mate badly, looked increasingly unhappy and started walking his box as if he sensed what was at stake. With the exception of race days it was the first time the pair had been apart for over two years, summer and winter. They are definitely good pals. If you turn them out in a field with four others they always stick together. Kauto Star got so upset on his own after a couple of days that I eventually moved Noland beside him to keep him company. He then kept looking inquisitively at Noland as if to say, 'Who the hell are you?'

There are two standard ways of dealing with a fibrillating heart. One is to use regular doses of a drug called Quinidine to bring things back to normal. If that doesn't do the trick the next option is to kick-start the heart with a series of electrical shocks, which, I'd been warned, can prove fatal. Happily that was not a course we needed to take.

With the help of a stomach tube Celia administered doses of Quinidine at two-hourly intervals as she tried to temporarily stop all the abnormal electrical activity in Denman's heart for a millisecond. If the drug works the heart's pacemaker takes over and returns to a normal beat. That is what happened with Denman at the third attempt. It was a huge relief to hear that his heart was back to normal but he was far from out of the woods because there were deeply unpleasant side effects which prevented him resuming full training for fully two months.

The drug is so toxic it makes horses feel awful, much like chemotherapy affects human beings. We were thrilled to see him back at the yard after five days, but we had to nurse him like a hospital patient for several weeks. Listless and weak, he was much the same as someone recovering from a major operation. Sick and lethargic, he was only allowed out of his box for a gentle morning stroll and a pick of grass. At that stage none of us had much belief that he would be able to defend his crown at Cheltenham.

As I've never been a fan of summer jumping, it was quite a surprise to find myself heading the trainers' table in the early months of the new season. I knew the run couldn't last. By the start of July I was down to only three horses in training at Highbridge, including Oslot. He'd choked badly at Market Rasen in September the previous year but returned like a car with a new engine once Geoff Lane sorted out his breathing. Oslot quickly rattled up a sequence of victories before landing the Galway Plate, normally a ferociously competitive handicap, with breathtaking ease. Ruby Walsh was beaming from ear to ear as they came back. His first words to me summed up the mood of the day. 'Roll on the winter,' he said.

The one that excited me the most that autumn was Kauto Star, who appeared to be in the form of his life. History tells you that so many horses who run in the Gold Cup are never the same again yet those defeats at Cheltenham and Aintree had clearly not affected him. He was bouncing, absolutely full of himself. Some of his work was unbelievable for a horse that had been in so many battles. He was full of enthusiasm before I took him to Down Royal for the Grade 1 Champion Chase, though Clive Smith needed a bit of persuading to let him run.

As a precaution I put a sheepskin noseband on Kauto Star for the first time. At Cheltenham and Aintree I felt his jumping had become rather sloppy, perhaps because he was lacking a little bit of concentration. I hoped that the noseband would make him pay more attention to his fences. Ruby Walsh was all for it. He says every time I put a noseband on one of our runners it wins.

Whatever the reason, Kauto Star was back to his very best at Down Royal. He cruised round, jumping brilliantly, before easing into the lead three out and pulling clear without being asked a question. It was uplifting to see him running away with Ruby from start to finish. The champ was back, but unfortunately the trip to Northern Ireland and back by road and ferry took much more out of him than I realised. He was away for four days, which left things tight for me to freshen him up for his next target, the Betfair Chase at Haydock.

Our horses carried all before them in November. On the Saturday after Down Royal we enjoyed seven winners, five at Wincanton and two at Sandown. But you can never take anything for granted in this game and a serious injury to Ruby Walsh a week later at Cheltenham left us all downbeat on the anniversary of his dreadful fall on Willy-anwoody at the course. This time his fall on Pride of Dulcote didn't seem too bad but he collected a kick in the stomach as the horse scrambled to his feet and was in so much pain he was taken straight to hospital.

I always feel guilty if a jockey is hurt on one of my horses. When it happens to Ruby part of me feels injured in some ways, too. It is dreadful every time he hits the ground. That is why we pick and choose his rides a little bit. Tests showed that Ruby had ruptured his spleen, an injury that has forced some sportsmen on to the sidelines for six months. Surgeons operated that night, yet when I called to see him the next afternoon I found him walking around his ward in a dressing gown. That is Ruby. Normal rules of recovery do not apply to him. After that I knew he would be back much earlier than anyone imagined.

He was in hospital for six days, then flown back to Ireland on the Friday. The next day, can you believe, he twice walked the half-mile to the local shop and back again. When his own doctor came to examine him on the Sunday he was surprised to find Ruby fully dressed waiting at the door. That was all part of his plan to return in double-quick time. Plenty of well-meaning people were telling me not to push him into coming back too soon. The truth is that Ruby was the one doing the pushing. At first he was determined to be fit for Master Minded at Sandown only three weeks after his fall, which was probably mission impossible. If I had any say in the matter he would not have been there even if he'd been able to twist the arm of his doctors.

The previous year, when Ruby dislocated his shoulder, he should not have been allowed to come back at Christmas though it didn't stop him winning the King George on Kauto Star. To this day I have no doubt he wasn't fit to be riding. That is why I wasn't prepared to let him anywhere near Master Minded at Sandown. It would have been too soon. In the end common sense prevailed and he was persuaded to wait another six days.

Ruby's enforced absence left the door open for Sam Thomas to take over again on Kauto Star in the Betfair Chase. It was not a happy reunion. I fully admit that I made a pig's ear of that race, yet Kauto Star would probably still have won but for losing Sam after sprawling on landing at the last fence upsides Tamarinbleu. For some reason the horse didn't sparkle in the week leading up to Haydock. Maybe the long journey home from Ireland had left its mark.

We were racing for a massive pot and I thought we'd get away with it but everything went wrong. In particular our tactics were faulty on a course that is much more a speed track since they started using portable fences. Given the chance again I'm sure Sam would make much more use of Kauto Star. Instead it turned into a sprint finish.

Sam's misfortune on Kauto Star was the start of a tough sequence of reversals for him that attracted all the wrong headlines. Next day he was dumped at the Chair fence by Gwanako at Aintree, then endured a series of falls culminating in another last-fence drama when he was unseated from Big Bucks while still in with a big shout in the Hennessy Gold Cup. I was fuming afterwards that he'd blown a winning chance by ignoring my instructions to keep him covered up close to the inside rail. Subsequent events suggest he would have been hard to beat.

When Sam hit the deck twice more on the Monday at Folkestone I found myself in a corner over widespread press speculation that he would not be riding Master Minded in the Tingle Creek at Sandown on the Saturday. Clive Smith was incredibly nervous about using Sam after such a luckless run. Given the way Sam was riding he felt it would have been the wrong thing to put him up on Master Minded. I wasn't going to get into a confrontation with Clive by insisting that he should back down. Instead, I tried to defuse the situation by taking time to make the right decision.

Sam has always been a very good back-up to Ruby, but at the time he was going through one of those lean spells that all sportsmen will recognise. If an opening batsman keeps making ducks or a striker cannot find the net he is usually dropped into the reserves where he can find his form again. Then away they go once more.

That is what I was tempted to do with Sam once it became clear that Tony McCoy was free to partner Master Minded. It made sense for Sam to go to Chepstow where he could ride five for me. It wasn't a case of jocking him off Master Minded, as some papers suggested, because the horse had never been his ride. Sam had ended up on the floor at the third fence the only time they'd teamed up before. First, however, I sought the advice of a man who is a master of team selection. Sir Alex Ferguson sent me a text inviting me to ring him at home that night.

When we spoke Sir Alex pointed out the one key difference in our decision making. Unlike him I had owners to satisfy. He suggested that if they were twitchy or unsatisfied with a jockey I had to take their views into account and agreed that the sensible solution was to send Sam to Chepstow. My dad and Paul Barber felt exactly the same. It was really useful to talk to Sir Alex at a time when I was getting seriously stressed. With AP available at Sandown it was the right decision though I wanted Sam to partner Noland at Punchestown the following day. That was important to bolster his confidence during a difficult time for him.

After a tricky week of diplomacy it was a relief to see Master Minded win, in style, by ten lengths. Sam played his part on Noland by landing the John Durkan Memorial Punchestown Chase run forty-eight hours later than scheduled after snow covered the course on the Sunday.

To general astonishment, Ruby was back in action by the end of the week. He alerted me seven days earlier to say he'd been given assurances by the Irish Turf Club doctor that, provided he didn't suffer any setbacks, he could resume on 12 December, which was only twenty-seven days after his injury. It was a remarkable effort by Ruby but that is the measure of the man. What A Friend, owned by Alex Ferguson and Ged Mason, was running at Cheltenham on the 12th but I wasn't going to risk Ruby falling in a novice chase on his first ride back. So Sam Thomas won on What A Friend and Ruby had one ride on Mahonia, who finished second over hurdles. Typically, he couldn't understand what all the fuss was about. He looked light and white in the paddock but had to start somewhere and I thought Mahonia would win for him.

We minded Ruby over the next week, easing him back into things, trying to find him some winners before Boxing Day, choosing his rides with care as he steadily worked his way back to full fitness. He came to stay with me at Ditcheat for a couple of days, rode out and schooled as if he had never been away. I like having Ruby around, he's great fun and is so enthusiastic he is the best possible person I could have riding for me.

Ruby enjoyed two winners at Ascot on Gwanako and Red Harbour on 20 December. The one that really excited us that day was Celestial Halo who finished a highly encouraging second to the Champion Hurdle favourite Binocular. Another double for Ruby at Fontwell two days before Christmas might have seemed insignificant; not to me. The way he rode them convinced me he was right back to his best.

With Ruby fit once more I was increasingly confident that Kauto Star could achieve a hat-trick in the King George on Boxing Day. Others, though, couldn't wait to find faults in him. In my view this horse has never had the recognition he deserves. I don't mind fair comment, but was surprised and a little hurt at the way the critics were queuing up to write off Kauto Star. People were slagging him off unfairly. Some of the things said about him were ludicrous, total rubbish. Even in defeat he has run some great races. Take the 2008 Gold Cup where he was magnificent in defeat, as brave as a horse can be when he was up against it.

One of the daftest comments came from Channel 4's John McCririck on *The Morning Line* when he asked Clive Smith, 'Will you be retiring Kauto Star if he doesn't win today?' Clive didn't see that one coming. None of us did. The question astonished me. What planet was McCririck living on?

I am passionate about my horses. That is me. I get fired up. Why keep knocking Kauto Star? I don't understand it. Much like a football manager whose best player is getting stick, I badly wanted to be there on the touchline defending him. That is why I couldn't wait for Kauto Star to set the record straight. Yet in the run-up to the race I do admit to moments of self-doubt. Perhaps all the critics were right and I was the one in the wrong? Perhaps Kauto was no longer as good as I believed. Maybe he'd passed his peak and was already on a downward curve. I was prepared for defeat but didn't think it would happen.

My dark thoughts didn't last long. Surely we knew him best. How could he win so effortlessly at Down Royal if he was in decline? Kauto is one of the reasons I can't wait to get up in the mornings. Everyone at Ditcheat is emotional about him because he has taken us to places most stables have never been.

I watched the King George in a little Tote betting shop that was almost empty and once Kauto started winging his fences down the back stretch I thought it was all over. I knew then what the result would be because he was super fit, looked superb and has always been a stayer. Nothing could match him that day. He turned for home like a ship under full power, did a fair impression of a Muhammad Ali shuffle as he put himself right at the last fence, and sailed home unchallenged to a heart-warming reception from the huge Bank Holiday crowd.

Watching him bouncing back to win that famous old race for the third time in a row in such fabulous style was one of the best moments of my life. Above all I was thrilled for the horse who, once again, had made his critics eat their words. Retire Kauto Star, Mr McCririck? I don't think so. On the way home from Kempton I sent Ruby a text saying I was immensely proud of the way he had come back to full fitness in time for that race. His enthusiasm matches mine. We are as bad as each other!

You are learning all the time in this game and I am still learning about Kauto Star. It took me a while to realise that with him less is more. In the past I've asked him to race too often and definitely made a mistake in running him at Haydock. Clive and I agree we'll campaign him more sparingly in the future. He's been so good we can nurture him now and he is usually at his formidable best first time out. After Kempton I'd give him a month off and then work him really hard in the run-up to Cheltenham.

It wasn't all good news that Christmas. Tatenen and Osako D'airy were both beaten in Ireland before Neptune Collonges fell at the second last fence in the Lexus Chase as he was being challenged by Exotic Dancer. But I was still buzzing after the soaring triumph of Kauto Star who was heading back to Cheltenham with all guns blazing.

His owner, Clive Smith, must have been in dreamland after his other superstar, Master Minded, delivered a command performance in the Victor Chandler Chase at Ascot on 17 January. Everyone was blown away by his breathtaking jumping and the power of his ground-devouring stride as he stormed sixteen lengths clear of Petit Robin. It left the bookies predicting he would go off the shortest-priced favourite at Cheltenham since Arkle won the 1966 Gold Cup at 10–1 on.

Ruby was in raptures afterwards as he told Clive the race was a bit like Manchester United taking on Leyton Orient. He described Master Minded as better than a machine, more an aeroplane, before adding, 'He is amazing the way he can jump so high in the air and still make ground. He knows he has unbelievable power and is willing to use it. He is on his own as a two-mile specialist. Different horses do wonderful things on different days. This fellow seems to do it every day.' I couldn't have put it better myself.

Our euphoria didn't last long. Next morning Clifford discovered an unsightly swelling on the outside of Master Minded's near fore tendon which left us fearing for a couple of weeks that he might not be able to make it to Cheltenham. At first glance it had all the signs of what we call a 'leg', an injury to the tendon that would put any horse out of action for at least twelve months.

Clifford and I were beside ourselves with worry, yet all the bruising was on the outside which gave us hope that the damage was no more than a bang. We retrieved the boot Master Minded was wearing at Ascot, put it back on and found a deep slash in the fabric over the point of the lump. It must have happened during the race. But for the boot he would have sliced straight through the tendon.

I rang Clive with the bad news straightaway, adding that Clifford and I both thought it was a knock that would probably heal in time for Cheltenham. Buffy Shirley-Beavan wanted to scan the injury, but after some debate we chose to let nature take its course and tried to help things along by hosing the leg with cold water for hour after hour. Serious exercise was out. Instead, Master Minded had one or two sessions each day on the horse walker, building up to three hours a day.

Normally I am the first to alert the betting public about an injury. This was one of those rare occasions when I stayed quiet, simply because I didn't want to set off alarm bells unnecessarily. That, in turn, would have put more pressure on me. There is a time as a trainer when you have to keep things to yourself. Clive was in the picture throughout as Clifford and I prayed that our diagnosis was correct. Crucially, Master Minded was never lame at any stage. There would be no announcement to the press.

Yes, it was a bit of a rush to get the horse to Cheltenham as we were training him with the handbrake half on. If, at any time, I'd felt we were losing the battle, that he was unlikely to make the Festival, I'd have issued a statement at once. Luckily it never reached that point.

Master Minded was ridden for the first time a fortnight after the injury. I thought he'd be fine but ended up tearing my hair out when he tied up so badly we had to put him on the easy list for another week. Because he has always been prone to 'tying up', a form of set fast, I keep him on the go seven days a week. The risk, if I give him a morning off, is that he will become tight, stiff, distressed and sweaty as the muscles in his body start to ache.

It used to be known in racing yards as Monday morning disease. The symptoms of pain are similar to cramp in human beings and can be caused by a build-up of lactic acid brought on by a combination of too much dietary protein and not enough exercise. Back in work again after a quiet week, the more Master Minded cantered, the quicker the swelling on his tendon was going down. The crisis was over.

One way and another Denman dominated the headlines as he continued his comeback from his heart problems. I drew encouragement from the knowledge that another of mine, Eurotrek, had recovered from a similar diagnosis to win two major races. Equally, Call Equiname was never the same after straining his heart from the supreme effort of winning the Champion Chase.

I had an open mind about Denman's chances of ever reaching the same peaks as before but that didn't prevent a wholesale gamble on him in January for the John Smith's Grand National. I thought it was crazy when the horse had so many questions to answer. At that stage Aintree was the last thing on my mind.

If you had seen how ill he was after his treatment you'd understand why I felt there was a chance he'd never race again. This was a different horse from the heavyweight champion I'd trained before. Normally I struggle to get the weight off him. This time it was like starting again, training him completely differently as I nursed him along before trying to build him up after a serious illness. Denman was ready to begin cantering at the end of October. As so much was at stake, I wasn't going to rush him. If he progressed as I hoped he might make it to Cheltenham. If not, we'd stop, give him a long break and have another go the following season.

By Christmas he was going well enough for a speculative entry in a handicap hurdle at Wincanton. Although he was never going to be ready in time for that, he needed a race before the Gold Cup. The one I had in mind was the Aon Chase at Newbury early in February, but I was forced to change tack when the meeting was lost and a replacement race, the Levy Board Chase, hastily rescheduled at Kempton on the same day.

Full marks to the BHA for moving so swiftly but the choice of Kempton, a right-handed course, increased my fears that Denman could make a winning return as he has always been much happier going the other way. Although he'd galloped well enough round Wincanton with Neptune Collonges eight days earlier, he had plenty to prove. The way I felt, if he could win first time out after treatment to his heart, it would be one of my finest achievements. Deep down I didn't know what to expect. Strictly on his recent homework, ridden by Georgie Browne, you wouldn't know how ill he'd been, but he still had to do it on the track.

Denman's comprehensive defeat at Kempton raised more questions than it answered. While I was relieved to see him finish the race, he jumped left-handed the whole way, clearly wasn't as fit as I'd hoped and was in trouble the moment the winner, Madison Du Berlais, served it up to him in the final mile. He was out on his feet by the end, beaten fully twenty-three lengths. I wasn't expecting fireworks that day, far from it, but seeing Denman struggle long before the finish hurt. It wasn't a pretty sight. Defeat of an outstanding horse is never easy to stomach. Nothing compensates for losing.

The inquest immediately began as I was surrounded by a large posse of pressmen and TV crews hanging on my every word. I didn't hide my true feelings as I admitted Denman might never be as good again, that he may have reached his pinnacle in the 2008 Gold Cup. Yes, he'd improve for the run but not enormously. The bookies reacted by making Kauto Star 7–4 favourite for the Gold Cup and pushing out Denman's odds to 4–1. I thought they had it right.

27

How long have I got?

I've learned that it doesn't pay to arrive at the Cheltenham Festival with outrageous expectations. Sure enough, I left the course empty-handed on the opening day in March 2009. It wasn't all bad news, though. Celestial Halo came within a whisker of winning the Smurfit Kappa Champion Hurdle and the next three days turned out to be as good as it can get for a racehorse trainer.

Celestial Halo was in the form of his life going to Cheltenham. I'd kept him fresh all season for this one target, his jumping had become increasingly slick and his homework top-class so I was hopeful that he could turn over the warm favourite, Binocular. What happens? Celestial Halo pips Binocular by a head but is beaten a neck by Nicky Henderson's other runner, Punjabi, in a barnstorming finish. Ruby rode him aggressively from the moment the tapes rose, was always in the firing line and set sail for home approaching the three out. His tactics were spot-on but Celestial Halo got in a little tight at the last flight and was immediately headed by Punjabi who just edged him out on the flat.

My initial reaction was one of disappointment and frustration. Yet it was an outstanding run for a five-year-old and I loved the way Celestial Halo fought all the way to the line. With any luck he will go one better next March because he can only continue to improve as he gains experience, though I think the competition will be red hot.

On Wednesday, Master Minded was the star of the show for the second year running. Given the nightmares involved in his pre-paration I was thrilled to see him looking so well as he strode round the parade ring before the Queen Mother Champion Chase. It was a bit of a rush to get him there, so he was maybe only 95 per cent fit, perhaps two weeks off his very best. That is far from ideal in a championship race but it was more than enough to see him home by seven lengths from Well Chief.

Some people were quick to point out that he wasn't nearly as impressive as the previous year, but I wasn't complaining. Frankly, I'm not interested in my horses charging home by record margins; all that matters is that they win. Master Minded is so exceptional we need to nurture him for the future, to save something for the years ahead in the races that count.

Twelve months earlier he was still a bit of a tearaway. Now he is much more professional, an uncomplicated, high-mettled racehorse who is a class apart. We also know him better. I immediately ruled out a return to Aintree and kept him instead for Punchestown where he just lasted home from Big Zeb in the Kerrygold Champion Chase after idling all the way up the straight.

Chapoturgeon set the ball rolling on Thursday by landing the Jewson Novices' Handicap Chase in a canter. He was one of my naps of the meeting and never gave his supporters an anxious moment. I fell in love with the horse on a shopping trip to France. He was a tall, gangly grey who had some filling out to do. I was determined to have him the moment I saw him and quickly did a deal to buy him for David Johnson who had just joined my team of owners.

Next up at Cheltenham was Big Bucks in the Ladbrokes World Hurdle. Although he was good enough to be joining my team in the Gold Cup the following day, I took the decision to switch him back to hurdles after the debacle at the last fence in the Hennessy Gold Cup. Andy Stewart thought I was bonkers when I told him before Christmas that I was targeting the World Hurdle, yet, for me, it was an obvious strategy. The horse, however, is not straightforward. He's a quirky individual and the key to him is Ruby Walsh. Since Ruby was welded to Kauto Star I saw no point in running Big Bucks over fences for the time being. A suitable trial for him was a three-mile handicap hurdle over the course on 1 January when, despite giving away lumps of weight, he beat Don't Push It comfortably.

I don't bet that often. But I couldn't resist having a decent punt on Big Bucks for the World Hurdle when I saw Hills quoting 20–1. A friend, Richard Webb, and I had £500 each way between us. First, though, he had to justify his place in the line-up by running well in the Byrne Brothers Cleeve Hurdle at Cheltenham on 24 January. We were definitely in business when Big Bucks stayed on powerfully to beat Punchestowns, who gave him eight pounds, and Fair Along, two of the leading contenders for the race in March. There was no more 20–1 available after that.

The French horse Kasbah Bliss was all the rage for the World Hurdle with Punchestowns fancied to beat us on eight pounds better terms. The Frenchman was in trouble long before the finish and Big Bucks, too, appeared to be struggling as the field approached the second last hurdle. That's him: he's naturally lazy and often hits a flat spot before engaging top gear.

One moment Ruby was pumping away without any obvious response. The next Big Bucks moved up menacingly to challenge the leader, Punchestowns, at the final flight. A mistake there briefly halted his momentum but, driven with strength and purpose by Ruby, he swept powerfully to the front halfway up the hill and won with something to spare. Although hugely talented, Big Bucks is one of those horses that only just does enough in front, so that mistake probably helped him. I thought Ruby's ride on him was perfection. Less than a month later they franked the form by landing the John Smith's Liverpool Hurdle.

The best part of it was the sight of Andy's son, Paul, greeting the horse in the winners' enclosure at both meetings. Paul suffered major back injuries in a snowboarding accident just before Christmas and has impressed everyone he's met with his steely determination to walk again, however long it takes. He spent six weeks at Stoke Mandeville Hospital before making encouraging progress while based at the Royal Bucks Hospital near Aylesbury.

Heading home from Cheltenham on Thursday night I told Richard Webb I was going to put all our winnings from Big Bucks on Kauto Star in the Gold Cup the next day. To suggest Richard wasn't too thrilled at my suggestion is something of an understatement but I was so confident by then that I couldn't see him being beaten. I'd already trained the winners of two championship races and Kauto Star was my nap of the week. Despite Richard's protests I contacted Hills' representative, Kate Miller, who did the business for us at 9–4.

Ruby Walsh rode his sixth winner of the meeting on American Trilogy, a 20–1 shot who hacked up by eleven lengths for me in the Vincent O'Brien Hurdle. The result was a bit of a shock to form students but not to Ruby, who assured me a month earlier that the horse was the ideal candidate for the race after he was well beaten on deep ground at Ascot.

American Trilogy gave us all the best possible start to Gold Cup day. With five runners in the feature race the pressure was on, but for some reason I felt much more relaxed in the run-up than the previous year. Part of it was down to the fact that I was far more confident about the outcome. This time I was so happy with Kauto Star I had no doubt he would win. He was a totally different horse at home, working the house down and doing everything right.

It took me a long time to twig that Kauto Star is best fresh, which just goes to show you are always learning about horses. In the paddock I encouraged Ruby to be positive. 'Try sitting in third or fourth, keep him jumping and if you are going well don't mess about. Let him roll,' I suggested.

The same could hardly be said of Denman who gave me more grey hairs than any other during the season. I had some serious talking to do with his two owners, Paul Barber and Harry Findlay, after his lacklustre reappearance at Kempton. None of us knew for sure if his all-out effort in the 2008 Gold Cup had left a permanent mark. One immediate change we agreed after Kempton was that Jess Allen would resume her previous role as Denman's rider.

The early signs after Kempton were encouraging. Bullied and cajoled by Jess, he began to put a bit more effort into his morning canters. Then, ominously, he showed no zest at all during a session in the outdoor school watched by Paul Barber. He jumped like a raw novice that morning and was really laboured. Paul hardly needed telling that we were in serious trouble. Maybe the horse was remembering his unhappy experience in the school in September. Whatever the reason, we were close to drawing stumps, to pulling him out of the Gold Cup.

Ruby Walsh suggested we tried schooling him over our line of fences at the top of the hill three days later. It was like watching a different horse. Denman took hold of his bit, attacked his fences and for one moment threatened to disappear over the skyline. In the final ten days before Cheltenham he also started to look a lot brighter in his coat. All was not lost, as he suddenly began to blossom, but I was still lukewarm about his chance and assured Paul and Harry it would be little short of miraculous if he managed to finish in the first four. There could be no repeat of the aggressive tactics employed by Sam Thomas on Denman in 2008. Instead, I told Sam to ride with more restraint or they would not last home.

The last thing I needed and racing wanted was anything happening to Denman. That was my one fear. I knew he was coming back steadily. If I'd had any doubt at all about his wellbeing I wouldn't have sent him to Cheltenham. One of my last instructions to Sam was to pull him up if he had no chance going out on the second circuit. Nor did I want him battering Denman to finish eighth.

Our third challenger, Neptune Collonges, seemed better and stronger than ever. I warned his jockey, Christian Williams, that he must play to the horse's strengths by setting a good pace. Neptune is an out-and-out galloper who just lacks the tactical pace that would put him up there with Kauto Star and Denman. In my view Punchestown suits him better. On the big day at Cheltenham the ground was a bit too quick for him. He is too slow to be fully effective on that course. If he won it would be brilliant for me to have cracked this race above all with three stable companions in three years.

My final two contenders, My Will and Star de Mohaison, were running in the Gold Cup in preference to heading the weights in the William Hill Chase on Tuesday. I'd been training My Will all year for the Grand National and hoped the Gold Cup would be an ideal prep for that. He was doing his best and I expected him to give young Nick Scholfield a tremendous spin. Star de Mohaison hadn't quite lived up to our hopes during the season, but had more than earned his place in the line-up.

Whatever happened I wasn't expecting a repeat of my 1–2–3 in 2008, even less that mine would fill the first five places this time. You don't go into the Gold Cup expecting a clean sweep. That was never going to happen. It was a different day, a different race and I anticipated a different result. In the build-up much was made of the statistic that not one previous winner had managed to triumph again in the Gold Cup after defeat in the race. That didn't bother me one bit. Kauto Star was the one I favoured and this time I didn't anticipate defeat. His last two bits of work had been with Master Minded and Celestial Halo. How many Gold Cup horses could manage that?

I watched more of the Gold Cup than I usually do on the TV beside my favourite little Tote kiosk. Liking what I saw from an early stage, I popped my head round the corner from time to time to keep up with the action on the big screen opposite the paddock. I was astounded to see Denman travelling so well. At the same time I realised that Neptune Collonges was flat out. He couldn't go any faster.

I could barely take my eyes off Kauto Star who was gliding along, full of himself and jumping from fence to fence. I didn't shout for any of them until it was obvious that Kauto was going to win. Then, like just about everyone else at Cheltenham, I was roaring him on as loudly as I could as he put an end to all argument with one of the finest performances ever seen in the Gold Cup.

I was so happy I was beaming inside as Kauto Star soared over the last fence and bounded up the hill fully thirteen lengths ahead of Denman. I thought it was a great result for racing. Next came Exotic Dancer ahead of Neptune Collonges and My Will. Clifford Baker rushed out on to the course like an excited schoolboy to greet the winner. He confided later that it was the best day of his life.

I found watching the closing stages a highly emotional experience. If you have once-in-a-lifetime horses you can't avoid becoming involved. I was dreading that I'd end up crying my eyes out if one of mine won and couldn't believe what I was seeing when Denman moved alongside Kauto Star on the final bend. I was close to breaking down as Kauto Star crossed the line, yet I was so elated with Denman the tears never came.

I was every bit as proud of Denman as I was of the winner. For him to come bouncing back like that after such a serious illness defies belief. To say his preparation had not been easy is to totally underplay all the problems he'd had over the previous seven months. He must be tougher than old boots.

Given the conditions I thought Neptune Collonges ran a blinder in fourth place. Towards the end he was just done for a bit of toe. Easier ground would have helped him. One glance at the face of his owner, John Hales, was enough to tell me he wasn't happy. I know from experience to count to ten before speaking to him at these times and we didn't get to have a chat about the race for another three days. The Hales family felt that Christian Williams should have set a stronger pace on their horse but the fact is that he could not have gone any faster. He ran exactly as I expected.

Obviously it is frustrating for them to own such a high-class chaser when there are two better in the same stable. Take them out of the equation and Neptune Collonges would have been winning a Gold Cup. They have always been great owners and took it on the chin without a murmur when I rang a few days later with the bad news that the horse had picked up a tendon injury during the race and would be out for a year.

In finishing fifth, My Will ran an eye-catching trial for the Grand National. The only disappointment of the race was Star de Mohaison who was never in contention and last of thirteen to finish. He is much better than that. The Gold Cup put My Will spot on for Liverpool, where he briefly looked like winning at the second last before keeping on to be third behind the 100–1 shot Mon Mome with another of mine, Big Fella Thanks, in sixth. After so many failures in previous years it was a novel experience for me to have two in with a shout in the last half-mile of the National. I'll just have to keep going back to Aintree until I win it.

Ruby and I will find it hard to do better at Cheltenham next year after sharing three championship successes and coming tantalisingly close to lifting a fourth in the Champion Hurdle. Ruby's incredible total of seven winners at the meeting set a record that will surely last for years.

I'm often asked where Kauto Star stands in comparison with the great chasers of the past. Obviously it is hard to judge horses from different generations. Even so, I honestly believe Kauto has achieved more than enough to be considered the best since Arkle, though up to now I've held back from saying so. Yes, he does get beaten from time to time, but so too did Arkle. You wouldn't believe the e-mails and texts I get from Kauto's fans. He has a huge following, though I suspect he'd be even more popular if he was grey.

It is beyond argument that he is a wonderfully talented and versatile chaser. What he has achieved is phenomenal. His total of two Tingle Creeks, two Betfair Chases, two Gold Cups and three King George VI Chases entitles him to be right up there with steeplechasing icons of the past. In addition, he is as good and as sound as he has ever been at the age of nine.

Despite his record over shorter trips he has never been quick. He amazed me in winning two Tingle Creeks because he is basically a stayer. I think he was in the form of his life when he won that race in successive years, yet I can remember Ruby saying he needed two and a half miles after his first success for us at Newbury.

After this year's Gold Cup I had so many texts and messages from well-wishers. One I really appreciated was from Henrietta Knight who handled Best Mate so brilliantly. Many came from people I've never met. Having two outstanding staying chasers in the yard at the same time is a bit like having two wives in some ways. How do you favour one over the other? It is a tricky thing. And can anyone explain how two as good as them turn up at the same time in adjoining boxes? They have both achieved greatness.

I am mightily proud of Denman. He is an aggressive character, always ready for a fight while Kauto is my mate and has been around a lot longer. He is always pleased to see you in the mornings with his head over the door, taking it all in. If I had one last apple I'd give it to him. Kauto Star is a fantastic horse, so good for racing. My task now is to keep him fresh with maybe no more than three races a season. Then it is easy for him as he doesn't get tired. If I look after him he could be running for another three years.

There is definitely more to come from Denman, too, no question. As he really came to life after Cheltenham I had no hesitation in sending him to Aintree for the Totesport Bowl. He might have won it, too, but for falling heavily at the second last upsides the winner Madison Du Berlais. He then galloped off loose and jumped the last fence riderless before being caught near the winning post.

By then he was bleeding badly from a cut on his off-fore elbow where he knocked himself. It was a bit like someone taking a sharp blow to the funny bone, extremely painful but not serious. Although the Aintree vets wanted to take precautionary X-rays, I was happy for him to travel home that evening. Next day he ate up and was virtually sound. The wound didn't need a stitch and he was back cantering within five days.

If Denman has a good summer there is no reason why he can't come back to where he was in the winter of 2007–8. My aim is to bring him and Kauto Star to the Gold Cup next March in the best of condition. That will be some rematch. People often ask me which one is the better. That's a bit of a googly, an unfair question, as I'm hardly able to split them. They are both truly exceptional and I'm so lucky to have them both at the same time. We will do our best to get them to Cheltenham for the decider but before then I'm desperately keen for Kauto Star to win a record fourth successive King George VI Chase.

At Sandown late in April I collected another trophy as champion trainer for the fourth time. We ended the season with 155 winners, our best so far, with a further seven in Ireland. By the time you added the prize money we collected in Ireland our horses earned in excess of £4 million for the second year running.

Although it is nice to receive some recognition I do find it all quite embarrassing and don't really see myself as the champion. It is very much a team thing. You set your heart on a goal, build yourself up towards the top level and everyone wants you to get there. Then you become top dog and suddenly you can sense people thinking, 'Not him again. Not another Nicholls winner.'

After being flat out for the best part of ten months I am completely lost when the season has run its course. All of a sudden, when things go quiet, I suffer severe withdrawal symptoms and don't know what to do with myself.

Looking ahead, if things go pear-shaped for whatever reason and I had to begin again, then I would relish starting at the bottom some-where else with a handful of bargain-basement horses. I wouldn't think twice about it. I've always enjoyed a challenge and would back myself to train winners bought cheaply as cast-offs from other yards. That is how I began in 1991.

There is another, even better reason for wanting to continue as I am. This year Megan, aged twelve, has made enormous strides since she started competing in pony races. My nephew Harry has shown the way over the past three years; now Megan is every bit as keen. She won on her debut on G Whizz over six furlongs at the Blackmore Vale meeting and topped that by triumphing on him again at Cheltenham in April. I was extremely proud watching her galloping home in front up the hill where I've enjoyed so many winners. Her success in the saddle has sparked her interest in how I train the horses.

Early in April, Megan told me she'd be leaving school at seventeen to work for me as my assistant. It was just what I wanted to hear. 'By then, Dad, it will be time for Dan Skelton to move on,' she assured me in all seriousness. Talk about long-term planning. It sounds as though Megan already has it all mapped out. How long have I got before she takes over?

It will be great to have my daughter as part of the team but I am sure she will understand in time that I am not planning to move aside. The way I feel right now I never want to retire. I couldn't walk away from what I have built up at Ditcheat unless the decision is forced on me. I pray that day never comes because the thought of giving up training racehorses frightens me to death. I can't even bear to think about it.

I couldn't begin to cope if I wasn't heading off to the yard first thing every morning. Without training I would be lost. It is the only thing I know and the only thing I want to do. That is why I want to go on and on for as long as I possibly can. Then, maybe, it will be time to pass on the baton to Megan and Olivia.

MY TEN FAVOURITE RACEHORSES

1. **Kauto Star**. He is so well named because he's a genuine star, jump racing's equivalent of Tiger Woods. Obviously every trainer dreams of having a horse in the same league as Desert Orchid. Kauto Star came along for me, has achieved so much at the highest level and is not finished yet. For me there will never be another like him.

2. **Denman**. Another wonderful horse, a big brute who astounded me by progressing from winning a maiden point-to-point to gaining an exceptional victory in the 2008 Gold Cup. He was awesome that day. I fell in love with Denman the moment I set eyes on him in Ireland. Seeing him bounce back from all his problems to finish a superb second in the 2009 Gold Cup was one of the highlights of my career.

3. **Master Minded**. A truly outstanding chaser, straightforward at home with an incredibly high cruising speed. His unique performance in winning the Queen Mother Champion Chase as a five-year-old may never be equalled and he continues to hoover up Grade 1 Chases over two miles.

4. **See More Business**. I shall always be eternally grateful that he came along at the right stage of my career and took me to all the best places. He was a right old bruiser, unbelievably tough and sound, won so many big prizes and was still full of enthusiasm at the age of thirteen.

5. **See More Indians**. In his box he'd snarl and try to bite you but there will always be a place in my heart for him as my first Grade 1 winner. He was also the first horse I bought at the sales and it was a

tragedy we lost him so early in his career. Who knows how good he might have been?

6. **Big Bucks**. I've always loved this horse, mostly because he's such a character. He is a bit of a softie, walks his box, gets a bit stroppy, has his quirks and keeps a bit to himself but he is all class and hugely talented. That is why he is so special. Last season I was confident he'd win the Hennessy Gold Cup. When that didn't work out he ended up proving himself to be one of the best staying hurdlers for some time.

7. **Azertyuiop**. Hard as nails and a bit of a loner, he was a horse you couldn't fail to like and proved to be the top-class two-mile chaser I needed. He had so much raw talent and would surely have achieved plenty more but for his career-ending injury.

8. **Call Equiname**. He probably gave me more sleepless nights than anything I trained. He was almost too soft to be a racehorse and had so many problems almost from the moment we bought him. Each time we'd patch him up and he eventually won the Queen Mother Champion Chase on his fifth run over fences. Unfortunately he was never the same again.

9. **Olveston**. A star in my eyes for providing me with my first winner as a trainer at Hereford in December 1991. The best part was that he was owned by my mum and dad with some of their friends and was named after the village where I grew up. I'd advised them to buy him as a youngster.

10. **Deep Bramble**. He was so laid back that all he wanted to do was eat and sleep so he needed lots of work. In fact, he was a pig when it came to eating but I remember him with enormous affection because, in the space of less than a month, he won two valuable long-distance chases at Sandown at a time, early in my career, when I was under a bit of pressure. He delivered the big winners I needed.

MY RIDING RECORD, 1981–1989

UK	Wins
1981–2	16
1982–3	23
1983–4	12
1984–5	7
1985–6	9
1986–7	18
1987–8	18
1988–9	15
Republic of Ireland	*Wins*
1988	1
Total	119

MY TRAINING RECORD, 1991–2009

Year	Prize Money Win and Place (£)	No. of Wins
UK		
1991–2	50,596	10
1992–3	81,528	20
1993–4	165,340	31
1994–5	164,925	28
1995–6	324,369	53
1996–7	359,318	56
1997–8	611,276	82
1998–9	1,192,566	110
1999–2000	940,495	71
2000–2001	1,129,499	83
2001–2	1,433,207	136
2002–3	2,205,056	152
2003–4	2,191,810	127
2004–5	2,754,205	153
2005–6	2,402,374	148
2006–7	2,972,659	126
2007–8	3,646,511	151
2008–9	3,473,326	155
	26,099,060	1,692
Republic of Ireland		
1998–9		1
2002–3		2
2006–7		1
2007–8		4
2008–9		7
		(15)
Total		1,707

INDEX